GW01255640

Ronnie Peterson

Formula 1 – Super Swede

By Johnny Tipler

Ronnie Peterson: Super Swede

Publishers Details

A Coterie Press Book
First British Edition August 2003
Published in the UK by Coterie Press Limited
6 Forest Hill Industrial Estate, Perry Vale,
Forest Hill, London SE23 2LX
Tel: +44 (0)20 8699 5111
Fax: +44 (0)20 8291 6463
coterieltd@aol.com

For other excellent books by Coterie Press why not have a look at our website: **www.coteriepress.com**

Copyright © 2003 Coterie Press Limited
Text Copyright © Johnny Tipler
Commissioned Photography Copyright © William Taylor
Other Photography Copyright © Individual Artist where applicable

All Rights Reserved
No part of this book covered by the Copyrights hereon may be reproduced, stored in a database or retrieval system or copied in any manner whatsoever without written permission, except in the case of brief quotations embodied in articles or reviews.

For information on this please contact the publishers.

ISBN: 1 902351 07 X

The Author & Publisher extend their special thanks for help in the preparation of this book to: Nina Peterson, Kenneth Olausson, Max Mosley.

Author: Johnny Tipler
Creative Director: William Taylor
Editor: James Bennett
Design: Scott Wilson
Printed by: Colorprint, Hong Kong
Originated by: MTA Group, London

All commissioned Photography is by William Taylor.
Other images courtesy of Kenneth Olausson, Nina Peterson, Ian Catt, Peter Nygaard, Robert Petersson, Jerry Booen, Ferret Photographic, Lars Berntson, Richard Spelberg, Ford Image Library.

The *'Ian Catt Collection'* of over 10,000 motor racing images is managed under licence by Coterie Press and is available to other publishers at the address opposite.

03	Contents
04	Foreword by Max Mosley
06	Introduction
08	**Chapter 01:** Ronnie The Man
24	**Chapter 02:** Country Boy Made Good
42	**Chapter 03:** Into The Big time
60	**Chapter 04:** Dawning of a New F1 Talent
82	**Chapter 05:** Mixed Fortunes
100	**Chapter 06:** A Very Special Year
116	**Chapter 07:** A New Team-mate
128	**Chapter 08:** The Bottom of the Barrel
144	**Chapter 09:** Back with the Old Firm
164	**Chapter 10:** The Six-Wheeler
178	**Chapter 11:** Ground-Effect
198	**Chapter 12:** The Tragedy Unfolds
210	**Chapter 13:** Aftermath
224	**Appendices:** Race Entries and results compiled by Kenneth Olausson, **231** Acknowledgements, **232** Index

FOREWORD

By Max Mosley

When we started March Engineering in 1969, our first car was a space-frame Formula 3 built mainly by Bill Stone in Graham Coaker's garage. By the autumn we needed someone to drive it, ideally one of the three outstanding talents in Formula 3 that year, Ronnie Peterson, Tim Schenken or Reine Wisell. It was Alan Rees who decided on Ronnie and persuaded him to join us. Despite a set-back at Montlhéry he quickly became part of March. That he was not just one of the top Formula 3 drivers of 1969, but one of the all-time great natural driving talents quickly became apparent later during a wet practice session at his first Monaco Grand Prix in May 1970.

It was impossible not to like Ronnie. He was easy-going, straightforward and completely honest. Although these are not the most suitable character traits for success in Formula One, his talent was so overwhelming that he was able to establish himself nonetheless. Had he been more ruthless and calculating, he would probably have won a world championship or two before his very sad and untimely death. Of all the drivers who passed through March in the eight years I was part of it, he was probably the one I got on with best. He was fun to be with, much more intelligent than people realised and someone you could trust.

When he came back to March in 1976, Robin Herd and I realised that he could and would simply drive round a car-handling problem. We therefore agreed that would work with Ronnie at the races while Robin worked with Vittorio Brambilla who, although not as quick as Ronnie, could give accurate information about the behaviour of the car.

There would come a moment during practice (it all counted as qualifying in those days) when no more could be done to improve the car. I would then simply ask him to do his best and he would put the car somewhere near or on the front row, no matter what was wrong with it. He would think nothing of turning the steering wheel of an over-steering car to the stops, holding it with his thumb on full opposite lock in a super-fast corner like the old Woodcote. It did not occur to him to come off the throttle.

Although he was with another team when he died, I missed him more than any of the large number of drivers who were friends but who died in racing accidents in the sixties and seventies. It still saddens me to think that had he had the protection offered by a modern Formula One car, he would have walked back to the pits.

Max Mosley

Above: Max Mosley left no stone unturned in his quest to secure Ronnie's services.

INTRODUCTION

By Johnny Tipler

The shy, good-humoured, mild-mannered Ronnie Peterson was, quite simply, the fastest guy on four wheels during the decade spanning the late-'60s to the late-'70s. A talent equal to Tazio Nuvolari, with a Formula 1 career brim full of potential but, like that of Stirling Moss, ultimately unfulfilled.

The Ronnie story is more than just an account of how the blond boy from a provincial town in the middle of Sweden made it from karts to being a Formula 1 star. There's a contradiction, a paradox about Peterson. On the one hand, his driving talent was mercurial, wild even, whether on the track or on the road. On the other, he was mostly a quiet, home-loving person, not especially given to excesses and wild parties – he hardly touched alcohol. Like Jim Clark, Ronnie was a man of few words, although he was without question Mr Nice, a sentiment echoed by everyone that knew him. 'Ronnie was not a great social animal,' said Jackie Stewart. 'He was very quiet and reserved, very Scandinavian in a lot of respects.'

Behind the scenes, his managers and race-team bosses helped elevate and manipulate his career up the motor racing ladder. But for the most part Ronnie lacked the managerial impetus and personal drive to become World Champions.

Aside from the successes, the on-track entertainment value and the love and adulation of his friends and fans, this also about the spoiling of innocence, the wasting of one of the world's greatest talents, and the injustice and the ramifications of that loss.

Ronnie's career began with karts in 1962, progressing to Formula 1 via Formula 3 and Formula 2, and spending eight years at the top level of the sport. He also drove Alfa Romeo, Ferrari and Lola sports-racing cars, and BMW touring cars. Having raced with stars of the '60s like Hill, Hulme and Rindt, as well as the likes of Jones, Patrese and Tambay who were better known in the 1980s, Ronnie experienced two eras of motor sport. He was a born racer who couldn't help but drive anything, but everything, absolutely flat-out; how a car's suspension and aerodynamics were set up often had no bearing on his lap times. Provided it held together, he would wring the most out of it. When the suspension settings of an analytical team-mate such as Emerson Fittipaldi were applied to his own car, he usually went faster still. That was intensely frustrating to team bosses like Colin Chapman. But it's a mistake to assume that Ronnie had no mechanical aptitude. In fact he understood it very well, adapting his style and technique to accommodate any shortcomings with set-up or defective mechanicals.

He told his friend Tim Schenken that there was only one way of driving: *'Flat out. I just like to drive flat out.'* Fundamental to the Peterson legend are the tales of the sideways powerslides, exemplified by how he dealt with the pre-chicane Woodcote bend at Silverstone, where at successive Grands Prix and Daily Express Internationals, race fans were treated to the spectacle of Ronnie barrelling through with his Lotus 72 on opposite lock and two wheels on the grass – at 160mph. That was a superhuman act, and typical Peterson. The fact that he always drove like that endeared him to spectators everywhere. It helped that his peculiarly English name made him immediately accessible to British fans – he was an honorary Brit. In his native Sweden however he was a national hero, easily comparable with the status of Jim Clark, James Hunt or Nigel Mansell in the UK. Notwithstanding the left-wing tendency that was rampant in Sweden around 1968 to dismiss motor sport as a symbol of gross capitalism, Ronnie was well-known to the national sports pages, and by 1971 he was a household name. Twenty-five years on, he'd not been forgotten. The Swedish national press still ran features about him, and on the 25th anniversary of his death his home town's museum sponsored a Ronnie exhibition and unveiled a statue of him. Other Swedish GP drivers like Jo Bonnier, Reine Wisell and Stefan Johansson weren't as successful and didn't capture the imagination to anything like the same degree.

In the Valhalla of Swedish folk heroes he ranks alongside World Heavyweight boxing champion Ingmar Johansson, cross-country skiing star Ingmar Stenmark, and, possibly their best-known sportsman, world tennis ace Bjorn Borg. He was better known than world champion moto-cross rider Torsten Hallman or rally champion Stig Blomqvist. Apart from Eric Carlsson, there hadn't been a Swedish motor sporting hero – Jo Bonnier was a gentleman driver from the old school – until Ronnie opened the doors to the glamour of Formula 1 that was blossoming with big-time sponsorship when he got his March contract in 1970.

The laconic Swede was so relaxed in public that sometimes he appeared to be in a dream. He would sit outside the Team Lotus Travco motorhome after a grand prix, signing autographs on race fans' programmes, and it was difficult to detect any stress.

Behind the wheel of a racing car he was magical, and that extended to road cars as well. He could make cars do seemingly impossible things. In the early 1970s, when the tobacco company John Player & Son sponsored Team Lotus and the British F3 and Formula Atlantic series, they also sponsored the British Grand Prix. To drum up advance publicity the JPS Motorsport press office invited journalists from the world's motoring press to Brands or Silverstone – whichever one's turn it was to host the GP – and I'd arrange with Lotus Cars for a couple of Elans and a Europa to be present. Then Ronnie and Emerson, or Ronnie and Jacky, would be on hand to whiz the pressmen around the circuit for two or three laps. That grabbed their attention in no uncertain terms, and column inches were guaranteed. Very often, the stunned journos had to be helped from the car afterwards (handed a JPS cigarette no doubt) and pointed in the direction of the bar. After the official guests had had their turn the staff could get a go and, unsurprisingly, a few laps of Brands with Ronnie in a Plus 2 Elan left an indelible imprint on the memory. As the Lotus swept over the brow of Top Straight and into Paddock Bend it was obvious that one was in the presence of a genius. No point in being scared; if anyone knew what they were doing, Ronnie certainly did. One could only watch in awe as he set the car up for the corners, controlling it with the throttle, going from lock to lock with just one hand on the wheel and the other on the gear stick, doing clutch-less gas changes, in a totally unconcerned and carefree manner. Tyres squealing, the car seemed to be sideways more often than not, especially all the way round Druids. To him it was obviously just a natural way of driving.

Ronnie had another quality that was not universal in top class motor racing, and that was honesty and integrity. He stuck with Team Lotus in an obsolete racing car in 1975 when others might have walked away. When he did return to Lotus in 1978 he dutifully played second fiddle to Mario Andretti because that was what his agreement was with Colin Chapman, even though he might have bested the American for the World title. There was no side to Ronnie. As his friend and fellow Formula 3 racer Picko Troberg commented, *'Ronnie was interested in just three things: motor racing, his beautiful wife Barbro, and his tropical fish. And golf too,'* he added.

The Peterson story ended in tragedy. Having survived several dreadful accidents during his career, Ronnie was involved in a huge pile-up at the start of the 1978 Italian Grand Prix. Despite serious leg injuries, he ought to have survived; a decade on he would have walked away from it, with chassis design greatly improved. But medical complications that set in after surgery brought about his death during the night. The Swedish nation went into mourning, as did the whole world of motor sport.

The tragedy didn't end there though. All through his top-line career Ronnie was accompanied by Barbro, who frequently acted as his timekeeper in the pits. Nine years after Ronnie's death, she too was dead, unable to overcome the profound depression brought on by his loss. But despite the shocking and wasteful nature of their respective endings, there is a positive outcome. Born in 1975, Ronnie and Barbro's daughter Nina is a talented and successful interior designer. In this respect she follows in her mother's footsteps, claiming to have no particular gift behind the wheel of a car.

Johnny Tipler

Ronnie Peterson: Super Swede

CHAPTER 01

Ronnie The Man

Race paddocks were accessible to anybody in the early 1970s, and you could rub shoulders with the stars. They were all at the Radio Luxembourg Trophy meeting European F2 Championship round at Mallory Park in the spring of 1973, some driving, some as spectators: Lauda, Reutemann, Depailler, Scheckter, Williamson, Mass, Pace, Birrell and Wollek, to name only a few. My attention was taken by the group of glamorous figures obviously enjoying themselves as they watched the racing at close range from the inside of the Mallory hairpin.

The tall blond one even sported a full-length fur coat. This cool coterie consisted of Ronnie Peterson, Tim Schenken, Dave Brodie and Frank Williams. Ronnie didn't look like a racing driver. He was a six-footer, gangly yet graceful, a fine figure out of the cockpit, with a boyish face and blond hair. Sometimes his laconic body language spoke louder than words.

All his racing life, the fans revered Ronnie, a following that grew larger and stronger as his career progressed. Snapshots from F3 to F1 show him signing autographs, or surrounded by adoring race-goers. For boy racers, regular guys, lovers of speed, beautiful women and tropical fish, he was one of us but exalted by his sublime talent. And that makes his failure to be World Champion and his tragic early death all the more poignant.

Seventies icon

Twenty-five years on, Ronnie remains the iconic driver's driver of the 1970s, just as Gilles Villeneuve is the man from the early '80s and Jean Alesi another half a decade on. Back in his hey-day, Denis Jenkinson described Ronnie in Motor Sport as, *'Not one for trailing around disconsolately at the back of the field, wittering about his tyres or his engine or the handling of his car. He is a racing driver of the best sort and earns every penny he gets.'*

Racing journalist Nigel Roebuck saw Ronnie as: *'One of the greatest chargers of all time, but also a lovely bloke, a loyal team member, a man of complete integrity and a thoroughly decent guy who honoured his commitments. If he said he would do something he would stick by it. He was never a textbook racing driver, in the Stewart sense of the word, but one who could make a car dance to his tune, a man of reflex and instinct. Rene Dreyfus once said of Nuvolari that understeer and oversteer were an irrelevance in his case; whatever the car's inclinations, it would do what its driver required. Ronnie was like that. He could drive around any problem his car might have, with the confidence to commit to a flat-out corner in the certainty that he could sort it all out.'*

In the pantheon of racing drivers, Ronnie undoubtedly ranks among the all-time greats. He combined phenomenal talent with absolute commitment and uncompromising bravery. *'He had wonderful car control, and sometimes he took chances when testing the limits,'* said Max Mosley. *'He wasn't the best of test drivers, because he could circumvent any problem with the car. When he had a bad day he would still go out and try his hardest. To take one example when he drove the March 761 at the Nürburgring in 1976. That circuit sorted the men from the boys, and although he started from seventh, he led on the first lap, and if you are quick there you are quick anywhere.'*

An ardent fan who became a close friend, Dave Brodie, thought *'he was the most stunningly gifted driver I've ever known, and I've known some good 'uns. He just had this fantastic balance.'* His March F2 and Lotus F1 mechanic, Keith Leighton, pinpointed what made Ronnie tick: *'there were so many times when you'd be just in awe. During practice at Silverstone in '73, Jackie Stewart came into the pits and said, "You want to go and watch your driver come through Woodcote." Ronnie had just gone out so I knew he was going to do four or five laps. So we go haring down to Woodcote. Next thing I'm watching Ronnie come through Woodcote, completely flat, sideways. Stewart's raving, he's never seen anybody with that much commitment. To see a multi-world champion like Stewart so excited, like a kid, was unbelievable. That was the ultimate compliment.'*

Driving ability

Ronnie drove in a slightly oversteering manner, so he'd really lean on the outside rear tyre, and put a lot of energy into that. He was harder on the tyres than, say, Emerson, who was more delicate and used the front aerodynamics to help the car into a corner. Ronnie was a physical driver who threw the car into corners and bounced it on the steering. *'Ronnie had pure self-belief,'* said his sparring partner John Watson, *'like Emerson, Jackie and Niki. They never questioned their talent; they always knew that they would achieve their goals. Ronnie tried to drive through problems, much more than Emerson or Mario. Mario sought to address a problem, rather than driving through it, working logically and progressively rather than just driving through it by sheer guts or bravado. In pre-ground-effect cars, that was enough, because all you had to do was fiddle about with rudimentary wings, and get good traction and good turn in. If you had a reasonably well-balanced car aerodynamically, you had good high-speed stability. Then you worked on the low speed mechanical side, which was about getting it to turn in and then getting good traction out of the corner.'*

It was the ability to modulate the throttle and balance the car on the throttle that made Ronnie so outstanding. Apart from the oft-cited Woodcote Corner at Silverstone, another turn where he was utterly spectacular was the 180-degree Curva do Sol at Interlagos, which was just below the pits. Watson recalled, *'Ronnie would go through it, the car balanced on the throttle, and there'd be no tyre smoke coming off the outside wheel because he had the car so well balanced. It was a hell of a thing to do, and the buzz you get from doing it is massive. But it is hard on a car, and if you have a potential tyre problem, either you overheat the tyre and the tyre de-laminates, or blisters. Jackie, for example, or Emerson, Niki, or Mario sought to reduce that style of driving to make the car more neutral, spreading the load across the four tyres, rather than knackering one particular tyre.'* It may be no coincidence that the very drivers Watson named won the Championship. Perhaps Ronnie's aggressive use of oversteer compromised his chances of winning in a fragile car over a Grand Prix distance, but that was the very reason why he was so incredible to watch in action.

Need to consolidate

The most astute team managers, drivers and mechanics acknowledged Peterson's genius at the wheel, but their admiration was tempered with a realistic appraisal of his flaws. In the early days, the charger lacked the strategic skills to cover the distance, pushing vulnerable components to breaking point. The quiet man didn't come to terms with the political nouse needed in the Formula 1 bearpit until it was too late. And finally, though he was immensely popular in the paddock Ronnie never quite managed to consolidate a team around him. Watson's view was that: *'Ronnie was one hundred percent racing driver. But your ability in the*

Chapter 01: Ronnie The Man

Opposite: Ronnie made his name in F3 in the Tecno. **Above:** The 1971 F2 champion balances the March 712 over the cobbles at Rouen's Nouveau Monde.

Ronnie Peterson: Super Swede

Above: According to March designer Robin Herd (right), Ronnie was bright and easy to work with. **Opposite: Right** Former team-mates remained good friends: Ronnie and Emerson in '74.

> HE HAD THE ABILITY TO ENTHUSE PEOPLE, YET HE WAS SO MODEST, SUCH A LIKEABLE BLOKE. HE WAS A PHENOMENAL DRIVER, WHO ALWAYS GAVE ONE HUNDRED PERCENT.

car is the least part of the process. It's the ability to create the structure around yourself and ensure that you get the team's undivided attention. Jackie did it at Tyrrell, Emerson at McLaren, Mario at Lotus, Lauda at Ferrari, Prost and then Senna at McLaren, Schumacher at Ferrari. It's a way that drivers can guarantee that they will not be challenged. But they also have to have the ability to see that there are some drivers who are better than they are, and certainly Emerson realised that the writing was on the wall as soon as Colin signed Ronnie. From then on, he was probably looking not to 73 but to '74 and on. Whereas Ronnie was looking at '73 as his chance to beat Emerson in the World Championship. Emerson realised that he couldn't beat Ronnie, as he was naturally a faster driver. But Emerson might have been a more intelligent man in a race car.'

James Hunt, whose confidence was irretrievably damaged by the experience of pulling Ronnie from his blazing car at Monza in 1978, made an acute assessment of their respective strengths in his Autosport column: 'I don't consider myself as somebody who's got enormous natural talent. I'd put myself in the second rank, behind people like Peterson. I can drive a car about as quickly as, say, the Fittipaldis and the Reutemanns and the Scheckters. Maybe I can't do one-off banzai laps in practice like Ronnie, but I reckon I can get the job done over 90 laps or so. Even Ronnie's got to drive a race distance like the rest of us mortals, and a Grand Prix is quite a strain, both mentally and physically.' But Ronnie had a core of personal stability that was striking compared to Hunt himself or, as Tyrrell designer Derek Gardner said, to Jody Scheckter. 'He was very different to Jody' said Gardner. 'Jody wouldn't be the same two days running. He needed the adulation of a team like Ferrari. Ronnie was a more complex man than most people were prepared to accept, though he was very reticent. If he answered a question he was monosyllabic and would never elaborate on it.'

It's often implied that Ronnie lacked the intellectual equipment and mechanical knowledge to be an all round champion. But that's not what Robin Herd, designer and co-founder of March thought: 'He had the ability to enthuse people, yet he was so modest, such a likeable bloke. He was a phenomenal driver, who always gave one hundred percent. People knock him and say he wasn't very bright. But that's just not true. He was a bright guy, easy to work with, and a competent test driver – certainly better than was generally thought to be the case, although not in the Lauda league.'

Mario Andretti was brutally frank. 'In '78 he did the first test ever with the Type 79 in Anderstorp, just before the Belgian Grand Prix, but he just didn't know what the car needed. He lacked that technical knowledge, and that hurt him because he couldn't really help himself. He could only make up for the deficiency with natural talent for so long, and that's why in many races he would be very quick but then fade back because he would over-tax the tyres or the gearbox.' Nigel Roebuck recalled that, 'Chapman always reckoned that Ronnie was at his best when partnered with a supreme test driver, and in two spells with Lotus, his team mates were Emerson Fittipaldi and Mario Andretti. Chapman said: "He'd mess around in practice, while Emerson worked on his set-up, then copy his settings - and nick pole position from him! Used to madden Emerson, that, and you couldn't blame him."'

March director Max Mosley was succinct: 'Ronnie wasn't that bad at set-up, but he wasn't one of those introspective, analytical drivers. He had so much natural talent that it was difficult for him for him to say that the car was doing something wrong when he could overcome the problem with his driving skills. But he could tell you what it was doing.' There's always the sense that Ronnie would give anything a go. Rex Hart said: 'He was not the easiest on cars but he went quickly. You can't have it all ways. He was quite hard on gearboxes. He didn't blow a lot of gearboxes up, but you certainly knew when the corners had gone off the dogs, and he was harder than Andretti on tyres. If the car was anywhere near right, Ronnie would drive the bloody thing, it was as simple as that.'

The back-room guys loved Ronnie in the same way that they loved Jim Clark, because he was a true racer and a man without airs and graces. The feeling was reciprocated. When the Lotus drivers visited Ketteringham Hall during 1978, as they did from time to time, Andretti confined himself to the business in hand, while Ronnie walked the floor. Rex Hart recalled: 'Ronnie used to walk around the factory, and not just where the fabricators worked, but seeing

Ronnie Peterson: Super Swede

all the other people. They didn't get many visitors, and that was appreciated. I don't remember Andretti walking round the factory at all. If there was a toss up whose car the fabricators were going to get stuff to first, I got mine before Andretti's guys.'

Video star

We have a poignant record of Ronnie on film, in the John Player sponsored *'If you're not winning, you're not trying.'* The story of the 1973 season when Ronnie partnered Emerson – who was in his third year at Team Lotus, it's a record of the way things were then; the relative informality, Chapman leaping out into the track and saluting his winning driver by hurling his *'Bob Dylan'* cap skywards; the joy of the mechanics, hugging after a victory, the resigned looks when the car broke. The fact that Chapman seemed to carry everything in his head, making spontaneous decisions about tyres or set-up; his irritation when Ronnie had three crashes at Zolder. We hear Ronnie accounting for his accidents at Zolder due to overdriving, and admitting a certain nervousness. He gives a lucid commentary of a lap around Monaco, and we hear him tell Chapman (in muffled tones through his helmet) about an accident to Emerson at Zandvoort, and Cevert's fatal crash at Watkins Glen.

Noel Stanbury was Team Lotus's commercial manager in the 1980s and half of the Stanbury-Foley partnership that handled JPS-Team Lotus promotion in the '70s and commissioned the film. Noel observed that, *'Ronnie was, at heart, a very shy and simple person. He never really realised just how much talent he had, or where it could take him. All the other drivers (Stewart, Lauda, and so on) feared Ronnie's ability – but would never admit it.'*

But there are other views on why Ronnie missed his rightful World Championship. That mistakes were made in his choice of teams and contracts as his career developed, and that he was let down by equipment failures which were beyond his control. There's rarely any point in staying in any job once things have reached rock bottom, and so it had been at Lotus. The trouble with F1 is that it's so close-knit, and the grass often looks greener in someone else's paddock enclave.

Ronnie was an honourable man who stuck to his word, nowhere more obviously so than at Team Lotus in 1978. And honour is not always rewarded in Formula 1. Perhaps he might have gone further with more aggressive managerial backing. Ronnie had his press agent, the jovial, larger-than-life Sveneric Eriksson, and business manager, Staffan Svenby. Staffan first met Ronnie in 1969. *'Ronnie didn't know anything about the money side,'* he said. *'He needed a new helmet, I got him a helmet, and he asked me if I would help him.'* Ronnie needed Staffan to protect him from all the *'shit'* associated with F1 (Ronnie loved the word *'shit'*...), and someone who could overcome his English language problems. Because he believed totally in his own ability as a driver, *'it never occurred to Ronnie to ask for special options or concessions in a contract, like, "I should have priority with one car or another,"* said Staffan. In the 1970s, the relationship between manager and driver was undeveloped. Drivers tended to negotiate for themselves, without relying on middlemen. That was fine for astute characters like Jackie Stewart and Niki Lauda, but Ronnie needed someone to advocate his case. There was no template for Staffan to follow; he was up against champion dealmakers operating at their peak in the cut and thrust of day-to-day racing, without much guidance from his client. On at least two occasions, Ronnie spoke directly to Chapman instead of going via Staffan – for example, he signed an option to go to Team Lotus for 1973 without negotiating with March or Lotus first. Said Noel Stanbury: *'What Staffan never achieved was a position for Ronnie where he could have become what he was capable of being – the World's Number One. He didn't go to races regularly and manage Ronnie's affairs. It was Sveneric that was present more often than not, but that was in a PR and journo role, not a get-your-man-the-best-deal role.'*

John Watson made the point that, *'when you sat down to discuss contracts with people like Max Mosley, Robin Herd and Colin Chapman, you needed someone like Staffan on your side. I mean, Ken Tyrell was no shrinking violet, believe me; Ken was as tough as they come, but he had a heart. If you're a racing driver, it's better to let someone else do the dirty work, fix the nuts and bolts.'*

Staffan acknowledged that, during his eight-year F1 career, Ronnie had

Opposite: In between races Ronnie & Barbro enjoy a days boating with Graham Hill and Carlos Pace. **Top:** JPS-Lotus mechanics Stevie May and Keith Leighton prepare Ronnie's 72 at Brands Hatch while Chapman muses. **Above:** Members of the 1974 F1 brigade (including Follmer, Edwards, Beltoise, Brambilla, Jarier, Wilds, Lombardi, Peterson and Ickx) take a trailer ride.

1969 – FALKENBERG

REINE o RONNIE

LEIF HANSEN o LENA

REINE LENA RONNIE

PICKO TROBERG

TORSTEN PALM

RONNIE LENA o OVE

INGVAR PETTERSON

Opposite: Sveneric Eriksson interviews Ronnie for Swedish TV at Anderstorp in '74.

sometimes been ill advised. 'We tended to be with the wrong team at the wrong time, apart from with Lotus at the end. He had a good start, but that period from 1975 to 1977 was not good. For 1976 there was really nowhere else for him to go except March, and sometimes on a chessboard you have to make sacrifices – you have to take a step backwards to make two steps forwards. I had a draft contract with Bubbles Horsley at Hesketh, but that didn't seem right, those guys all driving round in their Rolls-Royces!'

As for the quality of equipment, Keith Leighton summarised the problems: 'He wanted to be the best. Unfortunately in some situations later on in his career he didn't have the equipment to be able to do that, so he was probably overdriving. Like in the later part of his first Lotus stint, at Marches and even at Tyrrell. He was basically carrying the car. That was probably true throughout most of his career.'

Money

Peterson died a rich man by the standards of the day, leaving an estimated £1 million on his death in 1978. But if Staffan didn't feel comfortable with the Hesketh toffs, their apparent extravagance must have been anathema to Ronnie, who was always careful, not to say tight. In the early days his personal banker was his mother, Maj-Britt. Ronnie's friend and F3 compatriot Torsten Palm described the financial controls she imposed: 'In the Formula 3 days, Ronnie was very strongly influenced by his mother. He inherited her calmness too. On Sunday evening when he came home from races, she was on the lookout for the prize money. She looked after that side of it for him. When Reine (Wisell) won a race, there was a big party on the Sunday evening and there were girls and alcohol and everything. But when Ronnie won, he kept his money, never had a beer, going straight home, put the money on the table and went through all the figures. He inherited his mother's toughness on that, and he never spent a lot of money.'

'Ronnie was mean as hell,' said his friend Lars Berntson. 'We'd go to a restaurant and I'd say, "I'll pay today," but next time we went, Ronnie said, "Let's go Dutch."' Ronnie wasn't averse to standing his ground over money. One January when Team Lotus was about to fly out to Argentina, his pay cheque hadn't arrived. Ronnie told Peter Warr that unless he had a cheque the next day he wouldn't be going. 'Peter Warr turned up that night with a cheque,' said Lars. 'That's how tight it was. It didn't worry Ronnie unduly though. He knew his worth, and he was hot property at the time.'

Team Lotus failed to come up with a winning car in 1975, and Ronnie was obliged to rely on what, in F1 terms, was a museum piece. With no wins, his standing was therefore not so great by the end of that year, and there were even some who had written him off. Not so Count Ghughie Zanon. When Ronnie quit Team Lotus at the start of 1976, despondent at the lack of success and returned to March, his drive was funded by his wealthy Italian fan. The Count bankrolled Ronnie's 1976 season, and helped pay for his return to Lotus in 1978. Apart from his deal with Ghughie Zanon, Ronnie was making money out of racing car shows with Staffan. According to Brodie, *'He told me that he'd got more money than he could ever spend and it hadn't come from racing; it came from racing car shows.'*

Friendship

Ronnie Peterson had a gift for male friendship; his lack of pretension and his boyish exuberance meant that, again and again in the course of research for this book, people described him as a lovely guy. His F1 mechanic at March from 1971 to 1972, Peter Kerr, said, 'he was a gentle man, extremely honest and never went back on his word.' Kerr, a New Zealander who had been Jochen Rindt's mechanic at Winkelmann Racing during Rindt's reign as F2 maestro between 1965 and 1969, bought a house in Maidenhead with Howden Ganley and John Muller in 1967. He recalled *'the Swedes all arriving, including Ronnie and Reine, and dossing on the sitting room floor in sleeping bags, with the central heating turned full-on all night. I thought that was a bit odd for guys used to a cold climate,'* he said.

Howden described Ronnie as, *'the nicest guy you could ever meet; he remained just as polite and modest all through his life. His tremendous success never went to his head. Barbro was the same way – so nice, polite and modest. Having been very shy, Ronnie did become more self confident, but always in the nicest possible way. Ronnie was not the most co-ordinated guy out of the car, but once he got behind the wheel he became a superstar with all that timing, balance and judgement.'*

Racer Dave Brodie said, *'Ronnie was a blinding bloke to know, a proper bloke's bloke.'* But nearly all his relationships were within motorsport, the context for his whole adult life. Even the area where he lived in Cookham Dene was known as 'Racing Hill', because of the cluster of racing inhabitants, including Tim Schenken, Torsten Palm and Keke Rosberg, who lived in the same road.

Brodie was a legendary performer in an Escort special saloon and a Modsports Elan. He ran a very successful tuning business and was an early shareholder in Frank Williams' operation. Meeting Ronnie for the first time was an unforgettable experience for Brodie, not just because he was already a keen Peterson fan. At Mallory Park in 1973 Brodie and Frank Williams left the circuit after the racing in Brodie's tuned-up yellow Capri. Tim Schenken and Ronnie followed in a blue Plus 2 Elan. Brodie and Ronnie were driving. *'Frank made the big mistake of saying, "you won't be able to keep up with us," winding up Ronnie. I drove out of the circuit and there was a massive stream of traffic. Frank got the Sunday Times out, and tore a hole in it so he looked as if he was reading, but he could see through the trap door if an accident was going to happen. Basically, I made a second lane of traffic, and we ended up on the M1 with Ronnie glued to my bumper. The Elan could do over 110 mph, but the Capri was quicker. We were absolutely flat all the way down there. We were using the central reservation, the hard shoulder; there was no Armco in those days in the middle. I obliterated both carriageways with dust and shit, and in amongst all that was Ronnie with his pop-up headlights. We went past Silverstone at 90 with race traffic coming out, him still stuck on my bumper. We got to a roundabout near Maidenhead, and I went round it six times. But the seventh time I went off down my road, and he missed it. When we got back to my house, Frank said, "let's pretend this is how we always drive," so we got out of the car very nonchalant, Tim was going absolutely ape-shit, saying, "Fucking hell, I can't believe it, nobody drives like that!" Ronnie just said, "I don't understand, how can a Capri be as quick in the corners as my Elan?" I said, "it's called talent, Ronnie."'* It was the start of a close friendship between the two drivers. A postscript to this tale is that the French racers Jarier and Beltoise were arrested at Junction 15 on the M1 near Northampton because they were each in fast-moving cars, one blue and one yellow, and the police mistook them for Brodie and Peterson. They were locked up overnight, fined £50 and escorted to Dover.

Ronnie was a great explorer of back road shortcuts, as Howden Ganley recalls. *'On the way home from a test session at Silverstone in '74, we were in separate cars but ran more or less together, but then began taking different little short cuts, joining up again further on, then diverging. He was in a Lotus Eclat, I was in my BMW, and the speeds were really rising as each sought to keep in front. Eventually we reached the M40, and went from Stokenchurch to Junction 4 at High Wycombe at over 100 mph. We shot up the off ramp more or less side by side, round over the top where we came across some "enthusiast" trying out his new MGC, wandering about in the middle of the road. I went round the outside of him, and Ronnie dived through on the inside, and we then made that awkward left hander onto the A404 flat out, and off down the hill. We were some way down the hill toward the Marlow exit when the fellow in the MGC came after us. Not wanting to continue racing, we slowed down, and exited toward Bourne End. The MGC quickly overtook both of us, and then pulled up the sign in his rear window "Police – Stop", which of course we did. We pulled up next to each other and the two officers got out and came back to have words with us. We were both still in our overalls, just as we'd got out of the F1 cars. Neither policeman expressed the slightest surprise, or even remarked on our being dressed like this. It was as if everyone they stopped wore Nomex. They just gave me a ticket (to my UK address) and gave Ronnie a verbal warning as he was a foreigner.'*

Ronnie's behaviour on the road was reckless. But it says much about his self-belief, his feeling of immortality.

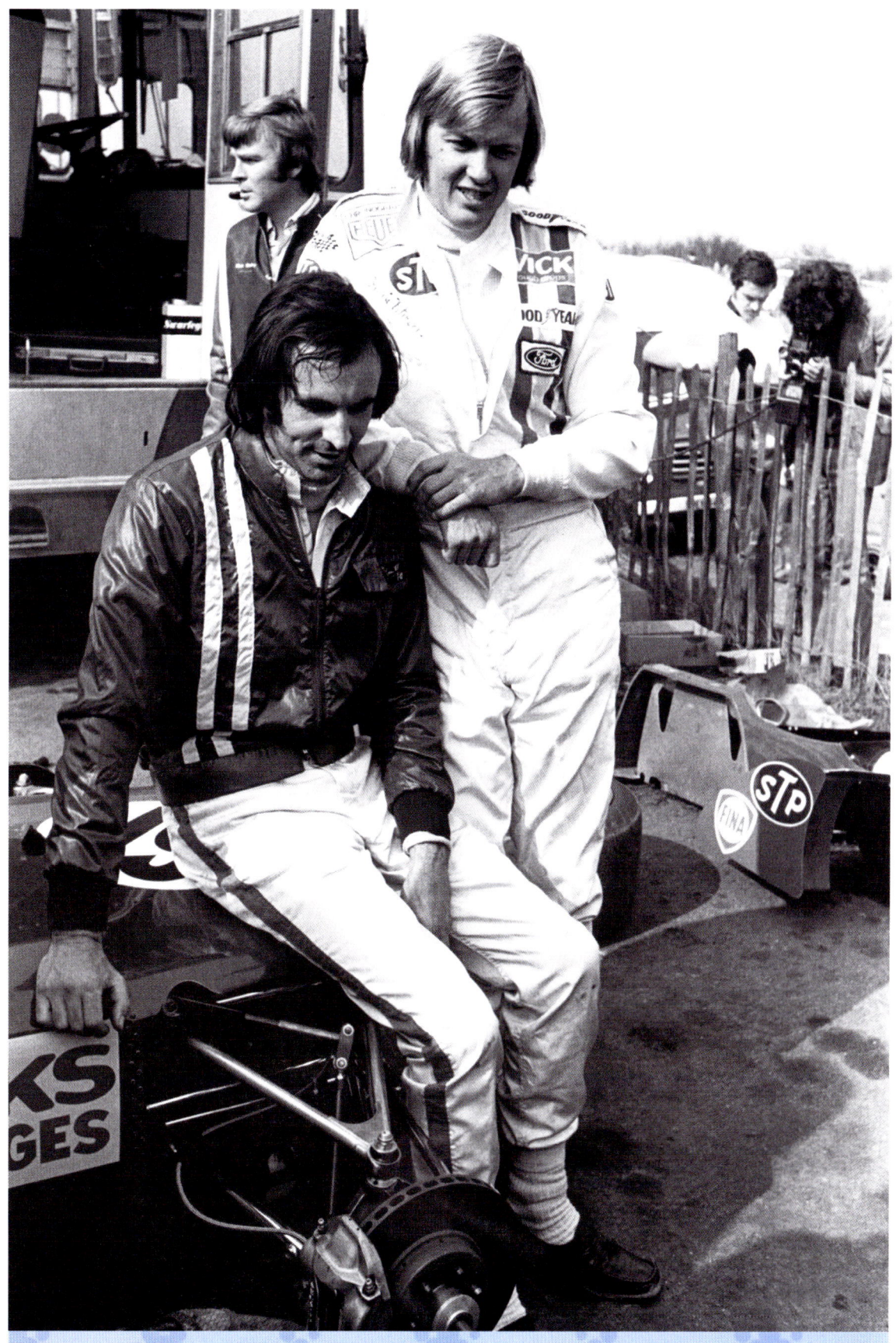

Opposite: At the Maidenhead GP, with Per Cewrien and Ronnie (in his helmet), Barbro creates an impromptu chicane. **Above:** Tim Schenken and Ronnie relaxing in the March enclave, 1971.

Ronnie Peterson: Super Swede

Above: Team effort - Ronnie and Emerson share a pedallo during time off at Monaco '73, while Barbro and Maria-Helena enjoy the ride. **Opposite Right:** Keith Leighton was Ronnie's mechanic at March and Lotus between 1970 and 1975.

RONNIE WAS THE BOY FROM THE STICKS WHO CAME GOOD, A TRAJECTORY THAT TOOK HIM FROM LIFT INSTALLER TO INTERNATIONAL HERO. A BOY LIKE ANY OTHER, BUT MADE MAGICAL BY HIS SUBLIME TALENT.

Regular guy

His great friend Tim Schenken said: 'Ronnie was just a regular guy. I spent some time with him, living with his family during the off-season, in Örebro, staying at his parents' house. He seemed almost embarrassed at the recognition and the fame that he had. He was never infected by his popularity, nor by the money he earned racing.' According to Keith Leighton, 'Ronnie didn't really have an ego. His ego was to be the best. And being the best meant it was against the stopwatch. He felt good if he was on pole position, basically. If he wasn't on pole he was very quiet, because he knew he could have done better. Usually in that situation the problem was overdriving, because he'd end up with too much oversteer; which seems impossible for him, but that would be it. If things went wrong, he would sulk a little bit, but not get cross. A lot of it would be inside himself. It would be self-reproach, thinking, "I shouldn't have done that."

Off duty, he was one of the boys. His mechanic at Lotus, Rex Hart, described the scene: 'Mechanics and drivers socialised together when we stayed in the same hotels. It was more like a family then. Ronnie was good fun and Emerson was as well. We all went round Emerson's house when we were in Brazil and used his pool. They were good times. At a couple of hotels there were stunts like, buckets of water on top of the door. We teased him, and there's no doubt that he really enjoyed it, just generally messing around.'

Ronnie wasn't an instigator of practical jokes like Graham Hill, although, as Keith Leighton observed, he was frequently in on a prank. 'You'd probably get the talcum powder out of the toilet on the plane put on you. You'd wake up covered in all this white stuff thanks to Peterson.' His classic trick was when weather conditions were bad, for example on a freezing day. 'He'd take you out to the pub for lunch,' said Keith, 'and drive like a maniac, knowing full well he was going to scare the life out of you. Because he was unbelievable on ice and snow. His driving was 10 levels above everyone else from being brought up in Sweden. He'd always pick somewhere 20 miles away!'

Howden confirmed: 'Whenever we were going somewhere and Ronnie was driving, the rest of us would make a drve for the rear seats. Nobody wanted to be in the front passenger seat. We were amazed at the way Barbro would just sit calmly there as if we were doing 20mph in the car park, while the rest of us would be crouched down in the back.'

Small town values

Ronnie was the boy from the sticks who came good, a trajectory that took him from lift installer to international hero. A boy like any other, but made magical by his sublime talent. Even though his inherent ability was honed by experience and his temperament and tastes grew more sophisticated, his small town essence remained intact. Lars Berntson described him as, 'a very normal individual, who just happened to have an extraordinary talent. He was shy and didn't really like large groups of people.'

He would have liked to have a dog, but that wasn't a practical proposition. His hobby was keeping tropical fish, a contemplative, almost nerdy pastime, like James Hunt's budgerigar breeding. Said Torsten Palm, 'every time we went to see him we had to go out shopping for fishes for his aquarium. It was a saltwater aquarium. That meant it was difficult to manage, because of the mix of the water, and the colour of the fishes was very special. And it was a big tank, I can tell you.' To be precise, 250 litres, according to Kenneth Olausson. Lars Berntson confirmed this. 'He had two big passions in his life, and the other one was fish tanks. I had one before he did, but his was bigger, and he kept on asking me, "Lars, isn't it time you got yourself a decent fish tank?"' Piko Troberg recalled, 'My wife Lena and I used to stay with him and Barbro in Maidenhead, and all he thought of was motor racing, Barbro, and his goldfish. And golf.' Ronnie's aquarium occupied almost an entire wall of the sitting room at his Farthingales home in Maidenhead. He loved to spend hours with his fish, nurturing them and feeding them. By 1976, Ronnie owned several horses, the kind harnessed to lightweight racing sulkies. He stabled them at the Baltic town of Gävle, 200km north of Stockholm. The best horse was called Mogens Palaix, and the driver was Bjorn Svensson.

Child's play

Ronnie was happy fooling about with children, rolling around on the floor with Brodie's son, spraying each other with squeezy lemons as water pistols. After he crashed the March 712 at Mallory Park, one of the spectators to receive minor cuts from flying fibreglass was a small boy. Ronnie autographed a piece of the March bodywork and sent it to him. In the paddock after the 1977 Italian Grand Prix Ronnie and Barbro were relaxing in the Elf-Tyrrell enclave with friends and team members, a familiar scene after any event. At Monza the tifosi were so desperate for souvenirs and stickers that a rope barrier restrained those that had infiltrated the paddock's inner sanctum. From here they hailed Ronnie and implored him for his autograph, something he was normally happy to provide. So he sauntered over to the clamouring fans behind the cordon, signed a few programmes and returned to the motorhome. As he sat at a table, a tiny little boy who had crawled under the rope, about three years old, touched him lightly on the arm, proffering a pencil and paper. Delighted, Ronnie signed his name and the boy made his way back behind the barrier. The child was relieved of the pencil and paper by their owner, handed another set and ushered back to Peterson's table. The same ruse worked three times, as Ronnie was clearly amused by it. Then a teenager tried it, and that was the end of the game.

Constant companion

From 1970, Ronnie's constant companion was his girlfriend and, later, wife, the beautiful Barbro Edvardsson. She too came from Örebro, and they met in the town's Prisma disco around 1968. She worked as a secretary, and during 1969 went to New York as an au pére before returning for the 1970 racing season. The fundamental backbone of his life in the '70s was this enduring relationship, despite some casual womanising away from home. She accompanied Ronnie and the team entourage to the races, taking the vital role of his timekeeper, perched on the pit counter or pit wall, unfailingly friendly. Ronnie and Barbro made their home in England, first at Maidenhead, then nearby Cookham Dean; they took a flat in Monaco, and had a holiday home in Sweden at Askersund near Örebro. They were married in 1975, and their daughter Nina was born in November that year. Ronnie and Barbro stayed together from 1970 until his death, despite the friction that threatened to unbalance the relationship in 1978, mostly due to Ronnie's growing frustrations with his lot at Team Lotus. Ronnie's mechanic Keith Leighton also knew Barbro very well. *'I knew them right from when they were first dating in 1970. I think Rouen was the first race she went to, so I got to know her then, saw them getting married. They were together constantly. It was pretty neat.'*

Ronnie's death was also essentially Barbro's, since she never recovered from it and died in 1987, either deliberately or from an accidental overdose of drink and drugs, leaving their 12 year old daughter Nina.

Outside motor racing

Lars Berntson and his wife Hélène were just about the only friends that Ronnie and Barbro had outside of motor racing, and provided a Swedish home-from-home for them in England. Lars was managing director of the car body repair company Plastic Padding, and met Ronnie through Gerth ('Jack') Elverskog, managing director of Vick's promotions company Merrill Richardson who had first sponsored Ronnie under the Smog brand. He endorsed Plastic Padding for 'two-tenths of nothing', just for the fun of it and because he was extremely good friends with Lars.

Ronnie and Barbro were frequent visitors at the Berntson home, a spacious split-level house near Maidenhead built in the early 1970s. *'They would just turn up out of the blue'* said Lars. *'You'd just say, come in, sit down, and Barbro would grab some of the Swedish papers and magazines we subscribed to. We had a lot of fun in a normal sort of way. Ronnie would take my daughter for a spin on the garden tractor to teach her how to drive, and we'd have barbecues in the summer when he wasn't racing. Every Thursday in the winter they'd come round for the traditional supper of pea soup and punch.'* Like Brodie before him, Larsexperienced the forcefulness of Ronnie's road driving. In 1975 they went to Sweden for Christmas in convoy. *'We were catching a ferry from Felixstowe, and Ronnie asked to follow me as he wasn't sure of the way, even though it was in the direction of Lotus. It was very foggy, we were running late and I was driving as fast as I possibly could. The whole journey, his Mercedes-Benz was literally inches away from the boot of my XJ6. Every roundabout was a challenge. At one T-junction where we had to come to a halt unexpectedly, he swerved alongside me, looked out of the side window, beamed and stuck his thumb up. When we got to Harwich I was knackered. Barbro came up to me with Nina in her arms and said, "Lars, thank you so much for driving so slowly - I haven't been scared once!"* Barbro seldom put a brake on Ronnie's racing activities, though she was often terrified. She put her foot down when Ronnie was invited to drive in the Indianapolis 500, refusing to let him go. A little surprising that Ronnie submitted, given how careful he was with money and the potential earnings to be made at the 'Brickyard'. Eating out, Ronnie enjoyed a steak but his favourite food was Italian, and any pasta dish. He liked all pop music. But despite the attractions of Swedish liqueurs and punch, he hardly ever touched a drop of alcohol. Lars threw a party in March 1978, when Ronnie had just come back from beating Depailler at the South African Grand Prix. *'He was so happy about that,'* said Lars. *'We'd laid flares up the drive to stop people driving in,'* he said. *'Then all of a sudden, there was Ronnie's car right outside the house. I said, "What about the flares then?" and he said, "Oh, I thought you'd put the landing lights on for me!" We had a rum punch on the go, and he asked me for a glass. Until that day he'd never, to my knowledge, drunk spirits. It took him five minutes to drink it. He asked me for another one, and drained the punchbowl into his glass. Next time I saw him, he was reeling a bit. I think it was the only time I saw him a little bit drunk*

Barbro withdraws

Because she had been so completely absorbed in his racing life, Barbro was terribly lonely after Ronnie died. For four or five years she had a relationship with John Watson, but it never filled the gap left by Ronnie. A regular visitor to the Berntson's, towards the end of her life she began to withdraw. Lars said, *'we always invited her but we could sense that things weren't right. She would phone an hour before a dinner party and say she wasn't feeling up to it. Barbro was in love with only one person in her life. Ronnie was her hero and her only love. She needed the fatherly feel of John, and he wanted them to both sell up and move down to somewhere like Hampshire together. But she wouldn't, because her house was like a mausoleum after Ronnie died, with every trophy and every photograph on display.'*

Peter Warr also had a first-hand view of Ronnie and Barbro's relationship: *'The lifestyle she led and the happiness she found with Ronnie was totally irreplaceable. She wouldn't have found it with anyone else. They were made for each other, and they were just delirious that things worked out so well. They loved life and they loved each other.'*

After Barbro died, Nina went back to Sweden to stay first with Ronnie's brother Tommy and then with her Peterson grandparents, but she didn't get on with her relatives that well. *'She carried a lot with her, but she really got a hold of her life,'* said Lars. In the late 1990s she found a new family with the Kennedys, enjoying life with fiancé and now husband Calle-Johan and his siblings. They were mutual friends of the Berntsons and, Nina had actually met Calle-Johan when aged about seven at their house. Nina was one of a number of motor racing children from that era, such as Guido Schenken, Natasha Rindt and, and still keeps in touch with one or two of them. She has survived the loss of her parents with dignity and courage, and is now living back in Sweden.

Ronnie Peterson: Super Swede

CHAPTER 02

Country boy made good

Ronnie Peterson was born at Örebro in central Sweden on St Valentine's Day – 14th February – 1944. The family home was – still is – in Hjälmarvägen in the Almby district on the south-eastern edge of town. There's a campus university there now, and industrial estates have filled in some of what would have been green-belt in Ronnie's day. Almby is middle-class residential, and the older houses can't have changed much. They are typically Swedish, wooden-clad, often with mansard roofs, and painted dark red, white, yellow or pale blue.

Opposite: Early training with *'the thing'* on snow and ice ensured that Ronnie was happy going sideways.

A two-hour drive west of Stockholm at the end of Hjälmaren lake, Örebro isn't near anywhere in particular. It's a provincial city of about 200,000 people, with a magnificent castle and an old nucleus, and modern suburbs. The surrounding countryside is a mixture of flat, arable farmland and pine forest, though it's only half-an-hour's drive south to the enormous Vättern lake. In the early 1970s, Ronnie and Barbro bought a holiday home – traditional dark red wood with white windows – in the forest at nearby Askersund. Ronnie's brother Tommy (two years younger), an emergency optician, moved back into the family home after their parents died in the late 1990s. Tommy Peterson realised early on that his brother was the favoured son because of his extraordinary talent. *'He knew what Ronnie could do in a car,'* said Sveneric Eriksson, later Ronnie's media relations man. The Peterson brothers didn't get on that well, and Tommy was always overshadowed by Ronnie in terms of parental attention. *'At times that was hard to swallow,'* said Sveneric. *'He's still a bit resentful. That part of the Peterson family was not particularly happy.'* Tommy went along to the Scandinavian races in the role of helper rather than mechanic, and later attended some of the European F1 races such as Monaco. Tommy never did any circuit racing but rallied in obsolete cars, doing fairly well so long as he remained on the track. *'A number of friends have fond memories of "Wild Tommy" in a superb-sounding but very fragile Renault Gordini, applying incredible opposite lock in true Peterson family tradition,'* said Sveneric.

In the mid-20th century, the Petersons were prosperous bakers, and Ronnie and Tommy's father Bengt was a bakery technician who, armed with an engineering qualification, found ways to improve processing in the family business. Bengt was an inventor in the same mould as the fledgling Colin Chapman. One of his first creations was a single-cylinder 125cc front-wheel drive vehicle built for his boys that was a cross between a garden tractor and a go-kart. It was here that eight-year-old Ronnie got the taste for driving, hurling the precarious 8mph device – known as *'the thing'* – around the Peterson's back garden and the lanes south of Örebro.

Bengt was an amateur racing driver and scrambles motorcyclist, so it was only natural that Ronnie should become involved with his father's passion. Bengt and his associate Sven Andersson, who worked at a local Renault garage, built and raced mid-engined 500cc Formula 3 'midget' cars, which were popular in Sweden in the early 1950s, and this was Ronnie's introduction to motorsport. Sveneric tells the tale of young Ronnie making his presence felt at an ice-race. *'There was an event held every winter on a frozen lake near Örebro, attended by thousands of people. One year, Bengt Peterson and Sven Anderson were helping to get the course on the ice ready for the race, and they'd brought a Renault Frégate with them to race. Suddenly an engine started up in the paddock, being revved sky high. Who should it be but Ronnie, aged 10, who had jumped into the car and started it up. He didn't go anywhere, but Bengt had to fit new pedals as Ronnie had stood on them and bent them.'*

Also hailing from Örebro, Sveneric first met Ronnie at a combined car and speedway meeting where Bengt Peterson was racing his *'midget'* – a 500cc Formula 3 JAP-engined car. *'Bengt was reasonably well known and, as his son, 12 year old Ronnie was allowed to drive the car for three laps. But he ignored the signals and, much to the amusement of the 10,000 strong crowd, he kept lapping until he ran out of fuel. That was typical Ronnie, even then.'*

Ronnie was more interested in the bikes and, of the stunts that children do; he could balance on a stationary bicycle for a long time without putting a foot on the ground. He created a dirt track for bicycles in the school playing field. He hated football at school and deliberately walked, rather than ran, after the ball just to wind everyone up. So they put the action man in goal, which he loathed even more. He sometimes played handball, ice hockey and brenball (like baseball), and was quite good at high jump and long jump, but claimed he never had an eye for ball games. When he came to the UK in 1971 he played golf, tennis and squash, but still felt the ball was out to trick him – strange for one with such incredible hand to eye co-ordination.

'Ronnie was never into books,' laughed Sveneric. *'Emmo gave him his 'World Championship' book...and Ronnie just about managed the preface! He was no star at school. Best item on the school curriculum for him was the End of Day Bell.'* As far as girls were concerned, Ronnie was a slow starter, though he later made up for lost time. Said Sveneric, *'he was more into bikes, mopeds, karting and then proper racing cars. But no serious motor-bikes! He always said I would kill myself on my various Nortons, Velocettes, Hondas and so on.'*

Ronnie wasn't one for sitting around at home. *'I wouldn't say he joined a gang, exactly,'* said Sveneric, *'but he certainly had a bunch of friends he mucked about with.'* He quit school aged 16, as early as possible, electing to train as a fitter at the local Renault franchise. He bought a 50cc scrambles bike and did well in local competitions, and was on the point of trading up to a 250cc machine when the bike was stolen. Instead of borrowing the money to buy a new bike from his dad, Ronnie persuaded Bengt to help him get into karting. Toward the end of 1961, father and son began to build their vehicle. It was powered by a German 200cc Ardie engine, and christened Robardie – a combination of Ronnie, Bengt and Ardie. The name endured throughout the 1960s as Squadra Robardie.

First kart race

Ronnie belonged to his local motor club, B & MCK. Aged 18, his first kart race was at Höör, 25 miles north-east of Malmö in February 1962. It was a popular karting venue, with at least 3,000 spectators in attendance to see the very first race on tarmac; previously they'd raced on gravel. Ronnie won by three seconds after a close contest with local aces Conny Holmberg from Vaxjo and Åke Persson from Malmö. The latter was one of Ronnie's main opponents, with many victories to his credit. The day's final event was the Höör race, and Ronnie came fourth behind Sven Faijersson and Persson.

Meetings at Laxa, Malmö and Gothenburg followed, and Ronnie finished second to established star Ingvar Nilsson in the race that counted for the national championship. When Nilsson retired at the end of '62, Bengt Peterson bought his 250cc Bultaco engine and installed it in a brand-new home-made chassis. This was a lightweight device, made mostly from aluminium and titanium, with

Chapter 02: Country boy made good 26 | 27

Opposite Left: Having started on scramble bikes, Ronnie never lost his appetite for two wheels. **Opposite Right:** Ronnie's first kart was the home-built Robardie, powered by a 200cc Ardie engine.
Above: He learned his racecraft on karts, winning Swedish titles in 1963 and 1964 and placing 3rd in the world class A series in 1966

Ronnie Peterson: Super Swede

AFTER FIVE
SEASONS IN
KARTS, TAKING
IN AS MANY AS
35 MEETINGS A
SEASON, IT WAS TIME
FOR RONNIE TO GRADUATE
TO RACING CARS, AND
BENGT RESOLVED
TO BUILD ONE
FOR RONNIE
HIMSELF.

Opposite: Two blonde Swedes – Ronnie's main rival in F3 was fellow countryman Reine Wisell. **Above:** Oversteering wildly in the home-built Svebe. Peterson always gave 100 percent.

negative camber a new sophistication on the rear suspension. In 1963, Ronnie blew away the opposition to win almost every race he contested, using the mysteries of oversteer to great effect. At the end of September, he dominated the 30-lap national championship class D race at Kilafors, near Bollnaes in northern Sweden, beating Åke Persson, who was the only driver not to be lapped. Again, some 3,000 spectators turned out watch. By the end of the season Peterson's kart featured disc brakes and magnesium alloy wheels.

Emboldened by success, Ronnie and Bengt decided that for 1964 they would get into international karting, and entered Class A for 100cc machines with no clutch or gears and minimum weight limit of 115 kg. In the four national championship races, Ronnie dominated totally and would have swept the board, had he not hit engine trouble in the first race on 31st May at Aelmhult in Smaaland. He finished fifth, but smashed the opposition in the subsequent races.

Ronnie drove a twin-engined kart powered by a pair of 100cc units for the first time in a local meeting at Skövde on June 13th, entered in both the new C-international Class and the A-international Class. He won both events in his own inimitable style. Ronnie also took part in Class D of the Nordic championship for 200cc motorcycle-engined karts with gearboxes at the Knutstorpring on 8th August. He had a fierce battle with Leif Engström and they led the rest by more than half a lap. But 500m before the finish, Leif's crankshaft snapped and blew his engine, handing Ronnie the win and the Nordic title as well. Then in the national Class A championship race at Malmö on 17th October, Ronnie out-performed everyone in the final, placing third in the title stakes. By now he was working for BPA, a local firm of lift installers in Örebro to fund his karting.

Ronnie won the European Karting Championship in 1966, and set his sights on that year's World Championship as well. He went to Copenhagen for the final on 25th September with the title in his sights, and reigning champion Suzanna Raganelli the only rival who could snatch the crown away from him. Peterson's Bultaco engine misfired, and several changes failed to cure the problem. He and his father later discovered that the carburettor float was cracked. Although they'd swapped engines, they hadn't changed the carburettor. So Ronnie had to be content with third place, after a 15-lap qualifying race and three finals of 20, 30 and 50 laps respectively. Ronnie came seventh, third and fourth in the finals and trailed Suzi Raganelli by 14 points as she won all three finals. He compensated for his failure to beat her on the track by going out with her instead. Although she was some years older than him, it was an affair that lasted two or three years. Ronnie visited Suzi in Italy, and began to feel very much at home there.

Graduation to cars

Ronnie didn't give up on karts entirely. He did a few a 3-hour long-distance races in 1966 and 1967 with Lars Lindberg, later a competitive car racer in Sweden. In one such event at the Stockholm track of Upplands Vasby on 4th November 1967 they looked certain winners until Ronnie made a rare mistake and crashed while avoiding another kart, and they dropped back to finish third, three laps behind the winners.

After five seasons in karts, taking in as many as 35 meetings a season, it was time for Ronnie to graduate to racing cars, and Bengt resolved to build one for Ronnie himself. Before he could go circuit racing, Ronnie needed a competition licence, and so he had to undergo a course of instruction. The closest circuit to Örebro was half an hour west at Gällerasen, just outside Karlskoga. The instructor was Reine Wisell, another blond Swede, three years older than Ronnie and, since 1962, a saloon car racer in Mini-Coopers and a Ford Anglia. His best place was sixth in the national championship. In 1966 Reine bought himself an F3 Cooper, initiating three years of intense rivalry between the two drivers.

Ronnie turned up for his 'instruction' in his father's Mercedes-Benz, and Reine realised immediately that Peterson was something special – *'he was very quick and very brave'* – although he hadn't heard of him before then. Later that day there was a race for the new candidates in racing school F3 cars, which Ronnie duly won.

Ronnie Peterson: Super Swede

The car that Ronnie, Bengt and Sven Andersson constructed was a neat, no-frills copy of a contemporary spaceframe Brabham BT15, which they called the Svebe. *'It cost much more to build than it would to have bought a secondhand Brabham in the first place,'* said Sveneric, *'even though much of the chassis componentry was gleaned from old Swedish fighter planes.'* No wonder, then, that Ronnie always got on well with his mechanics, since he knew just what it meant to build a car from the ground up. The Svebe chassis weighed 41 kilos, with Brabham BT15 suspension and Triumph front hub-carriers. Dimensions were similar to the Brabham. *'I guess it's a copy to a large extent,'* Bengt told Kenneth Olausson. *'The width is a little larger and therefore the track is also wider.'* The Svebe was well made, and sufficient care was taken to have copies made of the Brabham wheels, stamped *'Svebe'*. By way of a guide at 1966 prices, an F3 Brabham cost £2,275, including a 116bhp 1.0-litre Cosworth MAE or SCA *'screamer'* with single sidedraught or, later, downdraught carburettor. And, if you were lucky, set up by Jack Brabham in person. The Svebe turned up again in 2003 and was all set to be restored by Steve Worred's Maverick Motorsport in the UK.

Ronnie's first F3 race was the inaugural meeting at the community-built Dalslandring, near Bengtsfors in western Sweden. Ronnie finished a good third, his best result in 1966 season. He campaigned the Svebe in other Swedish and Danish F3 events at Knutstorp, Mantorp Park, the Kinnekullering, Falkenberg, Karlskoga, the airfield track at Skelleftea, and Skarpnack, Stockholm. A significant mishap occurred when the mechanic Ove Hedlund, driving the VW pick-up truck carrying the Svebe, fell asleep on the return journey to Örebro and hit a bridge, scattering the transporter's contents all over the road. Another mechanic was Åke Strandberg, who became a life-long friend. A native of Örebro, he went to some of the kart and F3 races with Ronnie as his mechanic when Bengt had commitments at the bakery.

With suspension designs evolving each season, the Petersons' best bet was to buy a more modern car, and at the end of 1966, Ronnie acquired a Brabham BT18 from the German star Kurt Ahrens, known as *'the last of the late brakers.'* The one major modification they had to make to the BT18 was to increase the height of the roll-over bar at a race at Karlskoga, where scrutineer Lasse Backman wouldn't pass the car until a taller hoop was fitted. This order was thoroughly justified as Ronnie subsequently turned the car over. *'He was a bit slow off the line,'* said Sveneric, *'and he was catching up and passing slower cars. He wanted to brake at his usual marker for a particular bend, but the guy in front wanted to brake earlier. Ronnie went off the circuit, and he ended up upside down almost in the trees. He was very grateful that the scrutineer had made him raise the height of the roll-hoop, although at the time he was pretty angry about the accident.'*

The Brabham saw Ronnie through 1967, and his first proper encounter with the international F3 brigade at Karlskoga. New Zealander Howden Ganley was one of Ronnie's closest friends, and they met in 1967 when Howden started in F3. *'As I did quite a lot of racing in Denmark, Sweden and Finland, I got to know most of the Swedish drivers'* he said. *'Fortunately for me, most of them spoke English. Most of us were trekking from race to race, living out of our vans. Ronnie had an Econoline, a bit better than most. At that time the Scandinavian organisers paid reasonable starting money and a fair bit of prize money, so it was possible to scratch a living from racing there. Ronnie was a bit shy, and his English was not so good as say, Reine Wisell or Ulf Svensson.'*

F3 gypsies

The Formula 3 circus travelled all around Europe, gypsy fashion, taking in a race every weekend, some of which counted towards the European F3 championship. In the 1967 season there were 65 Formula 3 events up for grabs, sometimes supporting the Grand Prix events but more often at obscure tracks like Chimay in Belgium, Vallelunga near Rome, and Brno in Czechoslovakia. Most drivers operated hand-to-mouth, running one- or two-year old chassis on shoe-string budgets, with only a clutch of works (Matra), works-backed or wealthy teams (Charles Lucas) competing with state-of-the-art machinery. Start money was around £125, depending on reputation, and £140 for a win (at Karlskoga,

Opposite & Above: Through 1967 Ronnie used a secondhand Brabham BT18 in the Swedish series, coming 5th overall. He also took in European events in Portugal, Denmark, Germany, Finland and the UK. The most significant modification made to the car was extending and bracing the roll-over hoop.

Ronnie Peterson: Super Swede

Above: In 1968, Ronnie and Reine collected their new Tecnos. Although they were rivals, Wisell mostly raced abroad while Peterson tended to concentrate on the domestic series in 1968, winning the Swedish F3 title.

for instance – much less in the UK). Bonuses from tyre, fuel and spark-plug companies bolstered competitors' funds. To be in with a chance of earning decent prize money as well as start money, the journeymen drivers avoided the more important races where top-line contenders tended to clean up. Nevertheless, Formula 3 was highly competitive at all levels, and no place for the faint-hearted. Races were driven flat-out, on the limit, for the duration. The specification of the cars was near-identical, so it was all down to driver technique, skill and bravery. A missed shift or muffed turn-in allowed one, or several, cars past. It was the perfect school of hard knocks for aspiring Formula 1 world champions. The drivers needed sharp wits, emotional control and quantities of talent to win out. The ladder to Formula 1 was less complicated in the mid-1960s than it became in the 1970s when entry-level championships proliferated for Formula Ford, Formula Vee and other one-make series. Back then the bottom rung was Formula 3, with Formula 2 the equivalent of today's F3000. If you were ambitious to climb the motor racing ladder, you had to be a winner in Formula 3. Tim Schenken outlined the itinerary: *'In 1969, I was driving the works-assisted Brabham BT28 Formula 3 car, run by Rodney Bloor and Sports Motors, and we went into Europe where we raced at a lot of supporting events for F1 and F2. The F1 venues were Monte Carlo of course, Barcelona, the British Grand Prix, and in F2 it was the same, with races at Pau, Jarama, Hockenheim and Zolder, but really we raced all through Europe, right up to Scandinavia.'*

The leading light in Swedish F3 was Picko Troberg, who'd started in Formula Junior in 1961 and raced in F3 until 1967. *'I was a regular in F3,'* said Picko, *'racing against people like the Brambilla brothers, Jonathan Williams, Henri Pescarolo and Clay Regazzoni. We had fantastic times. People travelled from circuit to circuit, camping in tents, and making a small living out of racing. For a while Frank Williams was staying in my flat in Stockholm, wheeling and dealing. They were good memories.'* Picko's best result in 1966 was second to Peter Revson at Montlhéry in the Paris GP. He recalled Ronnie coming on the scene in the Svebe that year. *'Very soon we recognised that this boy would be very good,'* he said. Picko also drove the Swedish BMC importer's Mini-Coopers, and owned a Lola T70 as well. *'The Lola was too big for my liking,'* he said. *'So I gave Ronnie his first chance to drive a big car at international level. He raced the Lola T70 in France – at Magny Cours I think it was – and the Österreichring. He won in France but went into a ditch in Austria.'*

Several of the top F3 crews were invited to the 1967 Karlskoga race, including Chris Irwin in the Chequered Flag Brabham, and Roy Pike and Piers Courage in the Charles Lucas team's quasi-works Lotus 41s. Ronnie qualified 15th, and was involved in a dice with another Scandinavian driver when Pike came up to lap him. Ronnie politely moved over, only for Pike to edge him into the gully at the side of the track as they exited the corner. Ronnie recovered from his *'moment'* in the ditch and, pondering the American's tactics, contemplated whether to remonstrate after the race. Prudently, he decided not to make an issue of it, but it was another lesson in hard-nosed racecraft.

Another brush with the international elite took place in Finland. The Scandinavian countries occasionally invited the top F2 teams to race against home-grown stars, and in 1967 a combined F2 and F3 grid was assembled at Keimola by the king of F2, Jochen Rindt, and his Finnish father-in-law and F3 racer, Kurt Lincoln. Heading the entry were Jim Clark, Graham Hill, Jack Brabham, Frank Gardner and Alan Rees. Ronnie acquitted himself well in practice, attracting the attention of Rees, who ran the Winkelmann F2 team for Rindt and himself. This performance would stand Ronnie in good stead a couple of years later when Rees was forming the March team.

Foreign venture

In 1967, the dominant marque in European F3 was the two-car works Matra squad, with the ubiquitous Brabhams normally filling the rest of the top ten places and the occasional Lotus and Alpine muscling in on the results sheets.

Ronnie took in a couple of races abroad that year. To make his debut on the European F3 scene, he travelled to Vila Real in northern Portugal in July, but hit a kerb bordering the street circuit during practice, taking a wheel off the

Above: Racing the Tecno in 1969 brought many slipstreaming battles, culminating in the F3 win at Monaco that made his name, as well as the national and European titles. Ronnie always wanted a dog!

Brabham. By carefully pop-riveting the upright back together he managed to do three laps of the race before it collapsed again, long enough to earn the start money that would pay for his petrol back to Sweden. This event was won by Chris Williams, with Reine Wisell second. Ronnie's next foreign outing was at Brands Hatch, accompanied by the more experienced Swedish F3 aces Freddy Kottulinsky and Ulf Svensson. Rough seas delayed the ferry by almost a day, so practice time on the undulating Kentish circuit was negligible, and Ronnie failed to qualify. Otherwise, he was restricted to taking part in Swedish national meetings in 1967. 'He wasn't from a particularly wealthy background,' said Picko Troberg. *'A young boy couldn't afford to go out on the international circuit without backing.'*

Another contemporary on the Scandinavian F3 scene was Torsten Palm, younger brother of rally star Gunnar. Torsten bought his first car from Ulf Svensson at Bengtsfors, and he and Ronnie remained very close friends from September 1968 until Peterson's death ten years later. Said Torsten: *'I first met Ronnie in 1967 when we were both driving in Formula 3. At that time he was living with his parents in Örebro. There were no girlfriends, and he was very focussed on what he was doing. His father was always there in the pits, and they transported everything around in a blue and yellow VW van. In the autumn of '69 I got this van from him, because he bought a converted Mercedes bus. Half of it was for the racing car, half was a bed-and-breakfast area. He had a very good mechanic in 1969, Ove Hedlund from the north of Sweden.'* For 1968, Ronnie resolved to push the boat out. He learned that Reine Wisell intended to buy a Tecno and, knowing the Bolognese marque extremely well from his karting days, decided that could be the way forward. Among the F3 fraternity, Clay Regazzoni was making a name for himself with a Tecno, winning at Jarama at the end of 1967. Bengt and Ronnie went to see their bank manager, who agreed to a loan despite the fact that its intended use was unclear. It's more likely that house-purchase was mentioned rather than a new piece of kit for Squadra Robardie.

Ronnie and Reine travelled to Bologna together to collect their new Tecnos. Reine confirmed: *'the Tecno was the best F3 car at that moment.'* Showing that he meant business, Wisell promptly won at Jarama and Barcelona, placing second at Pau in south-west France to Pike's Titan. At the Anderstorp International meeting, Reine won again, beating the Titan of Trevor Blodyk and Ulf Svensson's Brabham. Ronnie was not so quick to show his hand. At the Monza Lottery in April '68 he came fourth in the flat-out slipstreaming maelstrom, while Reine came fifth. The winner was Jean-Pierre Jaussaud in a works Matra, and it was this experienced Frenchman who led the field home at the hotly contested F3 race that acted as curtain-raiser for the Monaco Grand Prix on 25th May. Jaussaud was in a Tecno this time, followed by Peter Gethin in a Chevron, while Ronnie was third. Close behind him was François Cevert in another Tecno. These were the hot-shoes whose names crop up again and again in the Peterson saga.

Ronnie's first win came in the Solituderennen held at Hockenheim on 21st July, the aggregate result of two heats. Ronnie and his Squadra Robardie mechanic Ove Hedlund devised a means of carrying extra fuel in the oil catch tank to avoid the possibility of running dry but, understandably, this was disallowed by the scrutineers. He and Freddy Kottulinsky schemed a strategy whereby they would tow each other along the long straights and pull away from the rest of the pack – normal practice in fact – although Ronnie came off best, beating his miffed countryman to the chequered flag. By this time Reine Wisell had notched up four wins on the international circuit, but Ronnie pulled off another one at Hameenlina in Finland on 18th August, seeing off local whiz-kid Leo Kinnunen and Ulf Svensson in the process.

Torsten Palm recalled a particular race involving Ronnie: *'One time, in Knutstorp in August '68, he was the hero, and I was really hungry to beat him. I came up alongside and gave him a nudge, and he was so angry at me, he didn't talk to me for a few weeks. He was Formula 3 king at that time. He left Knutstorp, which is in the south of Sweden, and went to the airport in Malmö, but he was so angry that he left his passport in the pits.'* This was in contrast to his later coolness under pressure. Kenneth Olausson observed that he learned to deal with such confrontational scenes and matured as his career progressed.

Left: The F3 field take off at Monaco in 1969. **Right:** Taller than average, (second from right) at the pre-race drivers' briefing at Monaco with, amongst others, Jaussaud and Pianta.

Meanwhile, other winners that year included John Miles in the works Lotus 41X, Jean-Pierre Jabouille in a Matra, Clay Regazzoni, Peter Westbury, Peter Gethin, Patrick Dal-Bo, Cevert and newcomer Tim Schenken.

Gearing up

The lanky Australian Schenken was to become his best mate after Tim and Ronnie had first met in 1968 at the Brands Hatch Guards Trophy meeting in October. Hailed as the next Jackie Stewart, Schenken had become almost unbeatable in Formula Ford that year, winning 27 out of 30 races in a works Merlyn. By mid-season he was also driving in F3 for Rodney Bloor's Sports Motors Manchester team in a Chevron, and won the 1968 Lombank F3 Championship as well as a Grovewood Award. 'One of the reasons why I was so competitive was that I was meticulous about the setting up of my car,' said Tim. 'The Ford-Cosworth SCA engines used a single-choke restricted carburettor and they were very high revving, up to 10,000 rpm. But they had very little torque, so the gear ratios were very important. The gear ratios one used were pretty much a secret, which everyone kept them to themselves. The cars only had four-speed gearboxes, so this placed even more emphasis on correct gearing.' Schenken recalled the Brands Hatch meeting. 'A young blond chap came up to me in the Brands Hatch paddock. He was a Swedish kid named Ronnie Peterson. He was running a Tecno, and he'd had a bit of trouble in practice. Like most Europeans or Scandinavians when they came to England, he had great difficulty in getting used to the English circuits, especially the Brands Hatch Grand Prix circuit. There was something in his manner and appearance that struck a chord, and he asked me for the appropriate gear ratios for the track. Even though I was very protective of my car's set up, especially the gear ratios, I gave him the information. And from that time on, we struck up a good friendship.' Schenken duly won that event from Tony Lanfranchi and Alan Rollinson.

Ironically, Brands Hatch became Ronnie's favourite circuit, his Woodcote cornering a treasured memory for race fans. Svenic Eriksson said: 'In those days it was more or less flat out, but there was also plenty of variety in the corners and ups and downs. It wasn't dangerous in the way the old Nürburgring was. He liked circuits that were challenging, and if they were difficult he could probably gain a tenth here, a tenth there. Whereas if it was a simple circuit, he couldn't really be bothered.'

Tim Schenken explained how his friendship with Ronnie blossomed: 'From 1968 onwards, Ronnie's path and mine followed very similar lines, the same with Emerson Fittipaldi, the three of us were racing in F3, then into F2 and then into F1. Formula 3 was close exciting racing and very popular, and Ronnie, as we all know, had outstanding skills. His car control was legendary. Whenever we were racing we were helping each other with circuit knowledge, and gear ratios and revs. I suppose that was data logging of a kind. You knew exactly what revs you were pulling out of all of the corners around the circuit, what revs you were pulling on the straight, you knew the gear ratios, and Ronnie and I would compare notes.'

Home-grown champion

Ronnie did enough to clinch the 1968 Swedish domestic F3 Championship, even if he hadn't impressed as much as Wisell on the international stage. Reine explained: 'I was under contract with Chevron in 1969, and we decided to continue to go international with F3 and sportscars with the B8. Being mostly in Europe seemed to have been the right way for me.' But the results counted where it mattered, in the Swedish media. This brought Ronnie to the attention of Per Cewrien who did PR for the Swedish branch of Richardson & Merrill pharmaceutical company. Their managing director was Gerth 'Jack' Elverskog, and he fixed Ronnie up with sponsorship from the SMOG brand of cough sweets. The SMOG sponsorship that year had enabled Ronnie to order a brand new Tecno from Bologna-based brothers Luciano and Gianfranco Pederzani for 1969 and fitted with one of their state-of-the-art 1.0-litre Novamotor-tuned Ford engines. During the course of the year he paid off the start-up bank loan and sold the VW truck to Torsten Palm to buy a more sophisticated Mercedes-Benz version.

Ronnie Peterson: Super Swede

Above: Jubilant at winning the prestigious Monaco F3 race in 1969. **Opposite:** Peterson's Tecno sweeps through the streets of the Principality.

Monte Carlo dust-up

The 1969 Monaco F3 race made Ronnie's future in world-class motor racing a certainty. Run in two heats and a final on the Saturday, between F1 qualifying, the event was expected to be confrontation between the Alpine-Renaults of Jabouille and Depailler and Jaussaud's Tecno. Instead it turned into a gripping showdown between the two Swedish aces, who'd won their respective heats. Peterson and Wisell charged off into the distance and no-one could stay with them. It was a close fought duel, with much wheel and tyre contact, kerb-hopping, and no quarter given; the lead changed more than ten times. The art of F3 slipstreaming was to avoid being in front until the very last moment, and Wisell was leading up to the last couple of laps when Ronnie forced him to brake just too late for the chicane on the harbour-front. The Chevron took to the escape road, and Ronnie was through to win by eight-seconds from his countryman. Jabouille was third and Schenken fourth. *'I had many memorable races,'* said Reine, *'but Monaco was a very good and hard race, perhaps a little bit extra as Ronnie was my greatest rival at that time.'* *'There was never a Formula 3 race like it, before or since,'* said Staffan Svenby, Ronnie's manager. Most drivers that win the Monaco F3 race go on to shine in Formula 1 – Stewart, Laffite, Pironi, Prost Kenneth Olausson saw the race and slept in Ronnie's Mercedes van: *'It was my first Grand Prix, and I remember thinking, "is it always as close and thrilling as this?" But of course it was not. That Monaco F3 race turned out to be one of a kind. When I came back to the van late that night there were a few envelopes containing telephone numbers under Ronnie's windshield wipers, which I gave to him the following morning.'*

The following weekend was the Spring Bank Holiday meeting at Crystal Palace in London. The F3 race became a contest between Peterson and his new friend Schenken. Time and again the lead changed as they ducked in and out of each other's slipstreams along Bottom Straight. Ronnie prepared to dart past Schenken as they emerged from the last corner but the plan was foiled by the presence in the corner of New Zealander Howden Ganley's Chevron which they'd come up to lap, and Ronnie had to stay put, ceding the win to Schenken.

In the paddock after the race, Ronnie was approached by Alan Rees, who was on the verge of hanging up his helmet to take on the role of team manager at March Engineering. He was still just running the hugely successful Winkelmann F2 team, and he invited Ronnie to take the second car for the remainder of the season. A nice thought, but Ronnie had already accepted another offer from Tecno. Alan Rees recalled the occasion: *'I first saw him in action in an F3 race at Crystal Palace. There were five or six drivers doing really well, Ronnie, Emerson, Reine, Howden Ganley, Tim Schenken and James Hunt. None of them were in F1, so it was just a question of trying to pick out the one most likely to succeed. In fact they were all pretty successful in the end, Emerson perhaps more than all of them. I liked Ronnie's style. In F2 I was a team-mate and a great friend of Jochen Rindt who had a particular style of driving, and Ronnie reminded me of Jochen. That's why I picked him.'* Rindt's F2 mechanic Peter Kerr agreed: *'Ronnie's style of driving was along the same lines as Jochen's, hanging the tail out, and Jochen was certainly a hero of Ronnie's in the early days. His sense of balance was incredible; he could stand still on a pushbike for ages. Those sorts of thing were easy for him.'*

The Monza Lottery for non-graded drivers in F2 cars was held on 22nd June, and this 45-lap thrash was Ronnie's first run in an F2 car – the works' Tecno, powered by a Ford 1.6-litre FVA unit. He was forcing his way up the field from a middling grid position, and led for several laps, until a brush with a barrier at the 140mph Lesmo curves obliged him to pit to have the tyre checked. He came seventh, still on the same lap as winner Robin Widdows. Thanks to the efforts of Alan Rees, Ronnie got another F2 outing at Albi in south west France on 14th September, this time driving Max Mosley's Lotus 59B under the Winkelmann Racing banner alongside Graham Hill and Jochen Rindt. Alan Rees: *'I was still with the Winkelmann team at that stage and we had Jochen and Graham Hill in the Lotus F2 cars. Max also had a Lotus F2 car and, after an off at the Nürburgring earlier in the year, decided he didn't want to drive anymore, and so we thought "lets make it a three car team for the last race at Albi." Ronnie drove that car. Graham won, Jochen was third and Ronnie was fifth. Jochen was very close to getting second and Ronnie was very close to getting fourth. So it was a good result.'* Ronnie was a couple of tenths behind Henri Pescarolo's Matra MS7, while Rindt was on the tail of Johnny Servoz-Gavin's Matra. There was another twist to this meeting. The Albi circuit consisted of three long straights linked by fast but bumpy corners. In practice Ronnie came onto the track in the wake of Stewart's Matra. He stayed with the maestro for five laps on the rain-drenched circuit, Stewart all the while wondering who's was the blue helmet. Said Mosley: *'I lent Alan my Lotus 59 and he put Ronnie in it. It was a wet practice, and Stewart was out in a Matra and Ronnie just followed him round. Stewart went faster and faster and Ronnie just sat there. That's the first time the world at large realised there was a big talent emerging.'*

Ronnie was active in other areas of the sport, and there were huge contrasts in the types of vehicle he handled. For example, he took part in the 1969 Swedish KAK rally in the ex-Bjorn Waldegaard VW 1600 TL. It was not a work's car, and not up to factory standard and certainly not well enough prepared to absorb Ronnie's driving style. He went off the road twice in the early stages, having to shovel snow for an hour in the first instance, then spending half-an-hour regaining the road, which points to high-speed exits on both occasions. The front end of the VW was damaged beyond repair, and Ronnie had to call it a day. *'It was a lot harder than I had anticipated,'* he commented dryly.

At Le Mans he drove a 7.0-litre Chevrolet Corvette in the GT category. Asked why the car appeared to be handling like a snake on the straight, Ronnie said, *'well, actually, I'm going flat out with the bastard, which won't go in a straight line.'* He retired after 16 hours with gearbox problems when lying 18th, having started from 26th on the grid. At six hours he was 19th, but a pit stop dropped him to 27th. This was the event won by Ickx/Oliver in a 5.0-litre John Wyer Ford GT40.

At the 1969 Kanonloppet meeting, Ronnie drove Jo Bonnier's Lola-Chevy T70 GT Mk 3B. He qualified third fastest and started from the front row alongside Brian Redman and David Piper, and led comfortably for nine laps until the heat in the cockpit became too intense. Both side windows were removed before the start to make it cooler, but Brian Redman's entrant, Sid Taylor, protested, so the windows were reinstated. After the race a sweating Peterson commented, *'it was maybe 70 degrees C in the car, so I had to back off, so Redman and eventually Piper came by.'* Ronnie was given water & grape sugar by the circuit medical team before climbing into his F3 Tecno for the main event. He beat Tim Schenken by four seconds, taking the European F3 championship honours, which was an unofficial title back then.

Wisell took his revenge at Brands Hatch in the Motor Show meeting on 1st Septemberber, beating the cream of British Formula 3 drivers, including Mo Nunn and Bev Bond. Qualifying for this event was the day after the F3 race at Knutstorp, where Ronnie came fourth in his Tecno. Scheduled flights from Sweden were in disarray, so a private plane was chartered to take Ronnie and Reine to Copenhagen airport. But Ronnie forgot his passport. Luckily the flight was delayed, so they made it to Brands Hatch after all. It proved impossible to air-freight his car, so Ronnie was lent an ex-work's Lotus instead. He finished 4th in the first heat and 2nd in the second, which meant he started from the fourth row. By one third distance he was lying fourth, and had just passed Jean-Pierre Jaussaud and Francois Mazet when the latter missed his braking point and mounted Ronnie's gearbox. And there he remained, while Ronnie was unable to dislodge him. *'I thought I'd loose him eventually,'* said Ronnie afterwards, *'but the damn Frenchman kept hanging in there on the back of my car.'* There was no alternative but to park up and get a marshal to lift Mazet off his car. He got going again, but the damage had been done. The throttle mechanism was sticking and the exhaust pipe was damaged.

Young guns in action

The most significant F3 meeting on the UK race calendar in 1969 was held at Cadwell Park, the wonderfully sinuous and undulating Lincolnshire track, on 28th September. It was the first international meeting there. The F3 cars lapped at around 85mph, and there were two 10-lap heats and a 25-lap final. Ronnie was

Opposite: Driving Jo Bonnier's Lola T70 to 3rd place at Karlskoga, 1969. **Above:** Tecno-crat - without doubt the dominant force in F3 during '69, Ronnie won 15 races in Sweden and Europe.

Ronnie Peterson: Super Swede

Top Left: After driving his Tecno all season, late in 1969 Ronnie drove the Winkelmann Lotus 59B at Albi alongside Rindt and Hill, coming home 5th. **Opposite:** He moved on to March for the F3 race at Cadwell Park, trying a full-face helmet for the first time. **Above:** In his usual style Ronnie hurls the Tecno to first place at Knutstorp in August 1969.

driving the brand new March 693-Novamotor, and recovered from a poor getaway in the first heat to challenge Schenken in the works Brabham BT28, only to struggle with a puncture that dropped him to fifth. This era marked the changeover from open-face to full-face helmets and, significantly, Ronnie's blue lid with its distinctive yellow peak was a full-face job, with a yellow band around the base. Heat two was led briefly by James Hunt's BT21 until he was demoted by the Chevrons of Wisell and Ganley. Schenken led the 22 cars away for the final, being passed by Charles Lucas and Wisell, with Peterson dicing with Hunt for fourth spot. After Lucas's engine blew, Schenken finally emerged the winner as Wisell spun off, with Ganley second and Peterson credited with fourth in an identical time with Hunt – the Cadwell timing mechanism couldn't split them.

Howden described the F3 scene in Sweden. *'We were over there for a series of races in late 1969, and Ronnie brought along his new girlfriend, Barbro. By then he was turning into a real star, and the "Ronnie and Reine Show" was in full swing, Reine with the Chevron, and Ronnie with the Tecno. They were pulling huge crowds at the races, and they were very helpful in ensuring that I also got good appearance money. The F3 European Championships were held at Karlskoga that year (the Swedes were the holders of the Trophy) and Ronnie won, Tim was second, and I was third, so it was good result for the old mates.'* Meanwhile, the UK's club-level Lombank F3 title was won in 1969 by Emerson Fittipaldi, who'd been driving the Jim Russell Lotus 59-Holbay.

A week after his dice with Hunt in the Cadwell Park F3 race, Ronnie took the March 693 to Montlhéry just south of Paris. The mighty banked circuit had a straw bale chicane, which Ronnie clipped as he challenged for the lead. The car flipped, snapping a wishbone, which pierced the fuel tank. As the car skated upside down along the track the spilled fuel ignited. It came to rest with Ronnie trapped in the cockpit. Fortunately, mechanic Ray Wardell had started running from the March pit the moment the accident happened. He, along with a couple of marshals, succeeded in extricating the Swede from the wreck. Ronnie spent two days in hospital with burns to wrists and arms, and returned to Örebro to recuperate. Max Mosley said: *'It was all quite a drama, but he recovered from that quickly enough.'*

In fact, Ronnie spent the long Swedish winter wondering whether he'd been right to commit to March, who were receiving a lot of flack in the specialist press for being over ambitious.

His first race after the Montlhéry accident was the Buenos Aires 1,000kms. The 1970 Temporada was for sports cars and sports prototypes, and Jo Bonnier offered Ronnie a drive in one of his two Lolas. He elected to drive the Lola T70 he'd handled at the '69 Kanonloppet where he'd come third in the stifling heat. Buenos Aires was no less warm, and Ronnie had to endure a hot cockpit, this time for 1,000km. But he survived, and took a fine third place.

A month later, the heat of Argentina was exchanged for the snow and ice back home. Ronnie wanted to have another go at the Swedish round of the World Rally Championship through the forests of Värmland, and borrowed a Porsche 911 from the importers Svenska Volkswagen. He was first away, chased by none other than rally ace Bjorn Waldegaard, also driving a 911 – but a work's car. Ronnie's co-driver was Torsten Palm. They'd done their reconnaissance and only went off once. It was a win or bust scenario and, as the previous year, Ronnie overdid it and lost it in the snow.

Ronnie Peterson: Super Swede

CHAPTER 03

Into The Big Time

March Engineering was an ambitious enterprise. The founders were erstwhile Clubmans and F2 racer Max Mosley, F2 driver and Winkelmann Racing team manager Alan Rees, amateur F3 racer Graham Coaker, and Robin Herd, ex-Cosworth and formerly McLaren's chief designer – hence the acronym MARCH.

This group of powerful personalities visualised not only an assault on F1, but also the creation of a business building F2, F3, Formula Ford, Formula Atlantic and CanAm customer cars. The Lotus group had been doing this sort of thing successfully for a decade, with Brabham and McLaren following suit.

The difference was that March seemed to be attempting it all in one go. That they brought it to fruition so quickly says much for their bravado, talent and dedication. In 1969 their F1 plans revolved around Jochen Rindt, a whirlwind who was as fast but less consistent than Stewart. The relationship between Rindt and Rees was based on a three-year association in the Winkelmann F2 team. Although contacted to Team Lotus, the Austrian also admired Herd, and sought to steer these elements of the March squad into setting up a Formula 1 operation catering just for his own requirements. It was a tempting prospect, but the March directors stuck together to pursue the commercial route. The first March F3 car, the 693 that Ronnie drove at Cadwell Park, was assembled in Graham Coaker's garage. Rindt, put out at Herd's rejection, sarcastically called it the Gremscheck, a corruption of 'Graham's shack.' 'We had no money at all,' said Robin Herd. 'Max had borrowed £10K, and Alan and I had £2.5K that we'd won by betting on Jackie Stewart to win the 1969 World Championship. Our total F1 sponsorship for 1970 was £10,000 from STP.' Ken Tyrrell paid £6,000 each for the 'customer' cars. 'It was a great adventure,' said Herd. 'We were young, everyone was keen, we were against the establishment, and people loved it.'

Mosley described the March operation in its early days: 'We didn't employ that many; it was a pretty small group of extraordinarily talented and hard working people. Plenty of all-nighters. It was like a war – a war on all fronts. We had no money, no time, very little facilities. The factory had only one pressing machine, so convincing people like Porsche (who were looking to buy Siffert a work's F1 drive) that we were going to produce F1 cars in three months time took a bit of doing. It was just non-stop. We'd just the one telephone that didn't really work because in those days you had to talk to the

Opposite: Impressed by his prowess in Formula 3, the March hierachy provided the means for Ronnie to move into F2 and F1.

Ronnie Peterson: Super Swede

operator if you wanted to make more than a local call, and we didn't even have a telex then. We were all kids by modern standards. I was 29, Robin was 30, Alan was 31. Graham Coaker was 37, and we thought he was a really old man. We thought everything was possible.' There were good reasons to believe it was, since the Robin Herd-designed CanAm McLarens had swept the board in 1967, and his McLaren M7A F1 car won its first two races in 1968. Meanwhile, Rindt was resigned to remaining at Team Lotus for 1970, where, frustrated by the performance of the new Type 63 four-wheel drive car and the ageing Type 49, he'd been pressuring Colin Chapman to get rid of his senior team-mate Graham Hill. When Hill had his big accident at Watkins Glen he effectively put himself out of the picture, leaving the Lotus stage free for Rindt.

With Rindt unavailable, March turned to the new generation. They were in competition with the established works teams, though. Fittipaldi was snapped up by Lotus, Schenken by Brabham, and Wisell and Ganley by McLaren. Ronnie had proved his ability beyond any doubt in F3, and shown sufficient potential in F2 to convince the directors to sign him up for 1970. Alan Rees: *'He had tremendous car control and he was a very straightforward person. He drove as his natural tendency was. To a large extent he would incorporate any faults with the car's handling into his driving style.'* As it turned out, events almost submerged Ronnie.

Star attractions

Good as Ronnie obviously was, it was clear to Mosley that the fledgling March team needed an established star for them to be taken seriously and to project their image. They hit on Chris Amon, the unluckiest driver in F1, who was fed up with his lack of success at Ferrari, which was over-committed in sports prototypes, F1 and F2. At 26, Amon was slightly older than Ronnie, but he'd been driving Grands Prix since 1963. Around the same time, Ken Tyrrell decided not to go with the Matra V12 engines that were on offer, preferring instead 3.0-litre Cosworth DFV power. So he ordered a pair of March 701 chassis for the new World Champion Jackie Stewart and his new recruit Johnny Servoz-Gavin.

(March chassis were identified by the year – '70 – plus the designated formula, in this case 1, to make 701.) Then Jo Siffert appeared on the scene. As a long-term contracted Porsche driver in sports prototypes, his German employers also wanted him to drive in a full works F1 team, which Rob Walker couldn't provide. But determined above all else to keep Siffert away from the temptations of Maranello, Porsche wanted to pay March to take him on board, an offer that was just too good to refuse. Finally, the STP fuel additives concern joined as major sponsors, and they needed a car for their man, Mario Andretti. This was effectively a customer car, and they chose a March on the basis that what was good enough for Jackie Stewart must be good enough for Mario. So by now, the fleet amounted to two works' cars, a quasi-works car and a couple more for Tyrrell. Ronnie was overlooked in the rush. Alan Rees: *'At one stage we probably did think of Ronnie as the main driver but we didn't realise how the whole March effort was going to take off. I simply envisaged getting into F3 and F2, and also an F1 team, but then things seemed to snowball. This is why we ended up with Chris Amon and Jo Siffert.'*

Max Mosley expanded on the driver situation: *'The original plan was to run Ronnie as the number two to Amon in our F1 team, but that went awry when Siffert appeared on the scene with enough money from Porsche to cover 30 percent of the budget. They wanted him in their sportscars so they were prepared to pay for an F1 drive. I then wanted to take Siffert and Peterson and not Amon because he cost money, but Robin and Alan outvoted me. Of course poor Chris ended up disenchanted with everybody. He was probably the most talented driver never to win a Grand Prix. He was fed up with Ferrari, and he was very friendly with Robin Herd, so he got the drive. In the end we lent Colin Crabbe a car and an engine in return for which he agreed to run Ronnie.'*

With the March signing, things had changed for Ronnie on the domestic front as well. He'd moved to England and bought a house in Maidenhead (3, The Farthingales – or the *'Fartingales'*, as he called it). Tim Schenken later moved to nearby at Cookham Dean, and Ronnie followed not long after, just up the road to the other side of the village, an area called Cookham Rise.

MAX MOSLEY
O RONNIE SKRIVER
KONTRAKT 1969.

FRANCIOS CEVERT

RONNIE MED SIN
TEAM-MANAGER
COLIN CRABBE

Above: Ronnie signs on the dotted line for March boss Max Mosley.

Ronnie Peterson: Super Swede

> 'I SAT IN THE BACK AMAZED, FASCINATED, WHILE BARBRO SPENT HER TIME WITH HER HEAD DOWN UNDERNEATH THE DASHBOARD IN THE FRONT SEAT, TELLING RONNIE TO SLOW DOWN. OF COURSE, HE DIDN'T.'

Above: The March 701 was a conventional design apart from its aerodynamic sidepods, and it worked well enough on straights and fast corners, provided the track surface was smooth. In 1970 Ronnie drove the seventh 701 chassis, run by Colin Crabbe's Antique Automobiles team, seen here in the paddock at Spa and opposite at the French GP.

March of time

Much midnight oil was burned by the 30 or so staff at March's brand new Bicester factory, with the first March 701 chassis under construction in mid-January. John Thompson who had built the Herd-designed Cosworth F1 car in 1969 was in charge of fabrication. The allied industries that supplied components to constructors were involved, including Girling, Lucas, Champion, Specialised Mouldings and Kent Alloys, not to mention Cosworth and Hewland. Two cars were made ready for a launch at Silverstone on 5th February 1970. One was for Tyrrell, and driven by Jackie Stewart, the other a red works car destined for Siffert, and Ronnie, along with several other test pilots, was to drive the latter.

It was his first taste of an F1 car – 3.0-litres of Cosworth DFV power as opposed to 1.6-litres of FVA in Formula 2. Mosley remembered the day: *'We had this great launch at Silverstone where we told everybody we were going to run the cars. The conventional wisdom in F1 was that it didn't exist, the whole thing was a hoax, this wasn't going to happen, and there was no way that we'd have two cars running, because we'd only rented the factory unit the previous September. So the whole of F1 turned up to watch, and happily the STP car ran as did Stewart's Tyrrell car, and then Amon and Siffert had a go. Andretti and Granatelli were there to announce the STP involvement. Then Ronnie was allowed a go, and that was his first run in an F1 car, on a freezing cold February day. He got it out on the straight and came back really happy because he said it would spin the wheels in any gear. He was completely astonished by the power, but of course he got used to it in no time at all.'*

Robin Herd described the 701 as being *'pretty conventional, conservative in design. We aimed for simplicity so the car could be built on time and maintained through the season. It wasn't particularly easy to drive – as even Jackie will tell you. It was bad over bumps and bad in slow corners; but it worked well in fast corners and down the straight.'* Apart from its flattened hammerhead shark nose, the most interesting aspect of the 701 was its side-pods, conceived by aerodynamicist Peter Wright at Specialised Mouldings, and the first stab at what would become known as the 'ground-effect' phenomenon. The inverted wing-shape of the side-pod acted in the same way as an aerofoil, but being closer to the track surface produced an area of negative pressure that drew the chassis downwards.

According to Jackie Stewart, *'the March 701 was never a particularly good car, but on the other hand Ken (Tyrrell) had no alternative, because at the end of '69 Matra decided that they wanted to go all French and nobody else wanted to sell us a car. Lotus wouldn't, Brabham wouldn't, and the only people that we could buy a car from to race were March. It was actually quite fast, because I was in pole position for its first Grand Prix in South Africa. Second time out, I won at Jarama. It was a very basic motor car with little or no sophistication.'*

The Silverstone test session gave March Engineering the ideal opportunity to announce its new, big-money sponsor: Andy Granatelli's fuel additives company, the STP Corporation. STP was known in Europe, having been associated with Team Lotus on its forays to Indianapolis. But there was some debate over what the initials STP stood for. Officially it was said to mean *'Scientifically Treated Petroleum'*, but this failed to satisfy some sceptics, who preferred to make up their own meanings. After spinning three times at Indianapolis in 1966, Jim Clark said it stood for 'Spinning Takes Practice', while Motor Sport's Denis Jenkinson thought that, in the case of March, it probably meant *'Siffert Takes Pole'*. Andretti's car was to be entered as the STP Oil Treatment Special.

Apart from a heady cocktail of talent on the March board, the senior mechanics included Bob Dance, ex-Team Lotus chief mechanic, Peter Kerr who'd been Jochen Rindt's Winkelmann F2 mechanic for four seasons, and Ray Wardell who looked after Derek Bell's Church Farm Racing F2 and F5000 cars for two years. *'We didn't have a chief mechanic,'* said Bob Dance. *'We were all in charge of a car, and there was the freedom to do what you wanted and in how you prepared it. March was a very easy going firm, and Ronnie certainly didn't make waves there.'*

When Stewart and Amon set identical pole position times for the South African GP at Kyalami a month later it looked as though the March 701 had all the makings of a winning car, straight out of the box. Stewart came third in the race, Siffert 10th, while Amon, Servoz-Gavin and Andretti retired. *'Kyalami was very hard on front tyres, and we should have won,'* said Herd. Things looked up for March when Stewart won the Race of Champions at Brands Hatch, ahead of Rindt's Lotus 49, and Stewart won again at Jarama in the Tyrrell-entered car's second Grand Prix outing, with Andretti third and Servoz-Gavin fifth. This race was the debut of the new Lotus 72, although Rindt retired and Miles didn't qualify.

Autobahn antics

In the layoff between Kyalami and Jarama, many of the racing fraternity attended the Motor 70 show, staged in Malmö by Staffan Svenby and Sveneric Eriksson. Tim Schenken remembers the journey to Sweden for this occasion all too vividly: *'Ronnie had a 280SE 3.5 Mercedes, and I joined him and Barbro to drive to Sweden in the winter of '69/'70 for the show. As we set off from Maidenhead the weather was foul, and we crossed on the ferry from Dover to Oostende It was so cold that the road was iced over, and we arrived at Oostende very late in the evening, and proceeded to drive to Brussels on the motorway. Well, any other car that had got out onto the autoroute was in the ditch. There were cars everywhere but on the road. But not Ronnie. It was 100km, and we went the whole way either sliding to the right or sliding to the left, with Ronnie just sitting in the front, one hand on the wheel, with his palm on the steering wheel, just putting opposite lock on and taking it off. And we'd drift for a kilometre one way and then it would go the other way and we'd drift back again. I sat in the back amazed, fascinated, while Barbro spent her time with her head down underneath the dashboard in the front seat, telling Ronnie to slow down. Of course, he didn't.'*

When they got to Malmö, Ronnie was presented with the Swedish media's 'Motor Man of the Year' accolade by Jackie Stewart. At the time though, it was beginning to look as if he wasn't going to get an F1 ride that year. To compound the agony, McLaren Racing ran Reine Wisell in an M7A at Silverstone for the Daily Express International Trophy. He could perhaps have taken consolation from the fact that Amon's STP March won from Stewart's Tyrrell-run March, although Wisell did well to come fifth, sandwiched between McLaren and Hulme in the works' M14s.

Ronnie got to drive one of the works' F2 Marches at Hockenheim on 12th April – the Jim Clark memorial meeting – but became embroiled in a first lap crash. Run by Malcolm Guthrie Racing, the 702 was not really race-worthy – Amon had a dismal time at the earlier Thruxton meeting, when Ronnie's car wasn't even ready – and established talents like Rindt, Stewart, Pescarolo, Bell and Regazzoni ruled the roost at these early season events. Peterson was not happy with the bulbous spaceframe March 702, dismissing it as a two-year-old design. It was, in effect, a modified 693.

Keith Leighton was Ronnie's F2 mechanic at March, and went on to be his mechanic at Team Lotus, alongside Rex Hart, up to 1976. *'John Thompson and I built the March 693 when we were both at Cosworth,'* he explained. *'I ended up doing the 1970 F2 season with Malcolm Guthrie. Basically, Ronnie was his team-mate, Malcolm supplied the money and Ronnie had the talent. That year, the car was hopeless. We only had six weeks to build an F2 car from scratch, which was a pretty heroic effort. Ronnie actually made that car look fairly good. There were some races, like Rouen, which is definitely a driver's track, where he excelled in it. He was probably overdriving the car, which was what Ronnie did. It was fun, 'cos every race we went to he was putting in one hundred percent in. During my whole history of working with Ronnie, you never doubted that.'*

By the Nürburgring round on 3rd May he'd taken part in three F2 meetings and finished two without completing a single lap. *'That was a really hairy one,'* said Malcolm Guthrie. Ronnie used his road car to learn circuits, and at the Nürburgring, he made a lasting impression on an unsuspecting passenger. *'I'd taken my friend around the Nordschleife circuit in my BMW,'* said Malcolm; *'he had his leg in plaster and he panicked at anything over 50mph, so it was a slow lap. Afterwards he stayed sitting in the car to read the paper while I went for a coffee. Ronnie then arrived and asked if me he could use my car to go* round the

Opposite: Pictured at Mantorp Park, Ronnie drove Malcolm Guthrie's March 702 in 1970. **Top:** One of his F2 contemporaries was promising Scot Gerry Birrell. **Above:** With the personal attention of the Pederzanis, Ronnie had a fitting for his new Tecno at the Bologna factory

Ronnie Peterson: Super Swede

THE THIRD RACE OF THE 1970 WORLD CHAMPIONSHIP SEASON WAS THE MONACO GRAND PRIX, AND OF COURSE AROUND THE TIGHT TWISTS AND TURNS, RONNIE FOUND THE 701 MUCH MORE OF A HANDFUL THAN THE F3 TECNO

Above: Ronnie was uncomplimentary about the March 702, describing it as a two-year old design, and even its designer Robin Herd was embarrassed by it – basically a modified 693, he said. Ronnie had 12 races in Malcolm Guthrie's car, with a best finish of 3rd at Hockenheim. **Opposite:** Ronnies March 702 still carries the RACC Scrutineering sticker from the Barcelona F2 race in April 1970.

circuit. I said, "fine," and he went off to find the BMW in the pits. Having asked my friend if it was my car, he got in the driving seat. My friend had no idea who Ronnie was, so he was rather astonished when they left the pits at 90mph. The following ten minutes was a complete manifestation of hell for him as he was mostly travelling sideways.' As far as Malcolm was concerned, *'Ronnie was the finest driver of his day. His idea was that you go everywhere flat out until you crash; then you slow down.'*

Ronnie had never been to the Nürburgring before that Eifelrennen F2 race. Keith Leighton described the events: *'The first day of practice he managed to get one lap in; it's raining of course – typical Nürburgring. He didn't come round again, and of course he'd gone off the road on a third gear corner. We fixed the car that night. The next day he goes out and this time he does a really good job, because he thought it was a fourth gear right hander, but in fact it's a second gear left hander. Put the car in a tree. We fixed it for the race, but he crashed in the race as well. So we had three out of three. It was his commitment. That was the way Ronnie drove.'*

In this case it was also down to the car. Malcolm was less than complementary about the March 702. *'It was the biggest load of junk that ever had four wheels attached to it,'* was his forthright opinion. He described how he wiped three wheels off his car in practice at Hockenheim, and Howden Ganley welded the suspension pick-up points back on overnight. Despite one wheel being an inch and a half off the ground, the car got a scrutineer's ticket after they'd fiddled with the spring and damper, and Guthrie managed to keep it going and came seventh. Back in the UK, the chassis was taken to Arch Motors to be rebuilt, where they claimed that only the roll-over bar was worth saving. *'Basically, March weren't interested in the 702. It had a spaceframe chassis that was an anachronism by then,'* said Malcolm. For his part, Robin Herd joked, *'I'm always astonished that Malcolm still speaks to me!'*

The Malcolm Guthrie team's transporter was later acquired by Brabham and Bob Dance enthused: *'it was painted white and had a huge winch inside that could pull anything. Malcolm had the transporter sideways on the motorway into Madrid once.'*

Grand Prix debut

During the first few months of 1970 Ronnie acted as van driver at the March factory, to-ing and fro-ing to collect the bits to make his F1 car. *'He would come in every day,'* said Robin Herd, *'and he'd see that the car had all its pedals or whatever, then come in the next day and find one of them had been removed because Stewart's car needed it. So it took a bit longer coming together.'* But March were as good as their word and the new 701 chassis, designated 701/8, was loaned to Colin Crabbe to run for Ronnie. Crabbe had a vintage car business operating under the name of Antique Automobiles, and among his treasures was a pre-war Mercedes-Benz W125 grand prix car. The previous year, Crabbe entered a Cooper-Maserati V12 for Vic Elford, but the talented Porsche driver was sidelined with a broken shoulder in a first-lap crash at the Nürburgring. *'Colin Crabbe did a decent job for Ronnie,'* said Herd, *'because he only had one engine and that did about 1,000 miles without a rebuild. A bit like the regulations that Max was pushing through in 2003, where one engine would have to do several races. We can say we've already done it – and came second in the Championship!'*

Max Mosley described the contractual arrangements with Ronnie: *'We signed Ronnie on a three year contract which I put together and agreed with his manager, Staffan Svenby. We had him signed up for '70, '71 and '72. So in '70 he struggled, but learned a lot with Colin Crabbe. But the whole thing was very under-resourced 'cos we had no money to support him with and Colin Crabbe didn't have a lot of money either, there was just that car and an engine. We did what we could to help, because we felt morally obliged to run him in F1, although not contractually bound to do so. Looking back, I think we made a big mistake. We should have said goodbye to Amon, which would have been easy because he was constantly asking for money. We should have run Siffert and Peterson. Siffert would have done a good workmanlike job and, in a works car, Peterson's talent would have come out in 1970. But that's all water under the bridge now.'*

Money matters

According to Staffan Svenby, Ronnie's sponsorship contract with Vick for 1970 was worth 15,000 SK, or around £1,000. For 1971 it went up to £2,500. The March contract for 1970 yielded £2,000, and in 1971 it went up to £5,000. In those days the drivers also got a percentage of the start and prize money, plus bonuses from Goodyear, Champion and the relevant fuel company. But it wasn't vastly more than, for instance, an average advertising executive's salary. As far as Ronnie was concerned, it was probably a good intro to Formula 1, since Crabbe's was ostensibly a private team; its Antique Automobiles nomenclature didn't exactly scream *'state-of-the-art'*, even if the 701 was a brand new car. There was only a single Cosworth DFV engine, and that wasn't necessarily rebuilt between races. So no-one expected too much in the way of fireworks. There was another anomaly, in that Ronnie's car used Goodyear tyres, while the STP Marches used Firestone, and the Tyrrell cars were on Dunlops. The third race of the 1970 World Championship season was the Monaco Grand Prix, and of course around the tight twists and turns, he found the 701 much more of a handful than the F3 Tecno he'd triumphed with a year ago. Nevertheless, he was very impressive, particularly in one wet practice session.

There were 16 starters and the Marches were looking good with Stewart on pole and Amon alongside him. Ronnie was 12th quickest putting the yellow-and-maroon Antique Automobiles 701 on the seventh row, behind Siffert and ahead of Surtees' McLaren. Early on, Stewart and Brabham traded places, while Ronnie was in amongst the second batch which included Hill in Rob Walker's Lotus 49, Oliver and Rodriguez in BRMs. They were soon joined by Stewart after his ignition metering unit had to be replaced, and in a race of typical Monaco attrition, Rindt woke up to find his old Lotus 49 in second place behind Brabham. In one of Monte Carlo's most dramatic finishes, he pushed Black Jack into a mistake at the Gasworks hairpin just before the end and, incredibly, took the win. Ronnie drove a solid race to come home seventh, two laps behind, and March's best finisher. He'd performed much better than Siffert in the second *'works'* March, who was four laps behind. At Spa for the Belgian Grand Prix on 7th June the factory team spent a lot of time working on the aerodynamics of the 701, which was primarily tuned towards exerting downforce on the nose to promote turn-in. They had yet to run on such a high-speed track so the desired characteristics were quite different to the Monaco set-up. The Antique Automobiles car was geared for an optimistic maximum speed of 195mph, (187mph on the Masta Straight was realistic) and when Ronnie found it wouldn't reach maximum revs in top gear, he simply left it in fourth, rather than waste time having the ratios changed. It was his first race at Spa but he was quickly up to speed on a circuit he had such little knowledge of, lapping less than ten seconds slower than Jackie Stewart who knew the circuit intimately.

Locked up

Ronnie nearly didn't make the start though. On his way into the Spa circuit, he had an altercation with the Belgian police. As his friend Kenneth Olausson recalled, *'The team was waiting in the paddock for him – Colin Crabbe and the mechanics, wondering if he was going to turn up or not, and he eventually arrived when the rest of the grid had lined up for the start. The reason was that he'd overslept, and he had to drive to the track in his Mercedes. By that time there was along long queue to get in, so Ronnie made a lane of his own and drove very fast right up to the front of the queue. The policeman on the gate was waving at him, which Ronnie took to mean that he could turn into the circuit. But as he did so, the policeman tried to stop him and he ran over the policeman's foot. He was chased by a motorcycle cop, stopped, and promptly taken off to the police station and locked up for a few hours. Finally, they realised he was meant to be in the race and let him go, just in time to make the start.'*

As it was he started from the fourth row of the three-two-three grid alongside Siffert in one of the works' cars, who was a tenth slower in practice. The race was led by Amon, then Stewart, from Rodriguez, Rindt, Ickx and

Above: As far as F1 was concerned, 1970 was a learning year for Ronnie, driving the March 701 run by Colin Crabbe's Antique Automobiles. The under-resourced team had just one DFV engine, and it ran for over 1,000 miles between rebuilds.

Ronnie Peterson: Super Swede

Above: Ronnie was fortunate to make the Belgian Grand Prix, having been arrested for a traffic violation outside the circuit. He came 9th in the March 701 on his first visit to Spa Francorchamps, despite a split exhaust.

Brabham. The BRM V12 was functioning as well as ever, and Rodriguez set a lap record (with the new Malmedy corner) at 149.5mph. Ronnie was running eighth when an exhaust manifold split, and Crabbe called him in to have it changed – no mean feat on a hot engine. Unfortunately he lost eight laps in the process, dropping him to 9th and last, and he was too far back to be classified. Not only that, the police were waiting for him, and he was banged up for two nights, still in his race overalls, until the case was dropped.

Le Mans beckons

One of the fascinated observers at Monaco during the 1970 practice was Ferrari team manager Dr Franco Gozzi, and on the strength of Ronnie's robust performance, invited him to pilot one of the 512S sports prototypes at Le Mans. He'd driven a Corvette there in 1969, and knew the score. Accordingly, he went to Modena to test the car around the town's even then decaying race track. Enclosed by high walls but with gates perpetually, Modena circuit was also home to the local flying school. Ronnie found the car *'big, fast and heavy,'* likening it to the Bonnier and Troberg Lola T70s he'd driven earlier. The closed cockpit was also cramped for the tall Swede, who had to keep his head tilted to the left. This made it difficult to set up in right-handers, although it was fine in left-handers. His co-driver for the 24-Hours was to be Derek Bell, then driving in F1 and F2 for Tom Wheatcroft and with Ferrari F1 and F2 experience under his belt.

This was the first time that the traditional Le Mans start was abandoned in favour of a rolling start and the eleven Ferrari 512Ss – including four works cars – were up against seven Porsche 917s and two 908s, with a trio of Matras and a quartet of Alfa Romeo T33s providing the wild cards. Although the 512S wasn't a bad car, a Porsche walkover was anticipated, partly because team discipline was stronger. But the rains came, cars spun off or broke down, and the Ferrari challenge fell apart with just three hours gone as Wisell, going slowly in the Filipinetti car because of oil on his windscreen, was hit from behind by Regazzoni's works 512S, in turn involving Mike Parkes'

works 512S, and the Bell/Peterson car blew its engine as Derek tried to avoid the carnage. Victors were Herrmann/Attwood in a 917. It was Ronnie's only drive for Ferrari in 1970, but the car had qualified well, and it wouldn't be the last. Just a week later another workmanlike F1 drive brought ninth place in the Dutch GP at Zandvoort, albeit two laps in arrears (the event where Piers Courage died) and made it two top ten finishes in his first three GPs.

At Rouen for the F2 race Ronnie put his works-supported Malcolm Guthrie March on pole for the first heat, bettering Rindt's three-year old lap record. *'I hated the place,'* recalled Malcolm. *'The 702 was terribly nervous there on those downhill sweeps.'* The heat was won by Siffert's BMW 270, with just a couple of tenths separating him from Peterson and Brabham, while Regazzoni beat Rindt in the second heat. In the final Ronnie battled with Wisell and led the last five laps from Siffert and Fittipaldi, only to spin off in the fast and furious twisty downhill section, wasting a 100-yard lead. He recovered to finish sixth behind Schenken, who set a new lap record. *'That was par for the course with Ronnie,'* said Malcolm. *'He kind of threw it away. If you relax or slow down, you loose your rhythm.'*

In F1's mid-season races, Ronnie's 701 suffered from a crown-wheel and pinion breakage at Clermont-Ferrand, and he was going well at Brands Hatch until he picked up a puncture in a front tyre and then had to have the clutch's hydraulic line bled, dropping him to ninth place, eight laps down. His engine gave up after 12 laps at Hockenheim, and it hadn't been rebuilt in time for the Austrian GP a fortnight later, which he missed. At Monza – where Rindt was tragically killed in practice – Ronnie was running in the leading bunch when his engine blew up as he passed the pits.

Ronnie missed the first practice session at St Jovite for the Canadian GP due again to an engine shortage, and was classified 13th in the race after loosing some 25 laps in the pits, an experience shared by Schenken, Brabham, Hill and Oliver. The Ferraris of Ickx and Regazzoni were triumphant, with Amon's works' March third.

The US Grand Prix was won by Emerson Fittipaldi in only his fourth GP, with his team-mate and Grand Prix debutant Reine Wisell third in the other Lotus 72C. Ronnie was 11th, four laps behind. As Mike Doodson said in his Motor Sport report from Watkins Glen, *'pictures of the four most prominent Formula 3 drivers were published earlier this year. They were Peterson, Schenken, Fittipaldi and Wisell: all four have now become established members of the Formula 1 scene.'* That said, Ronnie was one of a number of younger drivers (including Bell, Schenken, and De Adamich) who weren't invited to participate in the Mexican GP due to the organisers' limited budgets.

Piko Troberg hinted at a difference in temperament between the two Swedish rivals: *'When Ronnie got into Formula 1 he stayed on his feet, whereas it all went to Reine's head a little bit.'*

Ronnie borrowed Swedish driver Richard Broström's Porsche 908/2 for a sports car race at Karlskoga. He immediately took station behind leader Helmut Marko in another Porsche 908, but had to retire when a drive shaft snapped.

Ronnie rounded off the season with a couple more F2 races. At Imola, the European title race was still between Regazzoni and Bell, and it was the Swiss who came out ahead, with Fittipaldi second and Bell third, while Ronnie was fourth. At Hockenheim, there was a first lap incident at one of the chicanes, after which the leading bunch comprised the Tecnos of Cevert and Regazzoni, Fittipaldi's Lotus. Peterson's March, Quester's BMW and Reutemann's Brabham. This time it was the German who prevailed, with Regazzoni second and Ronnie third, just two tenths ahead of Emerson. Whilst the results don't suggest that Ronnie necessarily had the measure of his young opponents, his driving style and commitment spoke volumes.

Binding contracts

After the US GP, Colin Chapman made the first of his overtures to Ronnie. But he was tied to his March contract for two years, with an option for a third. Two races from the end of the 1970 season, the Tyrrell Marches were replaced with the Derek Gardner designed Tyrrell 001 and March had lost a major customer. The experienced F1 drivers had serious doubts about the 701's handling consistency. When Chris Amon decided to leave at season's end and join the Matra squad it came as no real surprise as he'd been ambivalent about the 701 all season, and often differed with Herd and Mosley about it. Then Siffert elected to go and join his Porsche comrade Rodriguez at BRM, disillusioned that he hadn't received number one status and guaranteed drives as opposed to having to qualify for races, while Andretti went to Ferrari. That left the March works' team with just Ronnie. Like Cevert in the number two Tyrrell-March, he'd no illusions about how it ought to handle; he simply adapted to whatever quirks the car manifested and got on with the job. And for 1971, that job was to be number one driver in the STP March team. Alan Rees: *'The time he spent with Colin Crabbe proved to be quite valuable because it got him some experience in F1, although not at the front of F1. When things changed around at the end of the year, it made him the ideal person to put in as number one March driver.'*

Max Mosley recalled the budgets for the 1971 season: *'In '71 we had no money at all and very little sponsorship, so Ronnie became the number one driver. The STP money was negligible. It looked big, and we made it look big, but the actual money was very low, but then again we didn't have to pay Ronnie very much under the terms of the contract. The car turned out to be a good one, and he started doing extremely well. He also did extremely well in F2 that year. That was the first monocoque F2 car, and it got us out of trouble actually, because by then we were in serious financial difficulty.'*

Mario Andretti remembered his time at March: *'I got on really well with Herd, Rees and Mosley. I had known them beforehand, and I thought it was quite an interesting venture and I was happy to be part of it. It was another chapter in my career. You go with untried machinery and, in fact it cost me, you know. It was a bit frustrating. I was not even in the factory team; I was there with the STP team. So it was a bit of a surprise realising that not all Formula 1 cars feel that great, because the experience I had before that was*

Opposite Ninth at Zandvoort in the March 701 was one of his better finishes in F1 during 1970. **Top:** Transmission failure at Clermont Ferrand was followed by 8th place at Brands Hatch (above).

Ronnie Peterson: Super Swede

BRASILIEN SEPT. 1971.

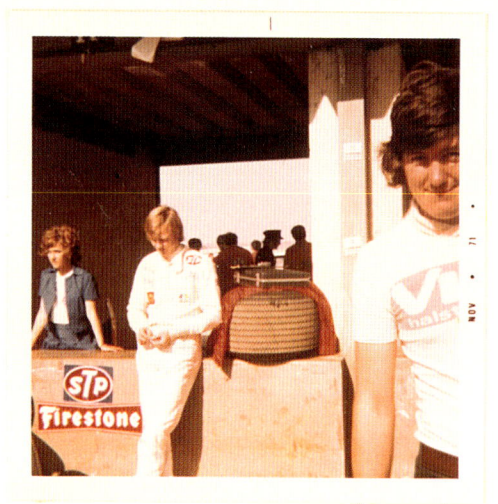

"BRIXIE"	KEITH	ANNE RIES
MIKE BEUTTLER	MIKE DOODSON	JEAN-PIERRE JARRIER & JOSE DOLEM
SAN PAULO	GUARAJA	

Opposite: Ronnie applies masses of opposite lock on the Antique Automobiles March 701 at Zandvoort's Tarzan hairpin

with Lotus, and the 49 was fantastic. Going to March, I was quite disappointed, but nevertheless it was a good learning experience.'

Of the March directors, Graham Coaker left, and was replaced by the Hon Jonathan Guinness, Mosley's half-brother. If the out-going works drivers were less than impressed with the 701, despite its initial promise, one particular customer was even more indignant. Max Mosley tells the story of German driver Hubert Hahne – a virtuoso in a BMW saloon car – who believed he'd been sold a duff March 701. 'Having bought a 'customer' car, he failed to qualify for the German GP at Hockenheim and, believing he'd been swindled, he had the March transporter impounded at the border.' Said Mosley,' in the end we agreed a settlement. We said if it can be driven round Silverstone at a certain speed, end of action. The court approved it. So Ronnie got into Hahne's car at Silverstone, and I think on his second or third flying lap he was well under the time that Hahne had said was impossible with the car. To be fair, Hahne took it in good spirit, because in a way it was terrible reverse for him. But Ronnie did the business.'

Another tale of Ronnie's off-track bravado concerned his regular commute from home in Maidenhead to the March factory. He could never resist a challenge behind the wheel and, according to Tim Schenken, 'Someone at March set a target time for where you turned off the A40 to Thame, through Thame and up (the B4011) to Bicester. And that was the way Ronnie always went to the factory, so he went and beat it. I don't think anyone could've gone any quicker. However, between Max Mosley, Robin Herd and Alan Rees, they spread the story around that someone had beaten Ronnie's time, and Ronnie would get to hear about it and go and beat it again. Now, God only knows what it was like being on that road if he happened to be trying to beat this bogey time. But whatever time the March directors put up, Ronnie seemed to beat it.' According to Sveneric, it simply served to make him more popular with the mechanics. 'It cemented friendships, because he was totally honest and he was a racer. The difference between Ronnie and Tim was that Tim had a book of excuses, whereas Ronnie just said, "Oh, the engine's gone bang," or "I overdrove a little bit."

Ronnie Peterson: Super Swede

CHAPTER 04

Dawning of a New F1 Talent

Sveneric and Ronnie went back to Örebro for Christmas 1970. 'Ronnie was good friends with Stig Blomqvist, and several years running he called up Stig and asked him for a ride in whatever Saab he happened to be driving at the time. The 240bhp Saab 99 Turbo impressed him a lot. One time they took Schenken with them. There was no back seat so he had to sit on the floor.

Opposite: In the March 712 with team manager Pete Briggs.

He'd never been in a rally car on a special stage, and afterwards he said to me, "Sven! You knew this! These guys are maniacs!"' Tim remembered the same incident, but was more focussed on Stig's technique: 'Stig took us for a ride through a forest which Saab owned – it was their test track, and we went in this Saab 96 2-stroke on packed ice, on studded tires. It was an incredible experience, his left foot braking, known as the Scandinavian twist, then the Scandinavian flick, where you turn the wheel the wrong way to unbalance the car before setting up for the corner, which was a style at that time only known to Scandinavian rally drivers.'

In the depths of winter Ronnie had actually driven a VW on the Swedish Rally early in 1969 and the following year, Porsche gave Ronnie a try-out in a 911. Said Torsten: 'We did some testing, but the night before the rally I was ill at the hotel in Karlstad where the rally starts. The hospital said, "you can't go on the rally as Ronnie's navigator," so they took another guy for the Porsche. He went off ten or 15 times, and finally didn't get back on again.'

Round and around

Early in 1971, Ronnie was back at the wheel of a Formula 2 car. It was the brand-new March 712, and he and Keith Leighton took it to Kyalami for evaluation. 'It was the first monocoque F2 car,' said Keith. 'Ronnie and I went to South Africa for three months, soon after Christmas in 1970. There was just me and him, and of course Barbro was there, and it was kind of their honeymoon, so I got to know them pretty well. We just used the car as a test bed. Everyday we went to Kyalami and simply ran it all day. He did between 3 and 4,000 miles just going round and round and round. By the end, his lap times were as quick as the Formula 1 cars'. He could have easily qualified a Formula 2 car in the top ten for the Grand Prix.'

'It was a whole learning exercise. We could adjust the car in every direction: we could make it wide or narrow track, alter the roll centres, and

Ronnie Peterson: Super Swede

Ronnie was asked to drive for Ford in the 1973 event; they had prepared an Escort twin-cam for him and Torsten Palm as co driver. The rally started in Karlstad and Tim Schenken went out with some friends of Ronnie's into the forest in the middle of the night to watch him come through the first stage. 'We must have waited there till 3 o'clock in the morning, freezing cold, and all the cars had gone through, but no Ronnie. So we went back to rally headquarters to see what had happened and, sure enough, he'd had an accident.' Torsten's version corroborates the story. 'The Swedish Rally of 1973 was the first winter rally ever that the cars were not allowed to have spikes. Just winter tyres. That is very tough in the winter. But he was so crazy driving, he went flat; I talked to him, "please be careful, here it is really a jump, and here a hairpin left," but he went full speed, we went up and down over the yumps with this Ford Escort. The windscreen popped out, and there was a lot of snow, and soon the whole interior was full of snow. I'll never forget how difficult it was to get out of the car, it was fully packed and we were bouncing up and down. We were going great guns on the first, second and third stages of the rally. And then we went off. The engine was still running, and Ronnie couldn't understand why we weren't moving. We got out and had a look and discovered that we'd completely lost the back axle. He was definitely not a rally driver!'

Ronnie declared in 1976 that he would like to have a go in the RAC Rally or the Texaco Tour of Britain, admitting that driving on snow and ice as he'd done in the Swedish Rally demanded a very different technique, which was not for him.

change all the handling characteristics. We'd run it for three days in one set up, and then he'd say, "let's try in a completely different configuration." So we'd spend a couple of days changing the whole car and then run it for three days like that. Eventually we'd exhausted every possible configuration.'

Throughout Ronnie's career with March, they felt he needed to have more of a feel for the car and tried to give him that. 'But every time, Ronnie would go out and drive the car as fast as it could possibly go, so he wasn't really feeling the differences in the car. He'd always give you the ultimate lap time, every time.'

Take off

The first race of 1971 was the Buenos Aires 1,000Kms, first round of the World Championship for Manufacturers, featuring Groups 5 and 6 sports-racing cars. Peterson was teamed with Jorge Cupeiro in the little Scuderia Filipinetti-entered 1.8-litre Lola T212-FVC. It was a race marred by tragedy, as Ignazio Giunti died when his Ferrari 312P struck the Matra 660 being pushed to the pits by Beltoise after he'd run out of fuel. Marshalling was haphazard, and in any case there was apparently a regulation forbidding drivers to push cars. Tentative attempts to stop the race were disregarded by press-on local drivers, so it continued, lap charts awry. On lap 129, Peterson's Lola got a puncture, causing it to veer off the main straight under braking; it hit the verge and took off, landing on its rear end, but fortunately without any damage to the driver. Said Sveneric: 'It amazed him that it all went suddenly so quiet. "All I could see was the scenery and this bloody tree coming towards me,"' he said. He was really cool about it.' Ronnie and Cupeiro were classified 12th, albeit 24 laps behind the victorious JW Porsche 917 of Siffert/Bell.

Tea-tray spoiler

The new March 711 was a low, ovoid-bodied chassis with side radiators and tall, narrow cockpit opening, but its most original feature was the tea-tray like front aerofoil. This mobile surf-board extended upwards from the rounded nose of the

HOCKENHEIM GP 1970

CAROLINE

JUNE o CAROLINE

Opposite top: Running the 711 without engine cover on the faster circuits such as Kyalami, gave a few more mph on the long straights.

Ronnie Peterson: Super Swede

> HE HAD A VERY SWEDISH TEMPERAMENT. HE RARELY GOT ANGRY, HE WAS A PRAGMATIST. IT DIDN'T PUT HIM OFF AT ALL, THOUGH HE WAS JUSTIFIABLY FED UP. THAT MALLORY PARK ACCIDENT WAS VERY UNFORTUNATE

Above: Ronnie drove the March 711 to 10th place in the South African GP at Kyalami. Because he could drive around problems with the car, and still go quickly, Ronnie was not such a good test driver. He found it hard to feed back information about what the car was doing, feeling its behaviour instinctively.

car on a single support. *'It projected up into the airstream, and was that much more efficient,'* said Robin Herd. *'But the downside was that it was very pitch-sensitive. In long fast corners, like at the Österreichring, it would lift, so it had to be adjusted. But on most circuits it was fine.'* Herd's original design, which had input from Frank Costin, originally had the engine faired in, but the aerodynamic side-pods of the 701 were absent. STP Oil Treatment continued to support the team to the tune of £20,000, and the cars were finished in that distinctive orange-red livery. *'The 711 was a good car,'* said Herd. *'Ronnie never spun it.'* Mechanic Peter Kerr's view was that, *'March should have put more money into it and made the monocoque simpler.'*

In a symbiotic arrangement typical of F1, March struck a deal with Alfa Romeo to supply its V8 engines in exchange for running a car for the talented Italian touring car and sportscar drivers Andrea de Adamich and Nanni Galli. These power-units were used in the Alfa Romeo T33 sports-racing cars, and had been tried in 1970 by McLaren, but the liaison proved unsuccessful and, in F1 guise, the engines hadn't been reliable. Ronnie's F1 mechanic was Peter Kerr. Not only was the experienced New Zealander a veteran of the Winkelmann F2 and Cosworth F1 operations, he went on to work at Arrows alongside Alan Rees, only retiring in 2001. Ronnie's other mechanic continued to be Keith Leighton, who was posted to the March F2 team for 1971 and run by team manager Pete Briggs. Kerr was then joined by Gary Sprague.

Alan Rees made one or two observations on suspension set-up: *'Ronnie wasn't as good at setting the car up as someone like Emerson. In that respect – setting up the 711 – he worked very closely with Robin. There wasn't anywhere near as much importance put on the car's set-up in those days. It was much more 'get in and drive it'. It was beginning to come that you played around with the chassis, but nothing like it is today, and no-one knew it was that critical either.'*
The 711s made their Grand Prix debut at Kyalami for the South African Grand Prix on 6th March. Ronnie had the Cosworth DFV-powered car, de Adamich the Alfa-engined version. Another DFV car was finished just before practice ended, for Spaniard Alex Soler-Roig to drive. Although Stewart came second in the new Tyrrell, it was a Ferrari dominated event, with Andretti winning. Ronnie was classified 10th, two laps behind, having struggled with a flat tyre. De Adamich was 13th, four laps down, although the Alfa Romeo engine was at least running at the end. At the Kyalami Ranch after the race, the March management showed their appreciation for all the work done to get the cars ready by throwing a big party. The resident band left their instruments behind, and the equipment was swiftly seized on by the team members. Ronnie played guitar, Alan Rees was on drums, and the whole entourage descended into mayhem.

Although Ronnie drove a March 711 at Brands Hatch in the Race of Champions on 21st March, it was actually the customer car built for Frank Williams that Henri Pescarolo would go on to drive. Since the car wasn't ready in time for practice, Ronnie had to start from the back of the grid and was carving his way through the field when a brake shaft snapped under braking for Clearways bend. The car promptly turned right, just like Rindt's Lotus had at Monza. There were real concerns about the 711's safety. *'Max and Robin asked me, "what do you think about these brake shafts,"'* said Peter Kerr, *'and I told them, "I don't think we can risk using them unless we know why it broke." I doubt the team principal would ask the chief mechanic's advice these days!'* Immediately, the other 711 chassis were converted to outboard instead of inboard brakes, just in time for the Questor Grand Prix the following weekend.

Most of the F1 teams were tempted to this event at the Ontario Motor Speedway in California by a substantial $278,400 prize fund. They were pitted against the cream of the American Formula A drivers – the US equivalent of European F-5000 and, in effect, a line-up similar to the Race of Champions. Jackie Stewart put the Tyrrell 001 on pole, and fastest F-A car was Donohue's Lola-Chevrolet T192. Astonishingly, Fittipaldi's Cosworth-Ford powered Lotus 72 shared row five with Follmer's Lotus-Ford V8 Type 70 – never a notably successful Formula-A or Formula 5000 car, and one place ahead of Wisell in the other works Lotus 72. Ronnie was back on the ninth row in March 711/2. There was a substantial banked section to the speedway, and the race got off with a rolling start. Ronnie soon lost the top of one of the March's dampers and spent a long time in the pits. He rejoined eventually and stayed with the scrap between Stewart and Siffert for second place, although he was well out of the running and ultimately unclassified in this extraordinary two-heat event, Andretti emerging a convincing winner for Ferrari.

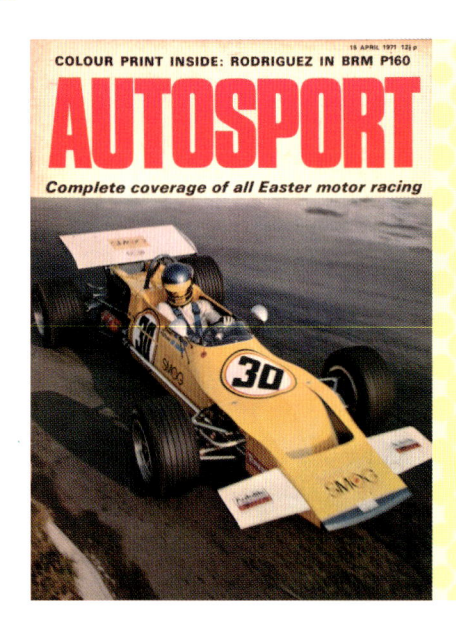

A near miss

On 14th March 1971, Formula 2 returned to Mallory Park after a four-year absence, and Peterson headed a first class entry for the non-championship event. In his report in Motor Sport, Andy Marriott said Ronnie *'dominated practice and his spectacular style was undoubtedly the high spot of the meeting.'* He was well in the lead of the first heat when, four laps from the end, a ball-joint on the end of a steering arm seized and the car turned sharp left at the Esses. It somersaulted onto the banking, shedding bodywork and coming to rest upside-down right up against the spectator fencing, and Ronnie was trapped underneath. He was released with nothing more than a cut hand. Said Alan Rees: *'He had a very Swedish temperament. He rarely got angry, he was a pragmatist. It didn't put him off at all, though he was justifiably fed up. That Mallory Park accident was very unfortunate – it wasn't his fault. It was largely down to the fact that it was a new team, and to a certain extent inexperienced. A mistake was made with the chassis that caused the accident. Not a design problem, but a preparation problem.'* Naturally, there was genuine concern about Ronnie within the team. Robin Herd was quoted at the time in Motor Sport, saying: *'If anything happens to Ronnie, I would seriously consider leaving motor racing.'*

The European Formula 2 Championship was where aspiring Grand Prix stars wanted to be after they'd made the cut in Formula 3. The power on tap from the ubiquitous Ford FVA unit was around 220bhp in 1971, a good stepping stone to Formula 1 where the Cosworth DFV was yielding some 400bhp. The cars were quick and feisty, and non-graded F2 regulars could mix it with the 'graded' Grand Prix stars. The latter weren't eligible for F2 Championship points, but being professionals, they would earn money from the races. The class of the field were the Rondel-Racing Brabhams run by Ron Dennis and Neil Trundle for Schenken and Hill; the works Tecnos of Cevert, Depailler and Jabouille; and the Bardahl-sponsored Lotuses of Emerson and Wilson Fittipaldi. The March 712 was, as yet unproven.

The first couple of rounds in the European Formula 2 series were the Jim Clark Memorial Trophy at Hockenheim on 4th April, where Ronnie set fastest lap and a new record in the March 712 but retired, and the Yellow Pages Trophy at Thruxton on 12th April. Graham Hill took the lead after Pescarolo retired and, despite huge pressure from Ronnie, managed to stay ahead of him – by a scant six-tenths – to the finish. Ronnie out-braked Hill at the chicane, but got balked himself on the following lap. Nevertheless, it was an encouraging result. Between these two races he should have been driving the March 711 in the non-championship Rothmans Trophy at Oulton Park (we were spoiled for F1 races then, weren't we?), but it was still at Bicester being modified after the Questor GP.

The second round of the F1 World Championship was around Barcelona's spectacular Montjuich Park on 18th April. The STP-March squad featured the same line-up as for Kyalami, although the car run by Frank Williams for Pescarolo had its suspension beefed up with gussets and stronger bracketry. Grid formations were still mainly three-two-three in 1971, and Ronnie shared row five with Cevert and Pescarolo. None of the Marches finished, Peterson's succumbing to an electrical fault on lap 24, de Adamich's two laps later with broken transmission, and Soler-Roig's after 46 laps with a broken fuel pipe. It was the first win for the Tyrrell, Stewart beating Ickx's Ferrari and Amon's Matra.

The busy schedule meant Ronnie was at Pau in the Pyrenean foothills for the annual street-race on 25th April, an F2 event billed as the 31st Grand Prix Automobile de Pau. He skated over a kerb in the wet practice session and cracked the gearbox casing. Keith Leighton welded it up, but it only lasted ten laps of the race, which was won by Rejne Wisell's Lotus 69. Jaussaud in another March was third, the March 712 proving competitive, *'even if Peterson's press-on driving style sometimes aggravated its more fragile points,'* as Alan Henry put

Top Centre: Donning his helmet while Peter Kerr fettles the March 711 for the Questor Grand Prix, Ontario Motor Speedway. **Above:** Peterson inherited Rindt's mantle as the king of Formula 2. He was the class of the field at Mallory Park's 1971 F2 meeting – until the steering failed.

Ronnie Peterson: Super Swede

Above: Practising the Alfa Romeo-powered 711 for the Daily Express International Trophy at Silverstone, Ronnie was never fazed by wet races. **Opposite Left:** The master of oversteer imposes his authority on the March 712 – running a special nosecone. **Opposite Right:** At Crystal Palace in May the handling of the F2 March proved a little difficult.

it in his Motor Sport race report. Tim Schenken recalled the meeting: *'His car control was legendary, and possibly nowhere more so than at Pau. It was wet on the first day of practice, and there was a very fast corner after the pits that Ronnie took almost sideways. After practice he was complaining that there wasn't enough steering lock on the March. He had the car going through there oversteering at such an angle that he'd run out of opposite lock.'*

At the much re-vamped Nürburgring on 2nd May, Ronnie as usual took pole position. In the race he set fastest lap in (a new F2 record), but broke a wheel rim, which punctured a tyre, in an avoiding action when the FVA engine in Bell's Williams-March blew up in front of him. He'd been dicing with Cevert and Bell for the lead at the time, and the Frenchman now led the F2 title race from Reutemann, with Ronnie third, thanks to his Thruxton points tally – Hill being a graded driver and thus not eligible. The second works March 712 was now being driven by the heavily mortgaged pay-driver Niki Lauda, who came sixth.

Another big shunt

Along with the Race of Champions at Brands Hatch, the early-season Daily Express International Trophy meeting at Silverstone provided a pointer to form in the coming European leg of the World Championship, as well as a chance to see new machinery in action. Ronnie was entered in the Silverstone race on 8th May in the Alfa Romeo powered March 711 normally driven by De Adamich and originally entered for Nanni Galli. The 440bhp Italian V8 easily revved to 10,000rpm, but wasn't happy higher than that. By comparison, the Cosworth DFV maxed out at 9,600rpm. Ronnie put the March-Alfa on the second row for the first 26-lap heat, but early in the race an electrical wire came loose and he had to pit to get it fixed. In the closing laps the throttle mechanism jammed open at Becketts, normally taken flat in third, and the car ran wide, disintegrating against the earth banking on the outside of the turn. As sometimes happens when open-wheel racers crash, the left-hand front wheel came off and glanced off his helmet, knocking him out for a short while. A photographer was first to arrive on the scene, then marshals arrived and released him. Thankfully there was no fire, but Ronnie spent the night in Northampton Hospital. Such was his tenacity that the following day he was on a plane to Spain for an F2 race – the so-called 5th Gran Premio de Madrid. When the organisers at Jarama realised he'd had an almighty accident at Silverstone only days before, they insisted on a full medical examination before they'd let him compete. In the race there was a hectic slipstreaming battle for the lead between Schenken and Peterson, lasting 21 laps until the March's FVA bounced a valve and Ronnie headed for the pits again. It was just one more retirement in what was building up into a long run of bad luck – he'd retired from the preceding F2 round at the Nürburgring – and Ronnie was becoming increasingly depressed and introverted. Two weeks after Jarama, Peterson and Schenken were soundly beaten at Crystal Palace by Emerson Fittipaldi in the Bardahl-Lotus 69, although they all shared the new lap record. Ronnie had been running second, but the March 712's handling was proving tricky as they were trying new damper settings and he understeered off on the last lap, allowing his Aussie friend through.

Ronnie's luck changes

A year on from his Grand Prix debut and two years after his F3 triumph, Ronnie arrived at Monte Carlo in optimistic mood. The weather was wet and about half the field didn't bother with the Thursday practice session. Ronnie did venture out, but was some six seconds slower than Wisell who was quickest. The best times were set on the Friday session, as Max Mosley observed: *'The thing that really impressed everybody was the early morning Friday practice in the wet, when Ronnie was second quickest to Ickx. It was obvious that there was a real talent there.'* With only 18 starters permitted, the March-Alfa 711/1 of Galli and Soler-Roig's 711/4 both non-started, the former with fuel starvation and the latter because a badly machined wheel came off. Ronnie was eighth quickest in 711/2, starting from row four of the two-by-two grid. Like the Lotus runners, Peterson's car was shod with a new compound of Firestones, reckoned to be stickier in corners but an unknown quantity over race distance. Alongside him at the start, Amon was delayed when the Matra V12 hit fuel starvation. As Stewart leapt into an unchallenged lead, Ronnie set about catching and passing those ahead of him; first Hulme's McLaren, then Rodriguez's BRM, who he forced into a late braking error at the Gasworks' hairpin; next he picked off Ickx's ill-handling Ferrari, and Siffert's BRM, all by lap 31. He began to haul in the canny Scot, but when it was obvious that he was unlikely to catch him, Ronnie eased off in order to settle for a dominant second place. That performance was enough to confirm what everyone had sensed all along – that Ronnie was going to make it in Formula 1, provided the car held together. Said Jackie Stewart: *'The first real impact he made on me was at Monaco in 1971 when he finished second to me. I'd had a difficult race because I'd broken a brake balance bar in the warm up lap, but everyone was giving him a lot of credit for that event, because he'd passed several of the top drivers. We saw quite a lot of each other after that.'* Keith Leighton amplified Ronnie's achievement. *'His exploits in F1 with the March 711 were unbelievable. You're not supposed to overtake anybody at Monte Carlo, and he overtook some of the top drivers of the day to come second. That was heroic driving. The design of that front wing wasn't the best thing in the world. Every time you braked you had too much front wing, and every time you accelerated you had no front wing. They didn't realise at the time, but it was not what you needed to make the car handle. Pitch sensitive is the word. In layman's terms it did the opposite of what you required.'*

The March team was jubilant. *'The '1971 Monaco race was a psychological breakthrough for Ronnie'* said Mosley. *'He said to me after the race that these big names had always been to him great drivers, and it came as a revelation that he could actually catch and pass them, especially at Monaco. I think that made him realise that he could do it, and he then went on from strength to strength. You see this with a lot of drivers; they have to get through that barrier of realising they actually have the talent.'*

It's a sort of oedipal situation, where a driver has to overcome his heroes to elevate his own status and self-confidence. Mosley continued: *'The top drivers all think that anyone could do it. When they come out of F3 they explain to you that any of the other F3 drivers could go just as quick as them if not quicker. They all think anyone could do it because it comes naturally to them. So it's always a bit of a surprise when someone who thinks he's got no special talent finds he can actually overtake the world's great drivers. Ronnie was a very modest sort of person in those ways. He could just do it. He couldn't explain to you how or why.'*

Sadly, one of the founders of March, Graham Coaker, didn't see the triumph. He had just died from complications following an F2 accident at Silverstone in which he broke a leg.

Taste of Martini

The European 2.0-litre Sportscar Championship was a hotly contested amateur series populated almost exclusively by open-top Lola T212s and Chevron B16s and B19s. On 5th June the annual Martini Trophy at Silverstone was a qualifying round, and Ronnie became a last minute entry in Bonnier's Lola T212 when Jo decided to opt out of the event on race morning. Ronnie, who hadn't practised and therefore had to start from the back with a ten-second penalty found himself vying with some of the top names in the field including Vic Elford, Chris Craft, John Miles, Ed Swart, Guy Edwards, Gerard Larrousse, Toine Hezemans and Helmut Marko. After a dramatic first heat with several changes of lead, Hezemans came through to win, with Peterson fourth behind Marko and John Lepp. Of the sometime leaders, Elford was eliminated when he struck a wayward starter motor and John Burton when he hit a hare – it was that kind of race. For the second heat, Ronnie was late out and once again obliged to start from the back. He was swiftly up with Hezemans and they swapped the lead f or a few laps, until Ronnie pulled away to a comfortable 10-second win. The Dutchman won on aggregate though, having a 17-second advantage over the Swede.

On 13th June the F1 circus gathered for another non-championship race at Hockenheim. The CSI (Commission Sportif Internationale) was faced with a three-week gap between Monaco and Zandvoort, having cancelled the Belgian GP because the old Spa circuit was considered too dangerous for F1 (even though the big sports prototypes still raced there). So the inaugural Jochen

Above: Impressive in wet practice, Ronnie started the 1971 Monaco GP from row four, passing the cream of F1 by lap 31 to claim 2nd place behind Stewart. Super Swede had thrown down the gauntlet.

Ronnie Peterson: Super Swede

Above: Starting from the back of the grid in both heats of the Martini Trophy at Silverstone, Ronnie came 4th and 1st in Bonnier's Lola T212, and 2nd on aggregate. **Opposite:** Waiting in the Zandvoort pit lane as suspension settings are fine-tuned.

Rindt memorial race was elevated from an F2 to an F1 event. The March enclave in the paddock was in crisis as one engine or another – Cosworth DFV and Alfa Romeo – was down on power, tired, or refusing to start. Ronnie had 711/2 and the new 711/6 at his disposal, the latter with an Alfa engine. Mechanic Peter Kerr described what happened: *'In the morning warm-up he practiced with the Alfa-engined car, but the engine packed up. So I worked frantically on the Ford engined car to prepare that while the other mechanics tried to get the Alfa engine going again.'* Kerr's efforts with the DFV motor paid off and, much to his relief, Ronnie drove his regular 711/2. As Ickx took an early lead, the battle for second place raged between the Swedes, Wisell and Peterson swapping places for 13 laps. Then brake trouble hampered the Lotus driver, and Ronnie went on to finish second to Ickx. *'I think if we'd have just used the Ford-Cosworth engine we'd have done better that season,'* said Kerr.

At Zandvoort for the wet and gloomy Dutch GP on 20th June, Ronnie had practised the Alfa Romeo-powered 711/6 but raced Cosworth-engined 711/2, as he was not happy with the feel of the new car. Sveneric thought Ronnie got on better in his first year at March because *'he adjusted himself to the car's behaviour instead of asking the car do what he wanted.'* In the race Ronnie passed John Surtees' TS9 and the two circulated in fourth and fifth places, which is where they finished up.

It was suddenly a different story in Formula 2, however. Having been a front runner all season, Ronnie's long overdue win came in the March 712M at the fast, sweeping Rouen-les-Essarts circuit at the end of June, where he won the final after disposing of Cevert's Tecno. *'Rouen was probably the most dangerous track we went to,'* recalled Keith Leighton. *'Everybody else had full wings on the car, but he'd taken all the wings off and was still flat out all the way down the hill. To make the car work on the limit, you've got to drive it on the limit. If you get a driver who thinks he's going to understeer or oversteer he's adjusting the car without knowing that it's going to do that or not. So Ronnie was making changes to the car because he knew what it would do, not because he thought it might do it. He was actually way ahead of the game, really. Somewhere like Rouen, another guy's going down the hill and he thinks it might get loose round there, so he'd be backing off the throttle. Sometimes if you do back off, it will make it loose. Ronnie wasn't like that.'*

He went on to win the Mantorp Park and Kinnekulle-ring rounds of the European F2 Championship as well, Cevert providing his main opposition. *'Over in Scandinavia, he was a man possessed,'* said Keith. *'He went there to win the races, and not just win, but to completely pulverise the opposition.'*

By mid season, March had built 20 units of the 712M Formula 2 car, more than any rival maker, and over half that number were active in the European F2 theatre. The yellow Vick-sponsored Peterson car bearing the SMOG logo had an advantage over many, in that his was powered by a Brian Hart-built FVA rather than an off-the-peg unit. Meanwhile, Ronnie tried out Schenken's Rondel Racing BT36 unofficially at Mantorp Park, and was impressed. Tim came second in the race ahead of Carlos Reutemann, Wilson Fittipaldi, John Watson and Gerry Birrell.

Alan Rees admitted that the STP funding was insufficient, and so March sought more F1 involvement with Alfa Romeo, since Cosworth engines were in short supply. Ronnie was unhappy about this, knowing that the torque curve and reliability of the Cosworth DFV was far superior to the significantly heavier Italian unit. But for the French Grand Prix at Paul Ricard on 4th July, he was given a new Alfa engine and chassis 711/6, while de Adamich took 711/1, also with Alfa power. Soler-Roig got the Cosworth-engined 711/4. It was clear that the Alfa engine was not up to the job, and Ronnie was despondent about his chances. His mechanic Peter Kerr recalled the meeting: *'Ronnie said, "I won't drive it in the race." He was adamant about it, so I said, "let's go and sit in your Mercedes and think about it." I said to him, "Just race it the once then everyone will know how bad it is. That's all you have to do." In the end he said, "OK." 'In fact, Ronnie put in a creditable practice time, starting from the fifth row, and was running eighth when the engine let go in the biggest way possible, spewing its oil all over the back straight, causing Regazzoni to go off. Pete Kerr's point had been proven.' After the race I said to him, "did you do a clutch job on it?"* (If you dipped the clutch, the revs soared and the engine could blow.) 'He said, "No, no need!"'

Robin Herd explained, 'we had to use the Alfa engine for that race as we didn't have any money. It was very much like Frank Williams' operation at the time, hand-to-mouth. Ronnie understood that if we didn't use the Alfa Romeo engine then we simply wouldn't be racing.'

Before the British GP on 17th July, March Engineering made a number of changes to the team, with Alex Soler-Roig (and his Marlboro budget) being replaced by Nanni Galli. Ronnie's regular 711/2 was sold to the Clarke-Mordaunt-Guthrie Racing team for Mike Beuttler, and the 711/6 chassis was fitted with a DFV instead of the Alfa unit. The Swede put it on the second row alongside Fittipaldi's Lotus 72, while the rest of the March runners were at the tail end of the grid. As Stewart swept away into the distance, followed by Siffert's BRM, Peterson, Schenken and Fittipaldi harried the Ferraris of Ickx and Regazzoni. By half distance the Ferraris' engines were finished and Siffert had been forced to pit, so Ronnie brought the March home in second place, about half a minute behind the Tyrrell team leader.

Autodelta drive

March's connection with Alfa Romeo enabled Ronnie to share a Group 6 Alfa T33-3 3.0-litre V8 sports-prototype with Andrea de Adamich in the Watkins Glen Six Hours on 24th July. One of the reasons for this was for Ronnie to evaluate the T33's transverse gearbox, which he liked. It had been a good season for the Milanese Autodelta squad, having won the BOAC 1,000-Kms at Brands Hatch and finished well up in other rounds of the International Championship for Makes. In the race, Ronnie battled with Andretti in the Ferrari 312P, averaging 120mph around the turns and dips of the Glen. The matter was settled when the Ickx/Andretti car refused to start after a routine pit stop, and Peterson/de Adamich stayed out for as long as possible on their Firestone intermediates until forced to pit for wet tyres. Their winning margin was two laps over the Siffert/van Lennep Group 5 Porsche 917, and they'd covered 279 laps or 677.4 miles at an average 112.77mph.

Clock watchers

An indication of the esteem in which Peterson was now held was that in practice for the German Grand Prix at the Nürburgring, most of the top F1 teams had a stop-watch on him as a marker against their own drivers' lap times. Max Mosley discovered this when Ronnie was given a suspiciously slow time of 7 min 32.4 sec, when somewhere in the mid-20s was more likely. When he did the rounds of the rivals' pit counters, this was corroborated, and he managed to persuade the timekeepers to issue a more accurate time of 7 min 26.5 sec, which put him on the fourth row with Fittipaldi. By comparison Stewart had set pole time with 7 min 19 sec.

At the end of the first lap, Ronnie was running fifth behind Stewart, the Ferraris of Ickx and Regazzoni, and Siffert's BRM. When Ickx went off, Ronnie was fourth. He was passed by Cevert, then had to pit to have the March's damaged right-hand radiator cowling removed, allowing Andretti's Ferrari by. The race ran out with Stewart the victor, followed by Tyrrell team-mate Cevert, then the two Ferraris of Regazzoni and Andretti, with Ronnie fifth and Schenken sixth. Before setting off for the Nürburgring, Ronnie's 711 monocoque had been reinforced with thicker gauge aluminium, vindicated by the fact that it survived intact while the other works March chassis buckled on the circuit's unique humps and crash-landings.

For the Austrian GP on 15th August, Galli's March was fitted with a DFV engine and hired out to Niki Lauda, who started from the back row. Max Mosley commented: *'Lauda turned up in '71 with some money looking for an F2 drive, so of course we said, "yes". And that's when he very bravely borrowed 2.5 million Austrian shillings, about £45,000, which in those days was a huge amount of money. Our budget in 1970 was £130,000, including paying Amon, and that's for a front running team – we were third in the constructors championship. That was for his F1 and F2 drives for 1972. We all thought he was a no-hoper because he was significantly slower than Ronnie. Lauda was the kid. I think they got on well, and Ronnie did his best to help him.'* Ronnie was halfway down the Österreichring grid, while Lauda was at the back. Peterson struggled in the race,

Above: A deal with Alfa Romeo saw cash-strapped March running the Italian firm's Autodelta drivers De Adamich and Galli in exchange for Alfa Romeo engines. The symbiosis included a winning drive for Peterson/de Adamich in a T33-3 in the 1971 Watkins Glen 6-Hours.

only managing eighth place with Fittipaldi, Schenken and Wisell following winner Siffert across the line.

Robin Herd remembered a test session at Thruxton soon after Lauda came on the scene. *'I put a wide-track on Niki's car and a narrow track on Ronnie's car. I told Niki to go out in Ronnie's car and do ten timed laps, which he did, and his best time was 14 dead. Then we sent Ronnie out, while Niki and I went round the back of the circuit to watch from a marshals' post. When he appeared, the car was sideways, the tyres were smoking, it was in the air over the bumps; and Niki took one step backwards and his face went pale. You could see all the spirit drain out of him, and he said, "Robin, I could never drive a racing car like that." On our way back to the pits I said to him, "your fastest time was 14 dead, what do you think Ronnie's time was?" and he said, "maybe 12.5, something like that." And Ronnie's fastest time was 14.3. And I thought, shit! We've got a potential World Champion, and we've got a pay-driver who's even quicker. Niki didn't realise how good he was at that point.'*

Formula 2 at Brands

Ronnie triumphed in a couple of late summer F2 meetings. The first of these was at Brands Hatch, where, for the previous four years, Formula 2 had been eschewed by the owning Motor Circuit Developments director John Webb in favour of the rumbling spectacle of Formula 5000. Astonishingly, the Swede put his March 712M on pole, 0.2 seconds faster than the outright circuit record then held by Brabham's F1 BT33, and a full 1.5-secs faster than Graham Hill's Rondel-Brabham BT36 which was second quickest. *'The time difference between Ronnie and Graham was greater than the difference between Graham and the back of the grid,'* recalled Robin Herd. The Swede muffed the start however, and at the end of the first lap was back in fifth behind Hill, the Fittipaldi brothers and Birrell. Thereafter he seemed to glide with ease past these front-runners to take the lead by lap 3, and cruised home to win by 15 seconds. *'Just to watch him there was unbelievable,'* said Keith Leighton. *'For him, Paddock Bend was totally flat; there was no thought of lifting, whereas most guys were actually braking going into it.'*

Opposite: Peterson's works March 712 leads arch rival Schenken's Rondel Brabham at a streaming wet Tülln-Langenlebarn. **Above**: Tops in Formula 2 – Mike Hailwood, Niki Lauda and *'Mad Ronald'*, as Hailwood called him.

Chapter 04: Dawning of a New F1 Talent 76 | 77

In contrast to the sweeps and dips of Brands' long circuit, the F2 circus acted out its next 200km round on the bleak, wind-blown airfield circuit of Tülln-Langenlebarn in Austria. The heavens opened on race morning, and the straw-bale-lined circuit was awash with huge puddles – the right recipe for aquaplaning. Completely un-daunted, Ronnie took command and won the first heat by 11 seconds from Schenken and Quester. In the second heat he was passed by Schenken, but got him back on the last corner to take a comfortable aggregate victory. Despite an unpromising start to the season Ronnie now looked good for the European F2 title. However, all was not settled, as he managed only sixth at Albi on 26th September after losing two laps with a serious oil leak, where Emerson won from Reutemann and Jarier.

The fastest ever, and the closest ever

Robin Herd recalled that he and Ronnie and Barbro drove to Monza that year in Ronnie's Mercedes, straight after the Brands F2 race. It was a non-stop journey and the two men shared the driving through France and over the Alps. *'With just a couple of hours sleep, Ronnie was out practising the March,'* said Robin. *'That was the way it was then. There was a much closer rapport with the drivers in those days.'*

The 1971 Italian Grand Prix remains (just) the fastest ever GP, with an average winning speed of 150.755mph, and the closest-fought finish with a mere 0.6 seconds covering the first five cars. The scene for what Denis Jenkinson described as *'the dice of the debutants'* was set by several teams trying out modified bodywork to minimise aerodynamic drag. Rindt's fatal crash the previous year was partly to do with the absence of a rear wing, and no-one ventured down that route again. But the Tyrrells had engine cowling and air ducting for rear-mounted radiators, BRMs had only stubby front wings, Surtees sported deflectors underneath their noses, while March did away with the 711's characteristic tea-tray front spoiler to produce a completely rounded nosecone providing minimal downforce. The front row was disputed between Ickx's flat-12 Ferrari 312B/1 and Amon's V12 Matra MS120B, pole given to the New Zealander after a protest. Cevert and Peterson shared row three behind the BRM pair of Ganley and Siffert, with Stewart and Regazzoni behind. No sooner had the front row come to a halt than the flag dropped and Regga's Ferrari surged up the inside to seize an immediate lead, vying with fellow Swiss Siffert in the V12 BRM. Amon and Ickx were swamped by the mid-field, and on lap four of the slipstreaming battle, Peterson took the lead, with Stewart following through. Regga was back at the front, and then Stewart took the lead, with Cevert taking his turn as his team-leader's engine blew. Siffert appeared briefly ahead. But the main contest centred on Peterson and Cevert, pushed by Mike Hailwood's Surtees TS9. By lap 45, with ten to go, Amon had hauled his Matra into contention and he led for five laps. But instead of peeling off just one tear-off visor, he pulled the lot off and, unable to see too well at close on 200mph, consigned himself to an eventual sixth place. Meanwhile Peterson, Cevert and Hailwood traded the lead, sizing each other up for the final run to the flag. Peter Gethin in the third work's BRM had caught up with this leading bunch, and he too slipped through to the front. It was anybody's race. As they crossed the line for the last lap, the order was Peterson, Cevert, Hailwood, and Gethin, with Ganley in contention if there was a major mishap.

On the back straight, Cevert led, Peterson outbraking him to lead into the 180-degree right-hand Parabolica and hold it for the dash to the line. He hadn't reckoned with Gethin. There was just enough space for the BRM driver to get his nose up the inside, by using a bit of the infield, and Gethin emerged ahead as they exited the turn. Peterson tucked in behind the more powerful V12 BRM, darting out of the tow with less than 100 yards to go to try and grasp the win. He'd left it a fraction too late, and Gethin got the verdict by a scant 0.01-sec. Cevert was third, Hailwood fourth and Ganley a close fifth. Ronnie had led for 23 out of 55 laps, and since bonuses were paid on a per-lap basis, Ronnie and March did rather well. *'The BRM was 85lb under weight,'* said Herd, *and we could have protested it. But that wasn't really done then.'*

"COMPLETELY UNDAUNTED, RONNIE TOOK COMMAND AND WON THE FIRST HEAT BY 11 SECONDS FROM SCHENKEN AND QUESTER. IN THE SECOND HEAT HE WAS PASSED BY SCHENKEN, BUT GOT HIM BACK ON THE LAST CORNER TO TAKE A COMFORTABLE AGGREGATE VICTORY."

Opposite: Ronnie so nearly won the 1971 Italian Grand Prix. Having led for 23 of the 55 laps, he was pipped on the line by Gethin's BRM. **Above:** The 711 ran at Monza without the tea-tray nose-wing for better straight-line speed. Max Mosley makes a point to Ronnie, who seems unimpressed.

Ronnie Peterson: Super Swede

Above: Late in 1971 Ronnie has a seat fitting in the brand new March 721 at the Bicester works.

Oily surface

March Engineering entered three works cars for the Canadian GP, and a new flatter nose with stubby fins and fared-in side-plates was tried in practice on Ronnie's car. The race was held in wet conditions on an oily Mosport Park surface, and was remarkable for a dice between Stewart and Peterson. The smooth and unflustered Tyrrell driver was passed twice by the more spectacular Swede, and the Scot tailed the March, waiting for him to make a mistake. None came, and Stewart had to exert his particular skills to retake the lead a dozen laps later. The fun ended when George Eaton let Stewart past and mistakenly moved over on Peterson, deranging his nosecone and rendering any further challenge out of the question. Ronnie hung onto second place, and only Mark Donohue making his Grand Prix debut in the Penske-White Racing McLaren M19A remained on the same lap as the first two.

Howden Ganley described the mood of the F1 graduates. *'By 1971 we'd all progressed from F3 to F1, and life was pretty good. Then for 1972 Ronnie and Tim were signed up for the Ferrari sports car team, and I remember them telling me about it (big secret) while we were at Mosport for the Canadian GP in 1971. I was thinking what a great deal it was for them, and musing that it would be nice if someone offered me that sort of deal. About an hour later Jabby Crombac came and offered me the Matra Le Mans drive!'*

At Watkins Glen for the final round of the year, Ronnie impressed in early practice only for his engine to expire. In spite of mucking about with suspension settings and tyres he couldn't improve on his times and started the race down in 11th spot. After sparring with Hailwood and Ganley, passing Stewart in the process, Ronnie finished third, four seconds behind Siffert, while Cevert notched up his maiden GP win.

Ronnie came second to JYS in the 1971 F1 World Championship. *'The trouble was, every time Stewart finished a race, was when Ronnie finished a race, and he always came second,'* said Robin Herd. But at Vallelunga on 10th October he secured the European F2 crown, taking his sixth F2 victory of the season by winning the 22nd Rome Grand Prix from Quester and Reutemann. But there was a sobering twist in the tail for Peterson's F1 fortunes. At the ill-starred Rothmans Victory Meeting at Brands Hatch, Ronnie tangled with Hailwood at Bottom Bend in a bid to wrest third place from him, and both spun off, Hailwood into retirement and Ronnie to a distant 16th place, in a race terminated at 14 laps by Siffert's fatal accident.

The new km Interlagos circuit at Sao Paulo, Brazil, was the venue for the end-of-term F2 Torneio races staged on 31st October and 7th November 1971. Local hero Emerson Fittipaldi won both events after battling with Ronnie Peterson and his own brother Wilson. Tim Schenken won a subsequent race at Cordoba, Argentina, from Carlos Reutemann. Sveneric Eriksson recalled the Argentinean's lesson in pronunciation: *'Carlos said to me, "It's Re-ootiman, Swen, Re-ootiman....."'*

Ronnie Peterson: Super Swede

CHAPTER 5

Mixed Fortunes

Now that Ronnie had proved he could take on and pass anybody in F1, he was hot property. As Denis Jenkinson observed in Motor Sport of February 1972, *'Peterson knows only one way of racing, and that is hard.'* He was hired by Ferrari to strengthen its already formidable driver line-up, handling the 312P Group 5 sports-prototypes. Being a racing driver was a profession, but in the early '70s it was also a hobby. *'The teams encouraged you to race in other spheres,'* said John Watson. *'One big advantage the drivers had at that time was there was very little testing.*

Opposite: Ronnie poses with Max Mosley and Robin Herd alongside the new March 721.

You might have had four or five test sessions during a year, maybe a couple of days at a time. The big test was always done down in South Africa in the winter. But you had free weekends so you could go racing, and you'd get paid for it. It's a boys' thing, you go out racing a sports car with your mates and have a bit of a laugh. To drive for Ferrari in a sports car was a great honour, and Ronnie was delighted to have been invited. Maybe Ferrari thought this was a way to get him into their F1 team. But it took Niki to bring Ferrari to a point where they became a World Championship team, and I don't think Ronnie could have done that. Emerson might have done, but then he would have been acutely aware of the politics of the situation.'

Same height

The 1972-spec monocoque Ferrari 312P sportscar chassis was wider than previously but still powered by the 440bhp 3.0-litre flat-12 engine. Ronnie was paired with his friend Tim Schenken who, conveniently, was much the same height, so no modifications were needed in the cockpit between driver changeovers. Said Tim: *'During 1971 it was often rumoured that Ferrari were going to run a sportscar team the following year with the change to the 3.0-litre formula, and many names had been mentioned in magazines as possible drivers, including Ronnie's and mine. I had a call at Monza that year to go and meet Mr Ferrari during practice to discuss it. Ronnie had already signed a deal. In fact he told me how much money he was going to earn, so I asked for the same amount. I think Ronnie probably was helpful in me getting the drive. It made sense to put two guys together who had respect for each others skills and got on well. So although in 1972, Ronnie and I were in different teams in F1, in sports cars we were together.'*

The first event on the calendar was the Buenos Aires 1,000Kms on 9th January, and Ronnie was fastest in practice. Opposition came from Alfa Romeo, of which Rolf Stommelen was quickest driver, with Chevron B19s, Lola T212s and T280s (one driven quickly by Reine Wisell), plus the odd

> **RONNIE BEING RONNIE DIDN'T DO THINGS BY HALF MEASURES. HE LIT UP THE REAR WHEELS OUT OF THE CAR PARK, SMOKED THEM ALL THE WAY OUT ONTO THE HIGHWAY.**

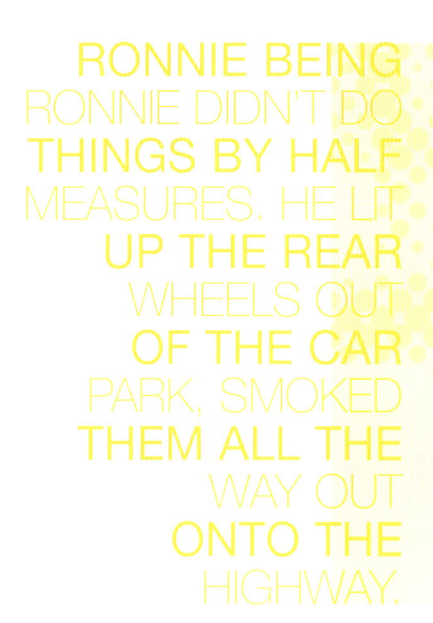

Porsche 908. After an early challenge from Stommelen, the three Ferraris crewed by Ickx/Andretti, Peterson/Schenken and Regazzoni/Redman held a comfortable lead. The Alfa challenge faded, partly due to inferior teamwork, and by half distance the only car to be worrying the Ferraris was Wisell's 1.8-litre Ecurie Bonnier Lola. He even overtook Peterson on acceleration from the hairpin, at which giant-killing demonstration the crowd threw their programmes into the air. The Wisell/Larousse challenge collapsed when a wheel hub seized during a pit-stop and, for the last 50 laps, Ferrari's new signings Peterson/Schenken enjoyed a lead of one lap over team-mates Regazzoni/Redman. There was more to winning for Ferrari than just crossing the line first. Tim recalled: *'Being Argentina, a Latin country, we were in the prize giving, and we must have had nine or ten silver cups, and when we came back to the Ferrari truck afterwards we said to Peter Schetty (then team manager), "What are we going to do with all these trophies?" And he said, "Well, if you really want to get on with the Commendatore – in other words, Mr Ferrari – what you should do is give him some cups." So Ronnie and I chose a couple of nice ones, which we gave to Peter, and he passed on to Mr Ferrari. And from then on, whenever we turned up at the factory, we seemed to be treated as his favourite sons; we had no problems at all. There were always great stories about the politics at Ferrari, but neither Ronnie nor I were ever involved in those. It was a wonderful time, 1972.'*

Almost a month later the second round of the World Manufacturers' Sports Car Championship was held at Daytona, Florida. Six hours long, it covered 194 laps or 1,189km, close to the 1,000km endurance events held elsewhere. Where it differed was that a whole gamut of machinery was eligible, from barely modified Group 1 sports GTs to out-and-out Group 5 sports prototypes. So the works Ferraris and Alfas shared the daunting Daytona banking with more humble vehicles like Mustangs, Volvo P1800s and MGBs; speed differentials were terrifyingly large. The Ferrari team consisted of six 312Ps, and the crews were the same as for Buenos Aires. Again, it was Wisell's Lola that provided the most serious threat to the Ferraris, and he was unlucky to collide with the flying engine cover from Regazzoni's 312P when it was torn off by a puncture – these two contesting the lead. Although stunned, Wisell was able to regain the pits. After that, the Ickx/Andretti car traded the lead with Peterson/Schenken, alternating as one car, then the other, made routine pit stops, the Belgian/American duo finally taking the win, after Schenken lost a couple of laps due to a puncture.

The pair nearly didn't even make the race though. Tim Schenken described their plight in the run up. *'We were staying at the Holiday Inn, across the road from the speedway, but got a bit bored with the food there so we decided to go down to one of the hotels on the beachfront the night before the race. Ronnie and I drove down there, had a meal, and we were coming back to the hotel. I was driving, as I was usually the mug that got caught if there was trouble, and as we were going along the esplanade, Ronnie saw some ramps leading onto the beach. It was quite legal to drive on the beach at Daytona. But he suggested we go down onto the beachfront and do it with a bit of style. So we took off from the main road, down the ramp, foot-to-the-floor and, in a glorious slide, onto the beachfront. Here, people normally went at 25 mph, but we were doing closer to 70. Right in front of a police car. The lights on the police car lit up, they came out and pulled us straight over, out of the car, frisked us and wanted to see some ID. All we had was cash, nothing else, so they arrested us, took us to the local police station and put us in the cells downstairs, along with all the other drunks and vagrants that'd been arrested that evening. It was getting late, and after a lot of talking, I convinced the police that they should let Ronnie go back to the hotel and get our ID because if we were able to show proof that we were competitors then they would release us, at least on bail. We were both getting a bit pissed off by this stage, because we had the race the following day. So they agreed that Ronnie take the keys of the car up to the car park to go back to the hotel. Now, Ronnie being Ronnie doesn't do things by half measures. He lit up the rear wheels out of the car park, smoked them all the way out onto the highway. As I heard the car disappearing, the police were immediately on the radio with an 'all cars' bulletin, to stop him. Sure enough, 10 minutes later, they'd arrested a very sheepish Ronnie and we were back in the cells together. So again after a lot of discussion we eventually convinced the police to ring Peter Schetty, the team*

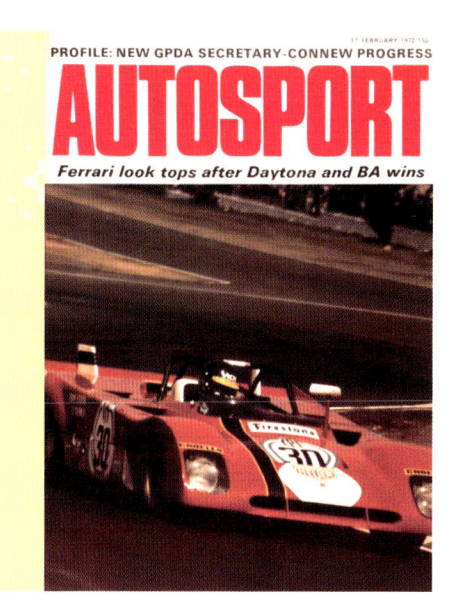

Top Left: The Peterson/Schenken 312P heads Ferrari team-mates Ickx/Andretti at Buenos Aires en route to victory. **Above:** Ronnie and Tim went on to take second at Daytona and Brands Hatch.

Ronnie Peterson: Super Swede

Above: On a publicity visit to a South African gold mine, Ronnie inspects the gold ingots. **Opposite:** The 721 promised more thn it delivered, and Ronnie struggled until the 721G appeared mid-season. Close friend Åke Strandberg gets him comfortable in the cockpit.

manager, to at least let him know what the problem was. I guess being in Daytona, and motor sport being a big part of the town and its history, we were lucky in that the police had some understanding of what the racing brought to Daytona Beach. Peter Schetty managed to reach Bill France who ran Daytona Raceway, and about 2 o'clock in the morning someone came down with bail money, and they released us. We were able to go back to the hotel. The following morning we were greeted rather icily by Peter Schetty who was not at all amused, and what happened to the bail money I don't know. We were supposed to go back and appear in court sometime later, but we didn't return, so whoever put the money up obviously lost it.'

The Peterson/Schenken partnership finished a fortunate second in the Sebring 12-Hours after Ronnie ran out of fuel three hours into the race because of a faulty collector tank on his car. It was got going again and looked set to take the lead from the oily Ickx/Andretti car, which had itself inherited the lead when Regazzoni's car expired in flames. But team manager Schetty ordered them to back off, which they resented as they felt they'd been robbed by team orders favouring the Ickx/Andretti car at Daytona.

The big spring sportscar meeting in Britain was the BOAC 1,000, and Ferrari continued its domination of the World Manufacturers' Championship with Ickx/Andretti winning for the third time from Peterson/Schenken, with two Alfa T33s next up. The three works' Ferraris all clocked identical fastest laps, setting a new record (1m 27.4 sec) in the process, and the two leading Ferraris crossed the finishing line together, although Ronnie and Tim were actually a lap behind.

As well as being a team-mate in the Ferrari squad, Mario Andretti was well acquainted with Peterson from the March F1 days, and he recalled his early dealings with him. *'I had known of Ronnie before March, and his reputation was that of an incredible driver with great car control who was spectacular to watch. We were team-mates in the Ferrari camp, but he was in the other car because he was so tall, and we wouldn't have been a good match physically. He was such an easy-going good guy. We'd be testing in South Africa two or three weeks before the race, as would many of the drivers, and after testing we would socialise, get to know each other and go do crazy things. Like, go to Kruger Park, and lark each other out of the car next to a lion or a tiger – they did that to me by the way – and we used to raise hell. We developed a friendship that was lasting and strong.'*

A new team-mate in F1

Meanwhile, the F1 World Championship got under way with the Argentine Grand Prix on 23rd January. Ronnie had damaged his 721 race-car in a testing accident in California between the Buenos Aires sports car race and the GP, but it was rebuilt at Bicester in time for the race. March's STP backing continued for 1972, the budget up to £25,000, but de Adamich and Galli were replaced by Lauda, who had successfully persuaded his bank to stump up another £35K to fund his drive. Alan Rees explained the driver status: *'When Niki came along, Ronnie was definitely the senior driver in the team, but Niki was, how can I put it, very keen to be up with him. And by mid-season he was getting very competitive. But Ronnie was always the senior driver.'*

Ronnie was also joined by his former F3 and karting mechanic, Åke Strandberg. *'At an F3 race at Mantorp Park, the March hierarchy asked me if I'd like to work for them,'* Åke said. *'I told them, "Only if you want me as a mechanic, not just because I'm a friend of Ronnie's."*

At this early stage in the season the March 721 still carried its tea-tray front wing and a brake problem in practice at Buenos Aires meant Ronnie couldn't put in as many quick laps as he'd have liked, so he started from row five alongside Andretti's flat-12 Ferrari. The main battle was between Stewart (who won), Reutemann, Hulme, Fittipaldi, Ickx, Regazzoni, Peterson, Cevert and Revson, but tail-ender Helmut Marko mistook Peterson for Lauda, who he was intent on blocking, and caused the Swede to spin at the hairpin, dropping him to sixth place.

At Kyalami, the 721 now had a new flatter nose with canard fins either side, and Ronnie started from the fourth row alongside Schenken's Surtees TS9B. Half the field was covered by one second, emphasising how close the racing was. It was hot, and hectic, and Ronnie came in fifth, totally exhausted. At the end of March, he was at Interlagos driving the March in a non-championship Brazilian Grand Prix, although only 11 cars started the race in front of packed grandstands. Appropriately, the Fittipaldi brothers created a stir at the front, while Peterson was hampered by a deflating tyre and an absence of clutch. He eventually came second to Reutemann after the local boys retired.

Good for business

March Engineering was on a roll. They'd taken orders for over 70 racing cars for 1972, from all over the world, worth £250,000. With more anticipated, they looked set to be the first racing car maker to top a £1m annual turnover. One of Ronnie's former sparring partners, James Hunt, led the works F3 team, along with Brendan McInerney, in March 723s.

Since Ronnie was runner up in the 1971 World Championship, even without a GP victory, it was inevitable that he'd receive offers of employment from elsewhere, and the March directors knew that they needed to come up with a very good car to ensure he stayed put. Robin Herd designed the March 721X. The suffix in the designation related to the location of the Alfa Romeo transmission, which was between the engine and rear axle instead of behind the axle line, a layout tried by A.T.S. ten years earlier. Ronnie had experienced this gearbox when he drove the Autodelta-built Alfa T33-3 with de Adamich at Watkins Glen. Herd's idea for the new F1 March was to contain as much weight as possible within the 721's wheelbase so the polar moment of inertia would be reduced. This ought to have made the car more responsive, and well suited to Peterson's remarkably quick reflexes. Autodelta manufactured the gears, which, like the casing, were identical to those used on the Alfa T33-3. In terms of construction it was bullet-proof, although hard to work on, according to Peter Kerr. Swapping the ratios meant a lengthy seven-hour operation instead of the 45 minutes needed for the ubiquitous Hewland unit, compromising Ronnie's penchant for trying out different ratio combinations. It also had a differential lock that made it very difficult to turn in to corners, and once the power was put down the back end would break away viciously.

Robin Herd was disparaging about his new design. *'I made an extraordinarily stupid decision,'* he confessed. *'The 711 was clearly the best F1 chassis, but I thought I could improve on it. One of the main things that made the 701 hard to drive was its high polar moment of inertia in relation to its wheelbase. The 711 on the other hand had a fairly long wheelbase with everything tucked inside it, and that made it easy to drive. So on the basis that more is better, I lengthened it even more by installing the Alfa Romeo gearbox ahead of the rear axle. Which was crap. But we managed to convince ourselves that the car would be faster. So we threw away the 711 and replaced it with the 721X.'*

Carlo Chiti who ran Autodelta, the sporting arm of Alfa Romeo, was difficult to deal with, and would only supply one set of ratios for the gearbox. *'Being the senior driver, Ronnie had first call on the ratios, and inevitably he wanted the ones Niki had,'* said Herd. *'The negotiations I had with them would have been good training for a barrister. I had to persuade Niki that the ratios he wanted just happened to be not the ones that Ronnie had. The intellectual battles at every race were just incredible.'*

The STP liveried car had inboard springs and dampers and a full-width nose but the engine cowling of the 711 was retained. All March 721s also had ignition cut-out buttons on their steering wheels since Ronnie's accident with the Alfa-powered 711 at Silverstone the previous year.

The other factor influencing the performance of the 721X was tyres. Sveneric commented: *'Goodyear stated that they wouldn't be producing special batches of tyres for 1972 and Robin Herd designed the March 721X on that basis, with all the weight in the middle for an extremely well balanced car. The trouble was, the tyre manufacturers went back to the special compounds. That meant everyone could have a car with a weight bias wherever the designer wanted it, and as a result the 721X was no longer a good car- it was a pig.'*

Ronnie debuted the 721X at the Race of Champions at Brands Hatch on 19th March, and the idea was that Lauda would take over the car and Ronnie

Chapter 5: Mixed Fortunes **88 | 89**

Opposite Left: The March 721X had its Alfa Romeo gearbox located ahead of the rear axle, and Ronnie debuted the car at the Race of Champions. **Opposite Right:** With inboard rear springs and dampers, the concept was all the weight was carried within a longer wheelbase and Ronnie finished 9th at the Belgian GP. **Above:** In close-up action at Station Hairpin. A minor accident in the wet Monaco GP found him back in 11th place.

Ronnie Peterson: Super Swede

Above: Although the March 721G reverted to Hewland transmission with outboard rear springs and dampers mid-season '72, designer Robin Herd regretted not having developed the 711, and a couple of 3rd places were scant reward for Peterson's efforts.

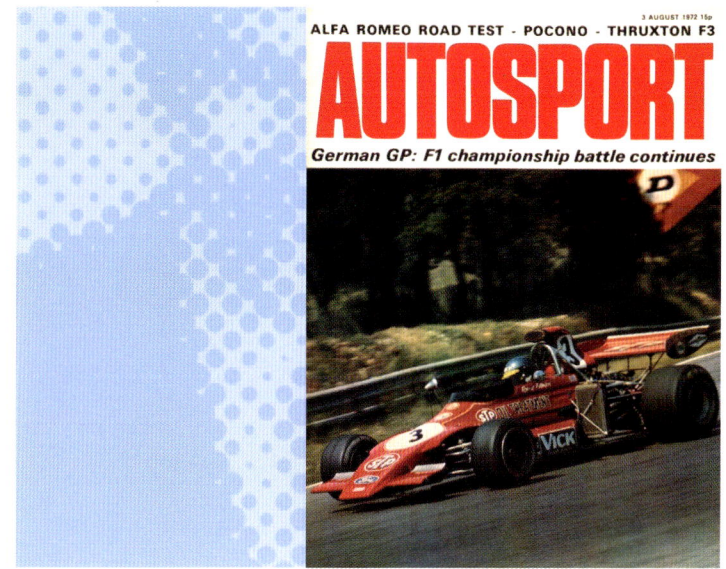

would be given a lighter version with titanium components. He experienced a number of teething problems and came 12th after a pit-stop. An engine blow up at Jarama and a minor accident in the atrociously wet Monaco race, then a battle way down the field with Stommelen's Eifelland-March (721/4) at Nivelles summed up Ronnie's mid-season in Formula 1. He was absolutely frustrated, telling Alan Henry, *'I just want the car fixed.'* STP were also beginning to wonder when the results of their investment would come.

At the non-championship Oulton Park Gold Cup, Ronnie drove the 721X with a Hewland transmission fitted, only to collide with Reine Wisell at the start. Both cars were eliminated, and Wisell sustained a broken finger due to steering kick-back. Peter Kerr commented, *'I'd worked all night to fit the Hewland 'box, and after the race I just put a new wheel on, drove it straight onto the transporter and went home.'* The bottom line was, the 721X just wasn't on the pace, and there was nothing Ronnie could do about it – his efforts becoming wilder the harder he tried.

Ronnie spotted that the stockbroker-sponsored March 721G of Mike Beuttler, a converted Formula 2 chassis, was quicker down the straight than his own car, and reported back to Robin Herd. In eight days he had an F2 chassis prepared, with Cosworth DFV and Hewland gearbox grafted on, and when Ronnie tested it at Silverstone using identical gear ratios to the 721X, he immediately found another three seconds a lap. Robin Herd grasped the nettle, removed the Alfa gearbox and replaced it with a Hewland unit, relocating the rear springs and dampers outboard; the result was called the 721X/2B. But Lauda's car, 721X/1 retained the central gearbox and inboard suspension. *'It still wasn't anything like as good as the 711,'* lamented Herd. *'If only I'd fine-tuned the 711 and spoken sweetly to Cosworth so we could get better engines, things might have gone better in '72.'*

While Lauda's car was not race-worthy at Clermont-Ferrand, Peterson's 721G performed well enough, and although a rear anti-roll bar mount broke, he was able to hold onto fifth place. He was less fortunate at Brands Hatch, crashing into Cevert's parked Tyrrell and Hill's abandoned Brabham when his

Ronnie Peterson: Super Swede

March's engine died as he set the car up for the daunting Paddock Bend. In Austria, fluctuating fuel pressure dropped Ronnie down the field, having been running fifth. He'd tried a new chassis with twin front radiators, an arrangement not unlike the *'lobster-claw'* Brabham BT34. At the Nürburgring, Ronnie started from the second row alongside Emerson's Lotus, with Stewart and Ickx ahead of them. Ronnie banged wheels with Stewart, who backed off and let him through, and on the fifth lap the Brazilian passed the Swede for second place. Soon enough, the Lotus's Hewland 'box burst, causing a fire, while Regazzoni's Ferrari was elevated to second place behind Ickx after tangling with Stewart. Ronnie thus came third after some heroic driving, earning the *'Jo Siffert Man of the Race'* award from Marlboro.

As the season progressed, Ronnie was growing tired of the promises made by Max and Robin, because even though he was driving his heart out, the results were not coming. By mid-season he was being courted by almost everyone and amongst the suitors was Colin Chapman, who approached Ronnie at the Nürburgring and got him to sign an option on his services for Team Lotus for 1973. Said Peter Warr: *'We had the best package and the best car to offer, and Ronnie always wanted to drive the best car. So there was a natural meeting of minds. No doubt, Ronnie was a prize catch, but he was having a poor season with March.'* Nevertheless Staffan and Sveneric were mad with Ronnie, who then reminded them that it was just an option. To the Swedish managers it looked like a binding contract. *'Colin paid £1,000 for the option,'* said Staffan. Perhaps Ronnie didn't fully appreciate the implications of an *'option'*. Headstrong or spontaneous, it's nevertheless surprising that he signed without consulting them. In certain matters, Ronnie apparently thought he knew better than his advisors.

No walkover

In the World Championship for Makes, what should have been a Ferrari walkover in the annual Monza 1,000Kms, turned into a shambles due to sheets of April rain that doused the circuit from the outset. Redman lost the back-end of his car against the barriers, while Ickx had electrical trouble, leaving Peterson in the lead, only to spin at Vialone, which necessitated the left-rear corner being replaced before Schenken, could take over. By half distance, the misfiring Ickx/Regazzoni car was back in front, with Peterson/Schenken third behind Reinhold Jöst's Gulf-coloured Porsche 908/3. Over 175 laps, cars get strung out, and Ronnie and Tim were nine laps down at the end because of the long pit stop, but still in third place. The Ferrari steamroller moved to Spa next, for the 1,000Kms on 7th May. Ickx and Regazzoni handled the number one car, with Peterson and Schenken in the second and Redman and Merzario in the third car. It was the latter pairing that would win. Alfa Romeo admitted they couldn't match the Ferrari's speed or driver line-up, while the main opposition came from the new Gulf Mirage M6 of Bell/van Lennep and the Lola T280 of Hine and Bridges. By lap 10, Ickx had lapped all the 2.0-litre cars, averaging a staggering 151mph. But in the final stint after lap 53, Regazzoni got a puncture, splitting the oil tank, which cost two laps in the pits while repair was effected. This handed the lead to Redman, who was lucky to keep the Ferrari on the road when he ran into an Ardennes rain shower. But Ronnie was less fortunate, spotting the changed road surface too late, sliding his car into the barriers and into retirement, 15 laps from the end.

Ferrari sent only one car to tackle the Targa Florio, and none of its top-line drivers was enthusiastic about driving. The Scuderia also ducked out of Le Mans in '72, having clinched the Manufacturers' title by June, as well as being faced with a strong challenge from the Matra team – which, in the event, provided Graham Hill with his swan-song Le Mans win. After an unexpected triumph by the Merzario/Munari pairing in Sicily, Ferrari returned in force to the Nürburgring for the 1,000Kms – six hours and 44 laps of the Nordschleife – with their star drivers back in harness. Ronnie was quickest in practice, joined on the front row by Derek Bell's Mirage M6. The majority were on wets in anticipation of a damp track, but Bell gambled on drys, and as a result had no grip at the start and was passed by hoards. While Peterson led from Merzario and Ickx, Bell moved up to fourth ahead of the two Alfa Romeo T33s of de Adamich/Marko and Stommelen/Elford. Well up were the Larousse/Bonnier Lola T290 (it was Bonnier's last-but-one race – the veteran Swede was killed at Le Mans a fortnight

Chapter 5: Mixed Fortunes

Opposite: Peterson and Wisell in pensive mood. Sharing the grid for the Spanish GP at Jarama with Reine's BRM.

Ronnie Peterson: Super Swede

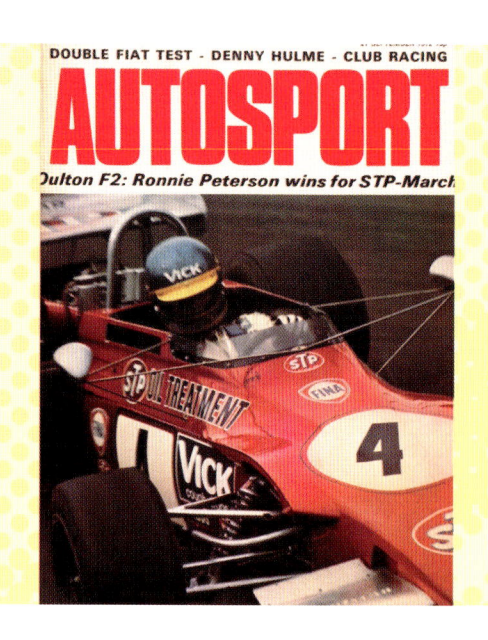

> WE HAD QUITE
> A SUCCESFUL YEAR
> IN THE FERRARI,
> WINNING TWO RACES
> AND BEING PLACED
> SECOND OR THIRD
> IN MOST OF
> THE OTHERS. BUT
> RONNIE'S SKILLS
> WEREN'T IN SETTING UP
> A CAR, THEY WERE
> IN DRIVING.

Above: Apart from successes in the Ferrari sportscars, main highlights of Ronnie's year in '72 were his F2 wins at Thruxton and Oulton Park in the March 722. **Opposite Left:** Testing a shovel nose on the 722 at Oulton Park. **Opposite Right:** Fastest in practice, the Peterson/Schenken Ferrari 312P made the right tyre choice and won the Nürburgring 1,000kms.

later) and the Red Rose Chevron of Bridges/Hine. Masses of Porsche 911s and Ford Capri RSs grappled for the Group 4 and Group 2 glory. With Regazzoni off, a tyre contest developed between the Peterson/Schenken Ferrari and the Bell/van Lennep Mirage – the former on intermediates and the latter on slicks. The Ferrari remained ahead. When the Merzario/Redman Ferrari was put on slicks, it caught up with the Mirage, such was the Ferrari's superior performance, and as they rounded South Curve on the penultimate lap, the Mirage's Cosworth DFV went bang, leaving a Ferrari one-two result. Ronnie and Tim won by over four minutes, averaging 166.68kph over 6hrs 1 min 40.2secs.

Tim recalled the differences in their respective techniques: *'We had quite a successful year, winning two races and being placed second or third in most of the others. But Ronnie's skills weren't in setting up a car, they were in driving. If it had four wheels he could drive it very, very quickly. Quite often he'd run the Ferrari first and set a time, and he'd be quite happy with it. Then I'd get in and find it would be quite difficult to drive – very difficult on some occasions. I'd then work with the engineers to make the car easier to drive, more to my style, and then I'd soon be producing competitive times. But when Ronnie got back in the car he'd still produce the time that he first established, so the set up of the car wasn't so important to him, and his natural ability more than made up for any deficiencies in handling.'*

The all-conquering three-car Ferrari squad showed up at Watkins Glen for the 6-Hours race on 22nd July, bent on making an impression even though after eight wins they could add no more point to their tally. But a Ferrari win meant better production car sales figures in the USA. By raising the tail struts three inches, the Ferraris found more speed – they now acted like wings rather than spoilers, and it was Ronnie that claimed pole position followed by the Ickx/Andretti car. Peterson/Schenken led comfortably for most of the race, as much of the opposition fell by the wayside. The third Ferrari 312P of Redman/Merzario blew its engine at 120 laps, while the Wisell/Larousse Lola retired when Reine was rammed by an errant Corvette. Then Schenken spun, before handing the car back to Peterson. Ten minutes from the end, Ronnie's brakes began to fade, and he was caught by the storming Ickx. These two were 14 laps ahead of the third-placed Gulf-Mirage of Bell/Pace.

High times

There had been some high jinks prior to the race, as Mario Andretti recalled. *'Ronnie was one of those that you just loved to have around. When he used to race Stateside, like, for example the Six Hours at Watkins Glen, I'd invite him to come and stay with us. We would go up to a sports park where they have all sorts of toys, and we'd get him so tired and so ruined! He would be crashing on motorcycles and all sorts of things. I remember he went back to the Glen and he was a total mess, twisted ankle, bruised chest, bruised chin, because he had flipped a 250cc Motocross bike. And we pulled him at about 50mph water-skiing and he had a huge flip on the lake and twisted his back a little. They were precious times believe me, the stories and laughs we used to have.'* Amazing, then, that Ronnie was in a fit state to race, let alone very nearly win.

Champ in a Matchbox

In Formula 2, Ronnie carried on much as he'd left off, winning the Easter meeting at Thruxton in the March-Cosworth BDF 722. Third place overall in the Jochen Rindt Trophy at Hockenheim on June 11th was the best of the mid-season results. Then on 16th September he won at Oulton Park, a drivers' circuit if ever there was one, from Lauda and Hunt. Another third place came at Hockenheim on 1st October. But it was not Ronnie's year in F2. That honour belonged to the consistent Mike Hailwood in the Matchbox Surtees, who'd notched up three wins and a host of podiums – Emerson had four wins but fewer point-scoring finishes.

Keith Leighton went to work at Rondel Racing with Ron Dennis in 1972, and he talked Ronnie into going to Rondel in October to drive four F2 races in the South American Temporada series. While wins went to Emerson, Carlos Pace and Mike Hailwood, Ronnie's engines blew up in every race. *'We had the biggest, baddest engines – belt-driven BDAs,'* said Keith, *'built by a Japanese guy called Itoh (who also went to Lotus in '1973). They were great engines, but there was something wrong with the camshafts; so they were fast, but didn't go very far!'*

Changing horses

The 43rd Italian GP at Monza was notable for the introduction of two chicanes, one just after the start, and another around the back at Curva del Vialone. In Saturday afternoon's practice, Ronnie overcooked it at the second chicane and badly damaged the March. This meant that his grid position was based on his Friday time, placing him on the back of the grid alongside Nanni Galli's Tecno flat-12. The chassis still wasn't as straight as it should have been and the handling felt odd. With adjustments made during the race to the aerodynamics to see if that would help, Ronnie finished ninth, a lap down. Emerson, meanwhile, clinched the Drivers' Championship with a win for John Player Team Lotus. He'd also won the Rothmans 50,000 at Brands Hatch a fortnight earlier. The purse being £50,000, it must have been galling to the sponsors that the Team supported by a rival cigarette company stole the honours. It was into this environment that Ronnie now committed himself, spurning the red March for the black-and-gold of John Player Team Lotus. Although he didn't drive in the Rothmans race, it was here that he signed Chapman's two-season contract. Though Max Mosley tried to dissuade him, Ronnie saw that his best chance of a winning car lay with Lotus. Mosley gave Peterson a hard time for the rest of the season, accounting for Ronnie's off-colour performance at Monza, but it was with Chapman that Mosley was really angry, for wooing his driver away. *'Ronnie very sensibly, but sadly, decided to go to Lotus,'* said Robin Herd. *'Funnily enough, Niki wanted to stay with us, but we didn't have the money. STP pulled out altogether, so he went to BRM. We did a deal with BMW to run the works March BMW F2 cars and had great success doing that.'*

Formula 2 mechanic Keith Leighton also went to Lotus for 1973. *'Ronnie told Peter Warr that he'd go if I went as well,* said Keith. *'I came walking into this restaurant near Maidenhead one evening, and there were Warr and Chapman and Ronnie. The next thing I knew I was going to Lotus.'*

Sveneric recalled the meeting between Ronnie, Staffan and himself with Peter Warr, Colin Chapman and his finance director Fred Bushell at the Heathrow Excelsior Hotel. *'Whenever we agreed something with Chapman and Warr, Bushell seemed to be against it! But we were just young 30-year old guys facing these businessmen who'd done everything. We were there three days, and every evening we were finished,'* he said. *'It was all we could do to get a hamburger or something. We had to watch every word that was said. When it came to how much money Ronnie would get, £25,000 this year, so much more the next, I turned to Ronnie and said, "What do you think?" He didn't know what to say. I said, "Haven't you been listening?" He said, "No, I've been watching those girls in the swimming pool!" It was flattering that he put his faith in Staffan and me. But Ronnie wanted to drive for Team Lotus, and he was happy to let us make the best of it. Nowadays managers are much tougher.'*

Because of the tax situation in Sweden, Ronnie was the first racing driver to have his contract written in such a way that his earnings were split between what he earned in the UK – being domiciled in England – and those that were earned outside the UK. Peter Warr elaborated: *'Although we'd had some experience with Jochen, with Svenby, we put together the first genuine contract catering for a racing driver living in England and driving in UK races, and one who works for a Swedish company and drives in all the other races. That was a novelty at the time, and that was why it took so long to sort out. Ronnie was effectively a company, the company was paid a retainer by Team Lotus, and he drew his salary from the company.'*

There was a definite buzz in the JPS camp when it was rumoured that Ronnie was coming for '73. *'We'd met Ronnie before '73, when he was with March,'* said Team Lotus mechanic Rex Hart. *'In those days drivers went around and spoke to other people. They just walked in and out of garages; there were no chains then. He was doing the right things to be a great driver*

Chapter 5: Mixed Fortunes 96 | 97

Above: A practice crash put Ronnie at the back of the grid for the Italian GP, and unresolved aerodynamic factors meant he finished only 9th.

Ronnie Peterson: Super Swede

RONNIE, TIM, HONDEN O NIKI.

FUSSI SOLER ROIG.

MARIA HELENA FITTIPALDI

CARLOS REUTEMANN

GIRLS

PUNTA DEL ESTE, URUGUAY

Opposite: Noted for his exploits in BMW saloons, Ronnie also had a couple of outings in Ford Capris – one in a celebrity race at Brands Hatch and the other (seen here) in a works Cologne Capri at Mantorp Park.

then and we were all pleased and excited once we found out he was coming to Lotus.'

Emerson was undoubtedly more circumspect about Ronnie's impending arrival in the team. John Watson reflected, *'Emerson recognised that Ronnie coming into the team was a major challenge to his position. So he started to talk to Brabham and McLaren and associated himself with Marlboro and, ultimately, he took Marlboro to McLaren. Bernie never forgave him for that, because they were talking to Bernie about Brabham becoming a Marlboro-backed team.'*

There was a precedent for Team Lotus having two number one drivers, and both World Champions at that. Back in 1967, Graham Hill joined Jim Clark. But their approaches were completely different, Hill deeply analytical and questioning, Clark the great natural talent. John Watson agreed: *'Graham might have been savvy and more streetwise, but Jimmy was quicker. And I would say in the place of Ronnie and Emerson, Ronnie was naturally quicker; but Emerson was more political.'*

Peter Warr expanded on the theme: *'Colin had always hankered after a return to the Jimmy Clark/Graham Hill days of equal number ones. We were slightly worried about Emerson after he'd won the Championship in '72. There were indications that he wasn't the team player we'd hoped he'd be; he started to think more about safety issues, and he seemed content not to be on pole, thinking that he could get the job done with a good car from further back on the grid. But that wasn't the way we went racing.'*

Some drivers follow teams because they've been successful in a given year, for instance Carlos Reutemann was driving for Brabham, but Ferrari won the World Championship so he went to Ferrari. Said Watson, *'The really smart people in F1 tend to look to teams that are not the winning team of that given year, but the team that's maybe just below that point. So when you jump on their wave, that wave crests and you're the guy on board, you control the championship. That's exactly what Emerson did at Lotus in '72, and then went on to do with McLaren in '74.'*

Twilight zone

The 1972 season drained away with Ronnie fourth at Watkins Glen, having been quickest in the appalling weather of Saturday's qualifying when only a handful of drivers braved the elements. For the first time, Ronnie's March was fitted with a rear anti-roll bar adjuster, controlled by a lever in the left of the cockpit, which the driver pumped to alter the roll bar setting according to diminishing fuel load. Determined to leave March on a high note, Ronnie put his 721G on the front row in Canada and led for a while before Stewart got by. The crowd was treated to the spectacle of Ronnie being blocked for four laps by back-marker Graham Hill, then in the twilight of his driving career, and in desperation, the Swede forced his way past, only to have the door shut on him mid corner. The March's steering was bent, while Hill's Brabham was undamaged. Ronnie was pushed back up the pit road and repaired, and out he went again, treating the former World Champion to a taste of his own medicine. Then Peterson was black flagged for the push backwards in the pit lane.

March made a last ditch attempt to win back Ronnie for 1973. *'They knew they'd lost the gold bullion,'* said Sveneric. *'We got a three-year contract from Max for '73, '74, and '75. It was probably one of the best contracts ever. We could do more or less anything. He offered us £100,000 (which matched what Ronnie was paid by John Player Team Lotus) and we could even put Ronnie's personal sponsors' money in our pockets. But by then though the train had left the station.'*

Ronnie Peterson: Super Swede

CHAPTER 6

A Very Special Year

Ronnie was buying into the Lotus legend, as well as into the more robust competitiveness of the Lotus team and its Type 72. But the crucial difference between Lotus and March was that Team Lotus existed to race and to feed Chapman's passion for motorsport, whereas March was also bent on building and supplying customer cars. Unquestionably they did this very well, dominating F2 and F3 in 1973. Ronnie's replacement in the March F1 effort, Jean-Pierre Jarier, was sensational in F2 but the F1 car was not on the pace.

Opposite: Ronnie appreciated the benefits provided by his long-term personal sponsors, Vicks.

By this time Lotus was not building customer racing cars, and the production car side was totally separate from the racing. So at Team Lotus, Ronnie was in a more focussed environment. The John Player-Team Lotus contract ruled out any sportscar activities, although F2 might be on the cards. Said Schenken, *'Because of contractual arrangements, Ronnie could no longer drive for Ferrari and I was paired with Carlos Reutemann. However our friendship was just as strong as ever, we played a lot of squash together, and spent our holidays with Ronnie and Barbro at their Monaco flat.'*

On the personal sponsorship front, Ronnie retained his support from Vick, and attracted the Swedish Polar Caravans concern as well. Chapman didn't want too many outside sponsors because of the arrangement for exclusivity he had with Geoffrey Kent of John Players. Texaco, Lotus's secondary sponsor, did well to have their logo in red and white rather than the regulation black and gold.

Ronnie opened his account at Team Lotus by getting pole position – for the first time in his F1 career – at the Interlagos Brazilian Grand Prix. His pole time was almost five seconds quicker than Emerson's lap record of the previous Easter. *'No matter how hard Emerson tried, Ronnie just went out and completely obliterated his times,'* recalled Keith Leighton. *'Imagine, you are a racecar driver, and you've done the best possible lap you can, let's say 16.6 or something like that. You come into the pits and you've got a smile on your face. Your team-mate is out there and he does a 16.2. I've witnessed that with Emerson, because I was pretty close to him too, and it was like, "how the hell did he do that?" The one which definitely got to Emerson was Ronnie at Interlagos in 1973. Emerson did what he thought was the perfect unbeatable lap, 2m 31.6. Ronnie went out and did 2m 30.5, more than a second quicker. Emerson was livid; he's got a Latin temperament, he wanted to be on pole position in front of his home crowd.'*

In the final session though, Emerson wasn't far off, being 0.7 second slower than Ronnie, with Ickx's Ferrari 312B2 completing the front row, nearly two seconds slower than the Lotuses. Emerson led the Brazilian race from start to finish, while Ronnie fought with Stewart for third, until the centre of one of his Melmag rear wheels pulled out, spinning him into the Armco. These pressed and bonded wheels were used by several teams, and such failures were not unknown. *'To watch Ronnie in the infield below the pits was unbelievable,'* said Keith. *'He'd be getting smoke off both rear tyres coming through some of the bends. Chapman loved it.'*

Now that Ronnie was at Lotus, commentators felt they had a yardstick by which to judge his mercurial performance, since the Type 72 was the quickest car and Emerson was reigning World Champion. The Brazilian pressed this point home by taking pole position in Argentina as Ronnie hit gearbox problems. Ronnie shared the third row with Cevert but by three-quarter distance, his race was over with a seized engine.

At Kyalami for the South African Grand Prix both the cars started from near the front of the grid but for the race Team Lotus miscalculated the angle of the Type 72s' rear wings, compromising their straight-line speed. Despite a strong showing though, Peterson's throttle linkage broke and he lost six laps getting it sorted in the pits, re-joining to finish in 11th place.

In another one of Ronnie's encounters with authority, Jackie Stewart remembered the F1 charter flight's arrival at Johannesburg for the South African race. *'The immigration people asked him "purpose of visit?" and he said he was going to a race meeting. He was bundled into custody because they thought he meant a "race" meeting. Here's this blond, Arian-looking man, and they thought he was attending some sort of racial meeting. He was kept waiting for about three hours at Johannesburg airport while they checked him out.'*

By the Race of Champions on March 18th, the JPS Lotuses had a fibreglass and foam sandwich cladding the sides of the car to comply with the new deformable structure regulations, and revised suspension manifest mostly in a wider front track, while new Goodyear tyres needed telemetry changes. After practice, they reverted to the narrower front track, which Ronnie preferred. This event was the curtain raiser to the European leg of the World Championship, even though it contained a strong F5000 contingent. The starter held the cars for so long that both Lotuses started to boil. Emerson's metering unit failed after three laps, and although he led the race, Ronnie's transmission lasted 18 laps before it broke. At Silverstone for the GKN-Daily Express International, the front of the grid comprised Fittipaldi, Peterson and Stewart, in order of practice times.

While Emerson's clutch burned out, Ronnie made the perfect start, and a battle royal began, both Lotus and Tyrrell right on the limit. After one lap, Stewart was past, only to spin at Beckett's. He was soon in pursuit of Peterson, hounding him for lap after lap, dodging the slower F5000 cars. An icy wind was blowing flurries of snow across the track, and it was cold enough to freeze on the track surface. Ronnie spun, as did several others, allowing the maestro through. SuperSwede, as he was known by now, recovered to claim second place ahead of Regazzoni's BRM P160E. Jackie Stewart commented: *'I had a good tussle with him in the Daily Express International Trophy race, which I won. He got round to Beckett's and spun off in the snow; I had the benefit of being just behind him, and was able to recognise the snow problem and brake earlier. But for these sorts of things, he'd have won more races. He drove at that time entirely by the seat of his pants, which was very good, but there comes a time when the head has to operate. I think he had the ability to be World Champion. He was always quick but he was fairly fast and furious at times, just because he was such a natural driver. Mike Hailwood used to call him "Mad Ronald". But I admired his ability tremendously. Any number of times, particularly in 1973, I'd follow him into a corner and think, "Uh-oh, Ronnie, this time you've overdone it, you're gone!" But he always seemed to get it back. It never surprised me that the spectators loved him – he was exciting to watch from where I was, too!'* The feeling was mutual. Sveneric Eriksson said, *'Apart from Rindt, Ronnie had no particular heroes. But he admired Stewart.'*

Chapter 6: A Very Special Year

Above: First race for Lotus at Buenos Aires ended in retirement (no4) **Right:** Ronnie's first pole position came at Interlagos (no2). Team personnel had never seen smoke coming off both rear tyres before. Publicity shot with Emerson. Mutual admiration society. Ronnie and Jackie on the grid before the Brazilian GP.

Ronnie Peterson: Super Swede

Above: Ronnie led magnificently at Montjuich Park, but the gearbox couldn't stand the pace. **Top:** Locking up a front wheel under braking for Loew's hairpin at Monaco 1973.

Super ace

Still the first F1 win eluded Ronnie. At Barcelona's Montjuich Park he claimed pole position and set fastest lap in the race, only for the transmission to fail after 56 laps. The imperturbable Emerson took the win. Even so, commentators such as Denis Jenkinson described Ronnie as *'a super-ace'* on account of his sub-1 min 24sec lap times around the undulating and spectacular Spanish park. Anyone under 1min 25sec was dubbed merely a *'hero'*. With no run-off areas, the Armco-lined circuit was a daunting proposition for anyone, yet Ronnie was fastest in all three practice sessions. In the race he'd lapped everybody else. As he walked disgruntled back to the pits, Ronnie completely ignored the cheers of the crowd. He had some justification in being annoyed as the gearbox internals had been renewed before the race. Mind you, the gravel surface of the Montjuich Park paddock left something to be desired – there was nothing remotely resembling the clean, clinical garages available to modern F1 teams.

For the next race at Zolder the newly-laid tarmac surface began to break up the moment cars began practising on it, and the GPDA wanted to remove the Belgian Grand Prix lock stock and barrel and run it at Nivelles. The voice of reason came from Hailwood and Ickx, who pointed out that everyone was in the same boat and they should just get on with it. Peterson did just that, logging another pole position, a second quicker than his team-mate who was down on row five of the grid. Remarkably, Ronnie had two bad crashes in practice, overdoing it on new pads and discs and then going off on cold tyres. He was required to have a medical check-over, while a car that he could drive in the race was built up by the long-suffering mechanics, from the remains of the two broken ones. There was no finesse about its set-up, but Chapman, clearly cross, took the view that, *'Ronnie will drive whatever you give him.'* So when the race started, Ronnie set off in fine style, although the serious challenge came from the Tyrrell twins. He dropped further and further behind with worsening handling and braking, spinning out backwards into the barriers on lap 43.

Mechanic Rex Hart spoke about car set-up: *'I was spannering on Ronnie's car from the word go, and he wasn't that good at set up. On the Type 72, that was Emerson's speciality. So we used Emerson's settings on Ronnie's car nearly all the time. And then we made a few other adjustments during the course of the day. But generally he just got in and drove the thing. It was as simple as that. Most of the time he was at Lotus he was pretty well quicker than everybody there. It was just the luck of the draw if he got the break in the race. He was a treat to work with, no question about that. He always came round and chatted if we were on an all-nighter.'*

They lined up at Monaco two abreast, with Stewart marginally faster than Peterson around the revised circuit – several revisions included the extension around the harbour-side swimming pool. The front row drivers were beaten away by Cevert and Regazzoni, but before the first lap was complete, Ronnie was in the lead. Suddenly his fuel pressure dropped, and despite switching on the electric fuel pump, the Lotus fell back. The battle at the front was now between Stewart and Fittipaldi, but a recovering Cevert came up from the rear of the field and placed the second Tyrrell behind his team leader, albeit a lap behind. The Scot was driving smoothly while the Brazilian's Lotus rode the kerbs dramatically as he attempted to keep the Tyrrell in sight. In the closing stages they came up to lap Ronnie, who might have balked Stewart to let Emerson have a crack at passing him. Cevert could have done the same to Emerson. But neither did, and Stewart won from Emerson, with Ronnie third but a lap behind.

The intimate and rather gauche John Player sponsored video *'If you're not winning, you're not trying'* was made during the 1973 season by TransWorld International. Wherever you went in pits or paddock, there was always a cameraman and a soundman filming some aspect of the Team, which was a novelty at the time. The film's title was a Chapman quote, and we see him and Warr plotting crucial tyre choices, wing and damper settings, amid brief asides to drivers and mechanics. Ronnie's parents went to some of the Grands Prix and are glimpsed in the film. Said Sveneric, *'Bengt would always have some suggestion to make to Chapman, which used to piss Ronnie off. Like, one time Bengt suggested to Chapman that the wheel centres should be fared-in to make them more streamlined.'*

At Anderstorp, Ronnie and Cevert shared the font row of the grid and Ronnie excelled on his home turf. A crowd of 55,000 packed the stands, and Prince Bertil was present to see how SuperSwede did. For much of the race the two black-and-gold cars were in charge, followed by the two blue Elf-Tyrrells. But in the closing stages, Emerson's gearbox failed and Ronnie was plagued by a deflating rear tyre. This allowed Denny Hulme's McLaren to ease by on the very last lap.

For this race the organisers billeted most of the teams at High Chaparral – cowboy city – some 20km east of the circuit. Sveneric recalled the antics driving back there after practice: *'you had to leave the tarmac and go in through the woods on a gravel road to get to it. Ronnie, Emmo, Peter Warr and Chapman had been loaned a Ford Granada each, courtesy of Gunnar Palm. I had a Lotus Europa, and I briefed them about the road – lots of hairpin bends, gravel surface, so I said to take it easy at first. Of course I was talking to deaf ears. We came to a place called Knutstorp, and there was a hidden alley they were meant to go down. Chapman saw it too late and spun into a farmyard. Warr did much the same, Ronnie tried to take the corner and went into a shallow ditch and managed to drive out again, while Emmo was laughing so much he lost it too. Every day for three or four days they raced each other, especially at that bend – Knutstorp Curva Grande. The team members had more fun with each other than they do today – it was more of a family thing.'*

That first GP win

Stewart had pole at Paul Ricard, with Scheckter's McLaren and Emerson also on the front rank, with Ronnie and Cevert behind. In only his third F1 race, Scheckter led for 42 laps, with Ronnie second, and everyone anticipating that sooner or later the *'upstart'* would be relegated to where he belonged. Only when Emerson tried to pass him did Scheckter get demoted, the South African slamming the door shut on the Brazilian, whose Lotus's suspension was damaged in the ensuing coming together. Emerson was very upset, as this was the first 72 he'd driven back in 1970 and until now it had never been damaged.

This little altercation allowed Ronnie to cruise blithely into the lead, riding the Ricard kerbs to an unchallenged victory. Everyone heaved a sigh of relief. He had broken his duck, and was rightfully a Grand Prix winner. Afterwards, only Ronnie seemed unable to believe his luck had finally held throughout an entire race.

In the wake of that first Grand Prix win, Ronnie began to endorse a product called Plastic Padding, the car body repair material of which company his friend Lars Berntson was managing director. *'He did it for free,'* revealed Lars, *'he said, "I'm not going to charge you. I'm doing it for fun." So he was the figurehead for two years or so.'*

'It's the classic thing,' said Warr. *'He'd learned how to win, and after that he won and won and won.'* So it was a freshly confident Ronnie that arrived at Silverstone for the British Grand Prix. Both drivers had the use of a spare car each, Ronnie's being 72/R6 and R8. It was during practice that people really sat up and took notice. The pits and the stands that surround Woodcote were the place to catch sight of the essential Peterson. As Denis Jenkinson put it, *'Peterson rose to the occasion and, in a display of driving that gladdened the hearts of the Silverstone old timers who thought the spectacle had died away with Fangio and Gonzalez, he snatched pole away from the McLarens with a lap in 1min 16.3, compared with their 1min 16.5sec. The first time the Lotus went through Woodcote at 145-150mph in an opposite lock slide, everyone said 'Good Lord!" The next time they said "Cor!" and when he did it on every lap even the most anti modern-racing enthusiast said "Good grief! It's fantastic!" And it was, because if he was driving like that on Woodcote corner, he was obviously doing the same thing on Copse, Stowe, Club and Abbey.'* Praise indeed from Jenks, not given to endorse anyone he didn't consider an out-and-out racer.

Peterson got away first, followed by Stewart but, first time round on cold tyres, Scheckter lost his McLaren, which skewed neatly head-on into the pit-lane wall, eliminating nine cars in the ensuing pile up. Miraculously, no one was hurt, except the unfortunate de Adamich who sustained a broken ankle. In the restart, Ronnie led again; this time from Lauda's BRM, but Stewart was soon challenging him. The Scot made a rare mistake, missing a gear, and plunged into the

1st Nice Won Ronnie! John Player Special

PETERSON ROSE TO THE OCCASION, IN A DISPLAY OF DRIVING THAT GLADDENED THE HEARTS OF THE SILVERSTONE OLD TIMERS WHO THOUGHT THE SPECTACLE HAD DIED AWAY WITH FANGIO AND GONZALEZ.

Opposite Left: At speed in the Lotus 72 in Sweden. **Opposite Right:** leading Hulme and Ganley at Monaco. **Top:** JPS sticker produced by promotions agency Stanbury Foley celebrates Paul Ricard success. **Above:** Ronnie again led at Monaco but falling fuel pressure dropped him to 3rd.

Ronnie Peterson: Super Swede

Above: Jubilation at his first win in the French Grand Prix, with JPS promotions guru Noel Stanbury, left, and Colin Chapman **Opposite Left:** Barbro clocks Ronnie's lap times at Silverstone, helped by a young Simon Hadfield. **Opposite Right:** The gloves are on for Ronnies maiden victory at Paul Ricard.

cornfield, narrowly missing photographer Charlie Knight, who snapped a sequence of memorable shots of the Tyrrell behaving like a combine harvester. Meanwhile, Ronnie was being hauled in by Emerson and Peter Revson in the works McLaren M23. As Emerson's transmission failed, Revson was through to take a well-earned win, while Ronnie successfully resisted pressure from Hulme in the other McLaren to finish second.

The Texaco Stars

Team Lotus had run the Type 73 Formula 3 cars with John Player backing in 1972 – Players also sponsored the British F3 series – and for 1973, they ran a Formula 2 team. Backing came from Texaco, and the cars were painted white and red rather than the black-and-gold of the F1 cars. The Lotus Type 74 F2 cars were billed as Texaco Stars, and were designed by Ralph Bellamy, also hard at work penning the 72's replacement. Emerson and Ronnie drove them, and former Lotus racing manager and chief mechanic Jim Endruweit led a dedicated team of mechanics. The cars made their debut seven races into the season at Nivelles, and both retired. It was that kind of a day. I was selling Texaco Star merchandise from a trackside stall, and sold perhaps half-a-dozen T-shirts out of a full Transit load.

Next round contested by the Texaco Stars was Rouen, part road course, part race track, with a very fast uphill section and long wiggling downhill part. Here, another of Ronnie's contemporaries, the talented Scot Gerry Birrell, was killed in practice. A chicane made of polystyrene blocks was erected half way across the track to slow cars down, but when Ronnie discovered how flimsy it was, it didn't last long, as everyone took bites out of it. On one such occasion, Ronnie went off, terminally, though in true Peterson style, he'd already set fastest lap. The Texaco Stars looked the part but they were far off the pace set by the March-BMWs or even the GRD, Elf and Motul-Rondel cars. Their Achilles heel was the Novamotor engine, based on the Lotus-Vauxhall twin-cam but built by the Pederzanis of Tecno fame. Keith Leighton pointed out that, *'the engine wasn't supposed to be a stressed member. But every time it went into a corner hard, the block would flex, and that would either do the camshafts or the crank. They just weren't up to it.'* Jim Endruweit said, *'Knowing full well that Steve Sanville at Norvic engines in Wymondham had been getting 220 bhp two years earlier out of a cast-iron head, I suggested going to him. But Peter Warr didn't let me because he said that the Old Man would go spare, because he and Steve had fallen out. The Italian-built engines kept running their big ends as well. We just couldn't keep them together long enough to do anything sensible. And when we did they didn't have any power. Nothing like the alleged 240bhp.'* Endruweit made several journeys to Modena to try and sort the problems, but they were only solved towards the end of the season by having the engines built by Norvic Racing Engines just down the road from Lotus at Wymondham. More fundamentally, the F2 team didn't do much testing so bugs were never ironed out, and both drivers' F1 commitments took precedence, so they missed a lot of races. While Emerson was clearly unmotivated, Ronnie managed a season's best, placing fifth at Karlskoga. At Enna-Pergusa, Emerson ceded his drive to charger Dave Morgan, who retired, while Ronnie finished seventh on aggregate.

Having worked with Clark, Hill and Arundell during the 1960s, Jim Endruweit had an intimate knowledge of talented drivers. *'Ronnie always turned up, ever the optimist,'* said Jim. *'He was the ultimate boy racer. Give him a roller skate and he'd race it. If you could keep the car running for long enough, if you could understand what he was telling you about the car in his fractured English, then you could do something with it, and you'd make an improvement. You'd point out that his lap times were the same as before, and he'd say "yeah, but its easier." So his actual times weren't very relevant, it was more what he thought of the car, which to me made a lot of sense, because I'd got used to that way of working with Jimmy (Clark). I always thought he was very much in the same mould as Jimmy; tremendously quick.'*

But things went from bad to worse with the Texaco Stars at Albi. Ronnie swapped from one car to another trying to get a better time, which prevented Morgan from qualifying, and ultimately Ronnie retired after eight laps with a blown engine. If he hadn't had much of a race on the circuit, Ronnie made up for it on

Ronnie Peterson: Super Swede

the road, recalled Jim Endruweit. *'We were coming back from the circuit at Enna in Sicily and we were sitting at temporary traffic lights by some road-works. Ronnie was driving and it was only an old Fiat hire car, and this Italian bloke comes up alongside. There's the two of them, sitting there waiting for the lights to change, and Ronnie's got to be first away. I thought, "Come on Ron, you don't need this." And anyway, we're storming up this hill approaching a hairpin and the bloody lights all went out in the car. Suddenly it's pitch black. And up ahead is a line of those pencil pines silhouetted against the night sky, indicating where the corner is. I'm thinking, "he's gonna stamp on the brakes any minute, or we're going to go over the edge." And he didn't do either. Just opposite-locked it round on the accelerator. I really thought we were a goner. Suddenly the bloody lights came on, and we were round the corner. How did he do that? He knew exactly where the bloody corner was. Obviously he'd worked out where it was, in readiness to give it the big one on the way round. Thank you Ronnie! He was a lovely bloke though.'*

The final dénouement for the Texaco Stars came at the October round at Vallelunga, where both Lotuses retired. Jarier was the runaway F2 champion and Lotus never built another F2 car.

No chance

Emerson crashed badly at Zandvoort when another Melmag wheel disintegrated in practice, and he was not really fit to race, having hurt his feet. But the Dutch Grand Prix was marked not so much by the fact that Ronnie led from pole position until his gearbox packed up and the engine failed on lap 67, but by the horrific accident that killed the brilliant Roger Williamson. The Tom Wheatcroft-backed driver crashed at 140mph and the barriers gave way, launching the March 721G into a roll from which it never recovered. While the race continued at unabated pace, only David Purley stopped to help, while the pathetically ill-equipped fire crews did nothing. Earlier in the season, Hailwood had succeeded in rescuing Regazzoni from a burning car. This time it was not to be. Purley seized an extinguisher from a reluctant marshal, but Williamson died in the blaze.

Stewart and Peterson lined up as the front runners for the German Grand Prix on the long Nürburgring circuit, while Fittipaldi was some 10 seconds back, feeling decidedly unwell. The Tyrrell two-some cut Peterson off at the South Turn, and Stewart and Cevert led the race from there to the finish. The Swede's Lotus's electrics gave up on the first lap.

At the magnificent Österreichring, a demonstration run by the Lotus pair was expected and, late in the first session of practice, it was clear that Peterson was fired up when he arrived in the pits with his rear tyres fizzing with bubbling blisters. Emerson went even quicker though and scooped the pole, with Ronnie alongside. SuperSwede made the best start, and found his main antagonist to be the veteran Hulme. It was a short-lived challenge though and after about 13 laps Hulme pitted with electrical gremlins, allowing Ronnie to ease off allowing his team-mate to close up. There were no team orders as such, but with Emerson ahead in the title points race, it was suggested that if Ronnie were able to, it would be nice if he supported Emerson in his bid to retain the Championship. Either way, Lotus would benefit from points in the Constructors' table. Sportingly, Ronnie waved Emerson by on lap 17, and the Lotus demonstration run continued. Then on lap 49 it all went wrong with the parting of a fuel pipe to Emerson's metering unit, handing the lead back to Ronnie, who took the victory by some ten seconds from Stewart.

Although the Lotus domination was maintained at Monza, it wasn't in the same league as modern F1 where, in 2002 at least, Ferrari supremacy was a foregone conclusion. Mechanical fallibility saw to that, back in the 1970s. If you were an Emerson fan, you'd probably say that one of the more controversial aspects of Ronnie's career was his win at Monza. There was nothing at all amiss with his drive. It was just that, with Emmo still in with a shout at the Championship, despite his Austrian retirement, Ronnie could have moved over again and let him by. The instruction was meant to come from Colin Chapman. But it never did, so Ronnie maintained station some 50

Opposite: Emerson soon lost interest in the Texaco Stars, although Ronnie persevered. F2 chief mechanic Ian Campbell discusses strategy with team manager Jim Endruweit. Barbro is more enthusiastic about prospects for the Texaco Stars than Ronnie. **Above:** the Ralph Bellamy-designed Lotus 74 Texaco Star looked the part but was let down by poor engines and no testing. Ronnie went well at Rouen – before the polystyrene chicane was demolished.

Ronnie Peterson: Super Swede

Above: Ronnie handed the lead to Emerson in Austria to help him retain the World title, but when the Brazilian retired, Ronnie took the win. **Opposite Left:** Fresh Goodyears – but Ronnie's penchant for oversteer sometimes blistered the rears while the fronts remained cold. **Opposite Right:** Wearing a hedge-sized laurel wreath after his win at the Österreichring.

yards ahead of his team-mate. It was the sixth win for Team Lotus, with three each to both drivers. However, it was to be Stewart's third World Championship, and he clinched it at Monza with one of the most astonishing drives of his career. He'd pitted with a puncture – a nail – on lap five, and stormed back through the field from 19th place, ending up fourth, gaining enough points to clinch the title. Keith Leighton expanded on the political situation within Team Lotus: *'Because Emerson had already announced he was going to McLaren, all bets were off from that point on. It wasn't yet official, but Marlboro let the cat out of the bag, which, him being a Player's driver going to Marlboro, backfired. So Ronnie wasn't being bloody minded by not letting him through, and Chapman didn't put the sign out for obvious reasons. Those years at Monza, 1973 and 1974, Ronnie completely destroyed the competition.'* This was echoed by Peter Warr. *'We got the message that Emerson was looking around for another drive, and was talking to John Hogan at Marlboro and John Goosens at Texaco and going for a tie-up with Teddy Mayer at McLaren. So it was understandable that we didn't ask Ronnie to give the last three races away so that Emerson could win the Championship.'*

Could Ronnie be motivated by someone else? Rex Hart: *'In practice at Monza we gave him a bollocking for letting Emerson go past in Austria. As far as we were concerned, we wanted him to win. It was never spoken about, but we did wonder if it stuck in his mind, because the next day he went for it and did the business, left everybody for dead.'*

With Stewart finishing fourth, Emerson not only needed to win Monza, but the two North American rounds as well, Stewart failing to score at either, a bit of a long shot. Emerson let it be known that, in any case, he was going to McLaren and taking the Texaco money with him. As to whether Ronnie was out of line in taking the win, he was a racer and probably felt that he'd done his bit for Emmo back in Austria.

In the event, Emerson was credited with second place in Canada and Stewart came fifth, which provided an answer of sorts to the points-scoring permutations. Except it wasn't quite as clear-cut as that. The race was started in extremely wet conditions, and when it dried out, everyone pitted for slicks. After that, the official lap charts got muddled up due to the wrong positioning of the pace car, and although Revson was given the chequered flag, many people thought Fittipaldi had won, including Chapman. Ronnie had been running second when he lost it on lap 15.

Then at Watkins Glen, what should have been a celebration of Jackie Stewart's racing career ended in despair with the death of François Cevert in an horrendous practice crash that virtually split the Tyrrell in half. It was small consolation that Ronnie, having taken pole, went on to win the US Grand Prix from James Hunt in the Hesketh March 731.

While Emerson had undoubtedly been the Team Lotus star during 1972, and held that spot for the early part of the 1973 season, the year as a whole belonged to Ronnie. More often than not it had been he who raised flagging morale by bagging pole position, despite crunching a few cars en route. Ronnie scored four wins to Emerson's three. Essentially, Ronnie was focussed on racing while Emerson was too often engaged in GPDA politics. *'Ronnie knew that given the same equipment he was quicker than Emmo,'* said Sveneric. *'But Emmo was better on set-up. From the word go at Lotus, Emerson always had a big family group of Brazilians around to pamper him. But neither Reine nor then Ronnie had that. They just had a few Swedish journalists following them around – although Ronnie had Barbro in his corner.'*

One of the reasons why Emerson's performance slackened was because Ronnie was invariably quicker. Lotus F2 team manager Jim Endruweit observed: *'They'd spend all practice with Emerson saying, "do this" or "do that" with the set-up, and Emerson would go out and do his quick time, and Ronnie would go out and go faster. And then they'd set Ronnie's car up and he'd go out and do the same time. You definitely got the impression that, pretty well whatever you did with the car, Ronnie would turn in much the same lap time, and he was constantly faster than Emerson. Which pissed Emerson off a bit.'*

Ronnie Peterson: Super Swede

> **1973 SHOULD HAVE BEEN HIS YEAR. HE WAS BY FAR THE FASTEST DRIVER, AND REALLY, HE THREW IT AWAY. BECAUSE OF NOT WANTING TO COME SECOND, HE DIDN'T BECOME WORLD CHAMPION. HE TRIED TOO HARD, BECAUSE THAT WAS HIS STYLE.**

It's always the problem with teams running two drivers of that calibre. Williams suffered from it with Piquet and Mansell; McLaren just about got away with it with Senna and Prost. It's great for the team because they have two drivers who drive each other harder, and between them they win the Constructors' prize. The downside is that it can compromise potential for one or the other driver to win the Drivers' Championship. Writing in Motor Sport in 2003, editor Paul Fearnley made a good case that Ronnie should have been World Champion in 1973 instead of Stewart. By totting up the points Ronnie missed out on for one reason or another he demonstrates that he could have overhauled Stewart and Fittipaldi in the second half of the season. Fearnley calculated that Ronnie led for 393 laps (1147.4 miles) compared with Stewart's 214 laps (676.1 miles) and led eleven of the 15 Grands Prix compared with six. He took nine pole positions that year to Stewart's three, and on average, his grid position was 1.93 to Stewart's 5.13. Hypothetically, if Ronnie had scored the points he deserved, he'd have finished the 1973 season on 92, rather than his actual 52, while Stewart would have had 65 instead of 71. Keith Leighton agreed: '1973 should have been his year. He was by far the fastest driver, and really, he threw it away. Because of not wanting to come second, he didn't become World Champion. He tried too hard, because that was his style. But if he'd just driven the car to win the race instead of to completely demolish the opposition, he'd have been World Champion.'

Peter Warr's view from the inside was that, 'one thing people forget about the 1973 season is the kick in the goolies we had at the end of the '72 season, when Firestone announced they were pulling out of racing. The Type 72 was designed specifically for Firestone tyres because of its radical weight distribution and other features; everyone else on Firestones was running on tyres designed for the Type 72. So at the start of '73, we went testing in Brazil with a 13in front wheel and a Goodyear tyre that was stiff enough to support the Forth Bridge, because the Tyrrell had so much weight at the front. And the car was undriveable. It took a hell of a lot of work to sort out, but by the beginning of the season it was blisteringly quick, and never faster than when being driven by Ronnie. What Ronnie did was drive the car to show up its technical weaknesses. We hadn't realised that it could be driven like that, where smoke was coming off both rear tyres, and perhaps it hadn't been designed to withstand that. He hadn't driven anything that quick, so he just revelled in it, every time he went out in it he was exploring the outer limits of its performance envelope. As we went from circuit to circuit he was exposing weaknesses in the car because it had never been driven that quickly before. The first half of the season wasn't down to Ronnie overdriving so much as weaknesses in the car.'

John Watson summed up, 'Ronnie could drive a car better than anybody, but Emerson was a more strategic driver. But what happened was both drivers knocked spots off each other and let Stewart win the championship.'

Opposite: Barbro does the lap charts in America. **Above:** Ronnie won at Watkins Glen, his biggest challenge came from James Hunt who was on a charge in the Hesketh March 731.

Ronnie Peterson: Super Swede

CHAPTER 07

A New Team Mate

Evidently Chapman was still not fazed by having two top-class number one drivers in the team, as no less a figure than Jacky Ickx was engaged to be Ronnie's team-mate for 1974. Having two of the world's best on board had worked against either of them winning the World Championship in '74, but Lotus still won the Constructors' title. It looked as though Emerson had made another shrewd move.

Opposite: The new Type 76 being fettled for testing at Goodwood by Lotus personnel including team manager Peter Warr, left, Stevie May behind car, Keith Leighton with foot on tyre, and designer Ralph Bellamy.

As John Watson observed, *'Instead of Ronnie, he had Denny, who was a super team-mate but wasn't a threat. But the big strength that Emerson had over at McLaren was that he'd brought Marlboro and Texaco to the show. It gave him an enormous resource, and he'd created another very good year for himself and, as it happened, a very good car.'*

Peter Warr explained the philosophy of joint number ones. *'Every good team wants to be in the position where, if one driver falls out, they're still in with a chance of winning with the other one. In those days, cars weren't that reliable, everyone had the same engines that they were taking to the limit, so you really needed to have a second car equally capable of winning.'*

A patrician character, Ickx had already built a formidable reputation in touring cars, World Championship sportscars, F2 and F3 with Tyrrell, and he'd won eight Grands Prix with Ferrari and Brabham, plus the Le Mans 24-Hours. The previous season he'd driven a works McLaren to third place in the 1973 German Grand Prix, having parted company with Ferrari. With Emerson gone, there was a similar sense of excitement about Ickx's impending arrival at Team as there had been a year before when it was known that Ronnie was coming. *'Ickx really was his own man,'* observed Rex Hart. *'He wasn't phased by anything He wasn't as quick as Ronnie, but he had better set-up abilities.'*

First round of the '74 season was in Argentina, and Ronnie wasn't messing about, putting his new Type 72 chassis 72/8 on pole. Ickx in 72/5 was on the fourth row, and both were flanked by Ferraris – Regazzoni at the front and Lauda on row four. Ronnie's car developed a misfire on the warming up lap, but led at the end of the first lap despite it. There had been a contretemps involving Regazzoni and Jarier that others got mixed up in. Ickx's transmission failed on lap 37, while Ronnie's efforts were hampered by a loose battery carrier, which cost him five laps so he was the 13th and last finisher. The second of the South American Grands Prix was at Interlagos, Sao Paulo. It was so hot that Ronnie suffered from dehydration and needed a glucose injection in the pits. His cockpit surround was adapted with a pair of cord supports attached either side

Ronnie Peterson: Super Swede

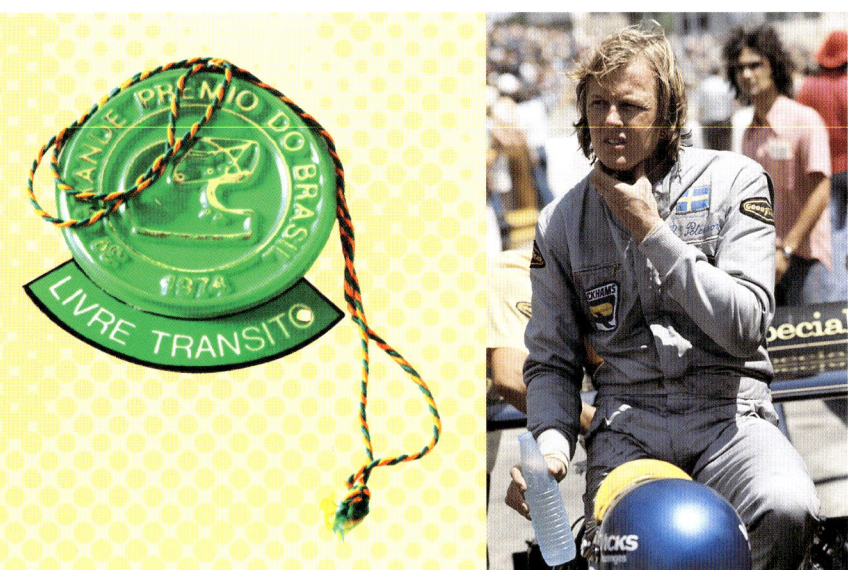

of his helmet to stop his head moving around too much in the fast corners and reduce the sickness he was feeling. A rudimentary forerunner of the modern HANS device. Under the circumstances he did well to make the second row of the grid. Reutemann made an excellent start, and Ronnie tucked in behind him, exerting pressure for four laps until he managed to squeeze past the Brabham. Emerson followed through, and it was a re-run of last season, except that the Brazilian was now in a red and white McLaren. All too soon, Peterson's car picked up a puncture, and he pitted on lap 19 for a wheel change. Ickx meanwhile threatened Regazzoni's Ferrari for second place, but he never managed it. So the Lotuses finished third and sixth, and Ronnie was immediately taken to hospital to treat his dehydration.

In mid-February, John Player Team Lotus unveiled the new Type 76 F1 car at the New London Theatre, Drury Lane. The first ever motor-show style launch for a Grand Prix car was hosted by TV personality Bill Franklin. Ronnie and Jacky were interviewed for the benefit of the suits about the new car's technical attributes which included an electronic clutch, activated by a button atop the gear lever, a V-shaped brake pedal for right and left-foot braking and a bi-plane rear wing. The drivers' road-going Elans were fitted with the electronic clutch so they could get used to them. As it turned out, these much-vaunted innovations were pointless, and they were gradually dropped until the car itself was sidelined in favour of the old Type 72s.

Chapman had an apparently cavalier attitude to driver safety, which Dave Brodie saw when the Type 76 was tested at Hethel for the first time. *'It was quite a cold morning'* Brodie remembered, *'and Ronnie drove the car round slowly in circles about half a dozen times. He said, "Ronnie, I want you to go back up to the beginning of the straight, drive down it as fast as possible, and, opposite that 50 gallon oil drum I want you to hit the brakes as hard as you can, but don't lock the wheels." So Ronnie took the car back, shunted it round, and off he went. When he passed the drum he hit the brakes. Within 20 yards the front wheels folded up around the front of the chassis. It torpedoed down the track – the front wheels weren't touching the ground – and it finally came to a halt about 100 yards past us. We all ran down there, Ronnie got out of the car and Chapman said, nonchalantly "build another set of front suspension one gauge up." Then got in his car and disappeared. He didn't say, " that was a near miss, Ronnie," or anything like that.'* Though Ronnie revered Chapman as a genius, Chapman had little respect for his driver's testing abilities. *'You could change a car quite fundamentally, and he'd still turn in the same sort of times! So you'd ask him how it felt different from before, and he'd say, "Ummmm, slides a bit more."' Where? At the front, the back, or both ends? And he'd say he wasn't really sure! Made me tear my hair out. Then, of course, he'd go and put the thing on pole position, so you couldn't really get too mad with him."*

By now an old-hand in F1, Jacky Ickx was protective of his set-up, which was a defensive necessity if he was to campaign his car in competition with Ronnie's. Rex Hart noticed that, *'So Ronnie didn't get to know his settings, Ickx would go out on the warm up with a particular set-up, and then at the last minute he'd change it on the grid to what he wanted. Lotus management were probably not aware of that. But certainly the blokes working on his car didn't know in advance what it would be, but they always took enough gear onto the grid to change whatever was necessary. I don't think Emerson ever resorted to that.'*

Team Lotus sent only a single Type 72 to Brands Hatch for the Race of Champions on 17th March, because the new Type 76s weren't ready for action. Jacky drove and provided bedraggled spectators with a demonstration of his absolute mastery of wet-weather car control. Lauda led in his Ferrari, with Jacky shadowing him, and on lap 35 of the 40-lap race, Ickx courageously drove around the outside of the Austrian on the notoriously difficult Paddock Bend to secure the victory.

The first time the new Type 76 was fired in anger was at Kyalami. The meeting got off to a bad start as the personable Peter Revson was killed in his UOP Shadow when the front suspension failed during practice. In the Lotus camp, all was far from harmonious, with Ronnie's new car presenting one problem after another, from jammed starter motor to oil leak, and it wasn't long

RIO DE JANEIRO

Opposite: Such was the heat at Interlagos that Ronnie suffered from dehydration.

Ronnie Peterson: Super Swede

Above: Racing the Type 76 in the Spanish GP, which he led until the engine blew after a pitstop. **Top:** Comparing practice times – Ronnie put the 76 on pole at Jarama, although the 72 was still on hand for benchmark comparisons with the new car. Team-mates for '74, Ronnie and Jacky make plans at Monaco. **Opposite:** Ronnie continued to receive the Vicks treatment in '74. The Swedish Royal family always took a keen interest in Ronnie's progress, with Prince Bertil checking things out in the pit lane at Anderstorp. Testing the Type 76 at Silverstone.

before both 76s had their automatic clutches disconnected. From being front runners, Ickx and Peterson were now back on rows five and eight. At the start of the race there was more pushing and shoving than usual, and as Ronnie's throttle stuck open he had nowhere to go but into the back of his Belgian team-mate, and both Lotuses ended up amidst the catch fencing on the first corner. They got going again, but Peterson's steering was damaged, while Ickx soldiered on for another 31 laps before retiring.

The Daily Express International at Silverstone on 6th April provided Team Lotus with the chance to get the Type 76 race-worthy and whereas Jacky had driven at Brands, Ronnie did the Silverstone honours. The novel gizmos (electronic clutch and brake pedal layout) were removed, but it still took a while to set the car up to Peterson's liking. At flag-fall, Mass took an early lead, but Ronnie soon pounced, and built up a commanding advantage. Hunt was on a charge, and by lap 22 he'd overhauled tyre-troubled Ronnie. No sooner had Hunt slipped the Hesketh 308 into the lead than the Lotus's DFV engine expired, ending the contest. Hunt's view of Ronnie at the time was that he was 'without doubt faster than anyone else in Grand Prix racing.'

Things looked more hopeful when Ronnie got his Type 76 on pole at Jarama for the Spanish Grand Prix, although the Ferraris were more consistent. There was still a long way to go before the new Lotuses would be functioning as well as the 72 in its hey-day. Ickx was hampered by a gearbox failure in practice, while Ronnie's fraught sessions were dogged by split exhaust manifold and malfunctioning brake master cylinder. A measure of the frustration was that he buckled himself into the spare 72, although he never actually went out in it. Drivers were expected to 'ride' the kerbs at Jarama, and no-one rode them like Ronnie – he had all four wheels over at one point at the last downhill right-hander before the pit straight. Race day was wet, the infield a mudbath, the outfield a flutter of umbrellas. Ronnie got away well and led the first few spray-hidden laps. By lap 17 the rain stopped and the track began to dry and Ronnie led the rush to get into the pits to change to slicks. During his stop the team forgot to remove the tape on the radiators and now that conditions had improved his engine began overheating and losing water, until soon after rejoining the race it blew up. He walked back, shortly to be joined by Jacky who ran out of brakes. Ickx's own tyre stop was fraught, being waved off when only one rear was done up, coming to a halt with no drive by the Trojan pit that was expecting Schenken at any moment. To compound the indignity, Ickx set the cockpit fire extinguisher off and the fumes prevented the engine from firing up.

Jacky Ickx had to start his home Grand Prix at Nivelles from row eight, while Ronnie managed row three, such was the difficulty in getting the Type 76 to function. By 50 laps, both Lotuses were simultaneously in the pits, having brakes bled, fuel leaks and oil leaks staunched, indecision over tyres and overheating. It looked hopeless and both cars retired.

With hindsight, Peter Warr believes Lotus were right to sideline the Type 76. *'The price we paid for Colin's design brief to Ralph Bellamy – design me a car with all the good points of the 72 and none of the bad, and 100lb lighter – was a very high one, because the 76 was as heavy as the 72 and didn't have all its good points either. So we had to fall back on the 72, which stood us in incredibly good stead, although it wasn't really competitive by then. My view is that we should never have let Maurice Phillippe go to Parnelli. The car he designed for them was the 72 but 100lb lighter and with all the latest technology on board.'*

Return of the 72

Realising that Monte Carlo was not the place for development work, John Player Team Lotus entered a couple of Type 72s for the Monaco GP. Ickx tried the spare 76 but immediately decided that the 72 was the better bet. Ronnie put his on the second row, while Jacky was back on the ninth row alongside Carlos Pace's Surtees TS16, having had a gearbox break during practice. As expected, the Ferraris of Regazzoni and Lauda led from the front row, with Jarier's Shadow and Peterson in hot pursuit. These four broke away from the rest – Ickx's front wings were deranged on the first lap – and Ronnie was soon

> THE TEAM LOTUS CAMP WAS OVERJOYED SINCE THERE HAD BEEN GROWING MUTTERINGS ABOUT *'TEAM SHAMBLES'* IN THE PADDOCKS. AND NO-ONE DESERVED A WIN MORE THAN RONNIE, WHO'D BEEN TRYING EXTREMELY HARD WITH RECALCITRANT MACHINERY ALL SEASON.

past Jarier. He spun on lap six at Mirabeau and Reutemann ran over the front of his car, damaging the Brabham but not the Lotus. Considering the confines of the Monaco track, Ronnie did well to recover at all. With 21 laps gone, Regazzoni overdid it and Lauda, Jarier, Peterson and Scheckter went by him. Four laps later Ronnie was ahead of Jarier again, and set off after Lauda. At 30 laps, the Ferrari's ignition failed, and Peterson was through. He reeled off the remaining 48 laps unchallenged, lapping even Emerson by the 59th tour. The Team Lotus camp was overjoyed since there had been growing mutterings about *'Team Shambles'* in the paddocks. And no-one deserved a win more than Ronnie, who'd been trying extremely hard with recalcitrant machinery all season.

'When there was a sniff of a win, he was back up there again,' said John Watson. 'As was proven at Monaco that year. Towards the end of the race, Ronnie came up behind me to put a lap on me, and here I am in a privately-entered (Hexagon of Highgate) one-year-old Brabham BT42, racing for fifth place against Emerson Fittipaldi in a works McLaren. And eventually he got through and went past Emerson as well. Afterwards he gave me a bollocking; he said, "you must never ever hold up the race leader," and I said, "Ronnie, I knew you were leading the race but, you know, I was involved in a battle for fifth place to score my first World Championship points." In my own excitement of finishing at Monaco, my first time there, in the points, I was thinking, "well, he can wait!"'

No renaissance

The Type 76 was wheeled out one more time at Anderstorp, and Ronnie tried it with huge side scoops to improve cooling, but settled for the Type 72 again. Jacky was closer now, the Lotus duo on rows three and four of the grid. There was to be no renaissance. Ronnie had a broken driveshaft on lap 9, while Ickx's engine expired on lap 28. It was some consolation when, on 11th August, Ronnie took a win on home soil, driving the March 742 in the 204km Circuit of Karlskoga F2 race, beating Depailler and Laffite in similar cars.

Between the Swedish and Dutch Grands Prix, Team Lotus called at Zandvoort to test the Type 76, and Ronnie had an accident when some experimental brake pads failed to do what they were meant to do. Brodie recalled: *'I got a phone call that he'd had a terrible accident at the end of the long pits straight, and gone through the catch-fencing and he'd hit a post and been unconscious for a couple of hours. I picked him up from being flown into White Waltham, and I couldn't do more than 50mph on the way home. He was sitting in the back of the Bentley and said his head was killing him. He spent the rest of the week in bed with the doctor coming in twice a day. He said when he got to Tarzan corner, the brake just went rock hard at 85 mph. It was like pressing your foot on a wall. Terrifying. I've had shunts like that and you get freeze frame memory; it seems to go on forever and you just know that you are going to have a terrible accident and you don't know whether you are going to get hurt, die or what. But I told him "When you're injured and paralysed, if you don't put something down on paper to Chapman, they are just going to say in court that you knew the risks and you were obviously prepared to accept them because you never moaned about them." So I phoned Staffan Svenby – Ronnie wasn't very bright about that kind of thing – and suggested he get a letter in to Chapman. I've no doubt Ickx had got one in.'* As we shall see, Staffan did indeed write such a letter to Colin Chapman, but never received a written reply.

Ronnie was fit for the Dutch Grand Prix on 23rd June. The Type 72s were wheeled out again, resplendent in a new coat of black-and-gold paintwork. Try as he might, there was no way Ronnie could get anywhere near the two Ferraris, and in the race they walked away from everyone, Lauda a full half minute ahead of Emerson's third placed McLaren. Ronnie had flat-spotted his front tyres by locking his brakes, and lost time pitting for a change, while Ickx's wheel-nuts came loose.

Above: Ronnie preferred to go with the 72 in the wet at Anderstorp, but it needed a manual lift to get axle stands underneath so the front corner could be replaced. Cocking a wheel at the Monaco chicane on the way to recording a great morale-boosting win.

Ronnie Peterson: Super Swede

Above: Ronnie started the British GP from the front row. He gets some advice from Chapman, but his battle with Regazzoni for 2nd was thwarted by a tyre stop **Opposite:** In relaxed mood with Colin Chapman, left, and Reine Wisell. Leaning heavily on his tyres through Dijon's fast curves.

Ray of sunshine

By Dijon and the French Grand prix in early July, it was officially admitted that the Type 76 was relegated to back-up car, and Jacky's spare was set up for Ronnie, just in case. It was evident that the Belgian ace was less than enchanted with his equipment at Hethel, especially in view of the success of Lauda and Regazzoni in his old team. Ronnie put 72/8 on the front row next to pole sitter Lauda, while Jacky was on row seven alongside John Watson's Brabham BT42. Another first corner mêlée caught out Pryce and Hunt, but the main race was between Lauda, Peterson and Regazzoni in the other Ferrari and in a processional race, Ronnie swept by Lauda on lap 17 and held a comfortable lead for the full 80 laps. The Lotus ran as sweetly as it had ever done, and a fully focussed Ronnie passed back-markers as if they were stationary. There was something absolutely right about the Peterson/Lotus 72 partnership. As Jenks remarked: *'The combination of driver and car seem to exude an overall personality and thought process. Although there are another twenty combinations on the grid, no thought processes are forthcoming.'* Meanwhile, Jacky Ickx was an uninspired fifth.

By dint of some heroic opposite lock driving around Brands Hatch's twists and turns, Ronnie equalled Lauda's Ferrari time and thus started the British Grand Prix from the desirable left-hand side of the front row. Ickx seemed more laid-back, content to play it cool and get himself a slot on the sixth row. Any chance of a Peterson-Lauda battle was thwarted by Regazzoni, who placed his Ferrari neatly between them going into Paddock Bend after the start. The Austrian simply drove away. The fight was between Ronnie and Regazzoni, but tyre stops eventually put paid to that Regga finishing fourth and Ronnie tenth. With two laps to go, when it looked like victory was in his grasp, Lauda picked up a puncture from debris on the circuit and had to pit for a tyre change. As he tried to exit the pits, his way was blocked by a mass of humanity and a course car waiting for the end of the race. So Scheckter got the win, from Emerson second and Jacky third.

In practice for the German Grand Prix, Ronnie was the victim of another rear wheel collapsing, and the car slid into the barriers, bending everything except the driver. He was luckier than his friend Howden Ganley, in hospital nursing a pair of broken ankles sustained in a practice accident in the Japanese Maki. The Lotus mechanics spent the night constructing a hybrid comprised of the Type 76 chassis with its latest forward-mounted radiators and front suspension, coupled with the Type 72 powertrain and rear suspension. So his race car was effectively a Type 76, but his grid position was based on the time set on the Friday in 72/8 since his outing on the Saturday in the Type 76 was some 10 seconds slower. Jacky Ickx in 72/5 was one tenth of a second slower than Peterson. Typically it was wet and dry in different parts of the circuit, and the two Lotus drivers were involved in a scrap for fourth place with Mass, Depailler, Hailwood and Merzario, and the Lotuses crossed the start finish line side by side to start the seventh lap. Although Jacky was in command of this scrap, it was Ronnie who emerged ahead, having got the better of the Belgian on the final straight, claiming fourth and fifth places. Ickx was unhappy, since in the battle for fourth place, Hailwood's McLaren had gone out of control into the barriers after the Pflanzgarten jump and, on the next last lap, Ickx had slowed down past the scene of the crash as marshals were still at work. Ronnie too had slowed, only not as much as Jacky. Meanwhile, Regazzoni, Scheckter and Reutemann occupied the podium.

By the time of the Austrian GP on 18th August, Team Lotus could provide its drivers with a Type 72 each and a Type 76 each as back-up. This tended to confuse matters, as when one model was performing well, the other one wasn't, and the upshot was that Ronnie started from row three in 72/8 alongside Scheckter – the two-by-two grids weren't staggered yet – and Jacky was in his Type 76, down on the eleventh rank alongside Graham Hill in his Lola. The race panned out with Ronnie running second, some six seconds behind Reutemann's BT44, until lap 46 when the Lotus broke a driveshaft universal joint. Jacky impaled Depailler on lap 44 when the Frenchman inadvertently got his Tyrrell sideways.

Initial signs at Monza were that the Ferraris and Brabhams would walk away from the rest. Team Lotus appeared to be relegated to the role of also-rans, since they elected to take both the Type 76s, and only one Type 72 as a spare. The respective status of the drivers was never questioned at the time. They were equal number ones. But Ronnie seemed invariably to out-qualify Jacky, and when he asked to use the narrow-track format 72 rather than his 76, his team-mate was left with no alternative but to go with the newer and more troublesome car. Which forces the conclusion that Ronnie was seen as the more likely JPS driver to bring a podium finish. In SuperSwede, Alan Henry quotes Ronnie as saying, *'I like Jacky very much. But he treats his driving as a sport these days. He's really an amateur driver who likes to drive in Grand Prix races.'* Although he went quicker in the 72 than the 76, it was only good enough to get Ronnie onto row four along with Hunt's Hesketh. Jacky put his car on row eight where he found Merzario's Williams. After 12 laps, Ronnie had claimed third place, much to everyone's surprise – he was going much better than practice had indicated. At 30 laps, Regazzoni took the lead as Lauda's Ferrari engine failed, and Ronnie was second, with Emerson breathing down his neck. Ten laps later Regazzoni's engine let go, and although Ronnie and Emerson swapped places one time, it was the Swede that led the Brazilian over the line, just as he had the previous year. Although Emerson seemed certain of the 1974 Championship, there was still, astonishingly, an outside chance that Ronnie could take it as well. It meant him winning both North American races, and none of the other contenders scoring any points whatsoever.

In Canada, practice at Mosport Park was dire for Team Lotus, with brake seizure and an off-course excursion for Ickx in both his cars, and a blown engine oil seal for Peterson. Both elected to race their Type 72s in narrow track format. But while Ickx was de-motivated, Peterson got up to fifth and harried Hunt's sliding Hesketh mercilessly. His car was dragging its nose fins on the ground having tripped over Mass's McLaren M23, and so had no downforce when close behind other cars or at full throttle on the straights. A forceful Peterson went on to harass Regazzoni for third place. When Lauda's leading Ferrari skidded off, Fittipaldi took the lead. Ronnie attacked the Swiss again, but Regazzoni managed to place himself ahead of back marker Mark Donohue in the Penske PC1 on the last lap, from which Ronnie had to settle for third. Although any chance of the title was gone, it was huge morale booster for Team Lotus, and he was said to be its *'biggest single asset'*. While Chapman carefully scrutinised the Maurice Phillippe-designed Parnelli, which Andretti debuted in 7th place, (the Lotus boss doubtless wondering how it differed from the similar Type 76,) Ronnie was sufficiently confident that John Player-Team Lotus would provide him with another winning car that he signed on for the next two seasons.

Ronnie's old friend Tim Schenken was drafted into the Lotus squad at Watkins Glen, getting the original Type 76 to drive on the understanding that he'd relinquish it if Ronnie needed it. Tim was having a bleak season in the Tauranac-designed Trojan. Although he failed to qualify the Lotus, it was acceptable for the fastest non-qualifiers to hang around at the back of the grid in case there were any non-starters. Andretti's Parnelli wouldn't start, and Schenken and José Dolhem tagged on the back of the field as the race started. Unfortunately for Tim, the organisers meant only the French Surtees driver to go, and he was black-flagged after six laps. For Team Lotus, it was a race best forgotten. Ickx brushed a barrier and damaged the 72's suspension, while the understeering Ronnie suffered a broken exhaust manifold and leaking fuel pipe.

Opposite Left: Victorious at Monza once again. **Opposite Right:** Soon after this photo at the Ring's Karussell corner, a practice crash in his Type 72 meant Ronnie's race mount would be an amalgam of Types 72 and 76. **Above:** Ronnie drove the BMW 3.0 CSL with Hans Stuck at the Nürburgring, Knutstorp and Kyalami, recording a win, a retirement and two crashes.

Ronnie Peterson: Super Swede

CHAPTER 08

The Bottom of the Barrel

The 1975 World Championship season was best forgotten, as far as Ronnie was concerned. The F1 World Championship got under way with the Argentine Grand Prix at Buenos Aires, and Team Lotus brought the *'old faithful'* Type 72s – 72/8 for Peterson and 72/5 for Ickx. Apart from bigger front brakes and thicker driveshafts they were exactly the same as they'd fielded 12 months previously. Behind the scenes, work was progressing on what would be the Type 77. But there was no completion date in sight for that.

Opposite: By 1975, relations between Chapman and Peterson had become strained. The Lotus boss thought Ronnie wasn't trying hard enough, while SuperSwede was frustrated by the lack of an effective replacement for the long-in-the-tooth Type 72.

Team Lotus's main sponsor, John Player, was, like all tobacco companies, obliged to cut back on the overt promotion of its products and, indeed, pulled the plug completely towards the end of the '74 season, only to re-sign before the '75 season began, albeit with reduced budgets. *'We told them that, without their funding, we'd be out of business,'* said Warr. So although Chapman still got the JPS money to run the cars, all promotional activity, including the press office, was suspended. . A side issue was that Ronnie was asked to take a cut in pay, which was hardly calculated to impress, especially as he was only too well aware of his status in the F1 hierarchy. The alarm bells started ringing.

During the winter lay-off, surreptitious attempts had been made to extract Ronnie from his Lotus contract and place him at UOP Shadow, effectively swapping seats with Tom Pryce. Funded by Universal Oil Products under prime mover Don Nichols, the Shadow team was run by Alan Rees, Jackie Oliver and designer Tony Southgate. Having nurtured Ronnie's career through F2 and F1, Alan Rees had an excellent rapport with him. Said Rees: *'Initially, when we started Shadow, I wasn't tempted to recruit him, as we had an American sponsor, and Jackie Oliver was one of the main reasons why we got that sponsor. So he was one driver, along with George Follmer, another American. Later on, for 1975, we got very close to him coming over to us, after the first Lotus episode. In fact it was virtually all arranged, and fell through at the last moment. He was pretty disillusioned.'* Indeed, Ronnie had a signed contract with Shadow, which he retained, in his files.

Dave Brodie was on holiday with Ronnie when he heard that Chapman was blocking the deal. *'Ronnie was getting more and more fed up the previous year. He hated it and he wanted to drive for Shadow. We were in Barbados. He got up from the game of gin rummy we were having and went and answered the phone. It was Peter Warr. Ronnie came back really upset, saying he couldn't drive for Shadow. He went away in tears, and I never saw him for the rest of the day. Warr gave him some cock and bull story about why he couldn't leave Lotus. Ronnie wasn't like a Lauda, who'd say, "what the fuck are you talking about, go and see a judge, tell him to tell me I can't drive."*

Peter Warr commented, *'the whole Shadow thing came about because he knew he was the fastest driver in the world, and he could see a car that was very quick. His instinctive reaction was, "I want to drive it." He just got spooked and thought, "I should be in that car." We were in considerable difficulties with car design and sponsorship, and there was a moment when, if Don Nichols had offered us £150,000 for Ronnie's contract, we'd probably have taken it. We went through the motions to a great extent, but back then, deals like that which have since become commonplace, weren't heard of. There weren't any buy-out clauses or deals where drivers' contracts could be bought out.'*

Meanwhile, Jarier put the new Shadow DN5 on pole at Buenos Aires, while Pryce in the DN3 was on row seven behind Ronnie – and two up from Jacky in the second Lotus. Ronnie had tried everything he knew to drag what was seen as a museum piece in terms of Formula 1 cars up the running order. That was his way. He hung grimly onto fifth place for the first few laps. But it was all to no avail, as his DFV's valve gear played up on lap 16 and he retired. Jarier was in for even worse luck than Ronnie. With new crownwheel and pinion installed on race morning, his Shadow got no further than the pit exit on the warm-up lap before it stripped all the teeth, rendering him a non-starter.

Two weeks later came the Brazilian GP. In the interim, new rear uprights were dispatched from Hethel in a bid to improve the Type 72's handling. Otherwise, there was an air of deficiency about the team. The only spare engine for Peterson's car had already been used by Ickx in Argentina; there was only one set of brake discs, and one of these was warped. The story of Ronnie's switch to Shadow surfaced anew as he had a fitting in one of the cars, and even declared he'd be driving it in the race. The fact that Lotus seemed to have come equipped with spares for only one car suggested to some that the second car was being made ready for a number two driver – who presumably would be Tom Pryce. It didn't happen, nobody jumped ship and, dogged now by acute understeer on account of the Lotus's new rear suspension layout, Ronnie qualified 72/8 on the eighth row, behind Pryce's Shadow, and even Ickx in 72/5. Pointedly, Jarier sat on pole with the Shadow. In the event, the French whiz-kid led the race for 33 laps until the fuel metering unit gave up, and Ronnie was 15th, two laps in arrears. Uncharacteristically, Ronnie was now grumbling about the car. He never normally did that, especially not in public. But though Team Lotus couldn't supply a car that did justice to *'the fastest Grand Prix driver in the world,'* nor was it about to release him from his contract.

Watch out

Next up was an outing to Daytona, where some of the top F1 names drove Chevrolet Camaros in the IROC (International Race of Champions) series alongside a galaxy of US superstars. All the cars were very well fettled by Roger Penske. It was 14th February, Ronnie's 31st birthday. Brodie was there as well, and observed a deliberate attempt to slow Ronnie and ensure an American victory. *'Every time he got in the lead – the whole straight in the lead – they slowed the race down and hauled him back in. I was in the crow's nest doing the commentary with Jackie Stewart, and I heard someone say over the commentary, "stop that Ronnie getting away, slow the race down, get the yellows (flags) out." A J Foyt was in the pits, and he said, "you haven't got a reason for it." Bill France, who ran Daytona took his Rolex off, threw it on the circuit, and said, "now you have! I want my watch back." Ronnie was quite miffed about it.'*

A flurry of mid-March snow greeted runners for the Race of Champions at Brands Hatch, and the Lotus pair looked in good form. Ickx took the lead initially, but it was Pryce who won from Watson with the JPS duo third and fourth a lap behind. John Watson recalled, *'The fact that I'd actually beaten*

Opposite: Third place in the early season Daily Mail Race of Champions at Brands Hatch was Ronnie's best result in the Lotus 72 all season.

'RONNIE'S STRENGTH WAS HIS BLINDING SPEED,' SAID WATSON. 'HE WAS A STRAIGHTFORWARD, MAN, WHEREAS JACKY IS AN EXCEPTIONALLY COMPLEX PERSON. JACKY MAY HAVE BEEN THINKING, WELL, "I CAN'T WIN THIS RACE, I'M NOT GOING TO DRIVE ANY HARDER"'

Above: Ronnie spins the Rondel March 752 in vain avoidance of a pile up caused by a back marker at Thruxton's chicane. **Opposite:** He retired from the British GP at Silverstone with engine failure.

Ronnie pissed Chapman off big-time, because he was absolutely outraged that a Surtees could pass Ronnie Peterson in a Lotus, and that's probably why I got the drive later on at the Nürburgring when Ickx didn't turn up. But the Type 72 was just old by then, and poor Ronnie was finding it very hard out there.'

Peterson and Ickx were temperamentally as well as skilfully different. *'Ronnie's strength was his blinding speed,'* said Watson. *'He was a straightforward, man, whereas Jacky is an exceptionally complex person. Jacky may have been thinking, well, "I can't win this race, I'm not going to drive any harder"'*

Ickx may have been stagnating in Formula 1, but he was still having fun in the less pressured environment of the World Championship for Makes, driving a Group 5 Alfa Romeo 33TT12 sports racer and knotching up a couple of podium finishes partnered by Arturo Merzario. Later in the year he won Le Mans with Derek Bell in the Gulf GR8, so it shouldn't be assumed that he was de-motivated. Just realistic.

At the end of March on Easter Monday, the fast Thruxton circuit hosted Britain's first F2 race for two years, with a healthy 30-car entry. Ronnie was driving one of the latest Herd-designed March-BMW 752s, and the car was entered by Ron Dennis's Rondel Racing Team. It proved something of a handful in practice, and he spun early in the first heat. As he made his way back up the order, he came upon a stalled Chevron back-marker stranded in the chicane, and in an instant, five cars piled into one another. Brodie remembered the accident: *'I jumped over the barriers and got him out of the car. He was lying on the ground, and he whispered, "Brodie, I've got to tell you something, my arms aren't working. I can't move them. Don't tell anybody. For about 20 minutes he couldn't move his arms, and then they came back again.'* In the race it was Jacques Laffite's turn to rule the F2 roost in his Martini-Schnitzer BMW.

At Kyalami, Team Lotus presented Ronnie with a brand new Type 72, chassis 72/9, which immediately confronted him with brake troubles. Jacky trudged along with the two locally run Team Gunston 72s of Keizan and Tunmer, and was thus down the back end of the grid. From the fourth row, Peterson made a demon start and was lying third at the end of the first lap behind Carlos Pace and Jody Scheckter. The new Lotus was still beset with understeer and Ronnie wore out his left-hand front tyre all too quickly, having to pit for a replacement. This cost him a lap, and he ended up with tenth place. The three other Lotuses followed him home, with Ickx in the middle.

Back home, the JPS squad entered two cars for the Daily Express International Trophy at Silverstone. Formula Atlantic star Jim Crawford, a driver in the fearless Peterson mould, was to make his F1 debut in Ickx's car, while Ronnie was third fastest in the 72 with its rear suspension revised yet again. Unfortunately for Crawford, he lost his Type 72 at Club corner on cold tyres and had a huge accident from which he was lucky to emerge unscathed. Ronnie was impressed. Then on the Sunday morning's untimed session, the Swede's engine blew, and although there was just enough time to install a new one, it refused to run. So both Lotuses were scratched from the grid.

Maidenhead Town Hall hosted a lot of F1 marriages, Tim and Brigitte Schenken, Mike and Pauline Hailwood, Judy and Howden Ganley and Ronnie and Barbro were all married there. In the April of 1975 Ronnie and Barbro's wedding was held, fondly remembered by Tim Schenken, *'I was Ronnie's best man at his wedding, and he was best man at my wedding. Barbro and my wife Brigitta were very close as well.'*

Barrier incident

The teams gathered at Barcelona for the Spanish GP on 27th April, and were pleasantly surprised to find that, instead of the cramped gardens behind the pits, the paddock now consisted of the decaying stadium originally built for the 1936 Olympics that were never held on account of the civil war. At first though there seemed little likelihood of a race taking place, as Emerson and the GPDA were out in force pointing out all the badly installed Armco around the circuit. A meeting was held in the Texaco hospitality truck and a strike

Ronnie Peterson: Super Swede

declared. The only drivers to boycott the affair were Jacky Ickx and Vittorio Brambilla, who did some slow laps on the Friday, while Ickx, Evans and Wunderink went out on the Saturday. The only solution was for the Constructors and mechanics to tighten up loose bolts on the barriers themselves. Even Ken Tyrrell was to be seen with sleeves rolled up brandishing a spanner. Reluctantly, the drivers emerged on the Saturday afternoon and the race was back on. In the race, Ronnie was driving his aggressive best, a couple of seconds off the Ferraris' pace, but he was squeezed into the unyielding barriers while lapping Migault's Hill GH1. Then one of motor sport's worst accidents occurred when Stommelen in the other Hill lost his rear wing at the notorious brow after the pits (scene of Rindt and Hill's 1969 crashes) and took off at about 150mph. The car was catapulted from one side of the track to the other, where it rode the guard-rail before pitching into the crowd, killing four spectators and a marshal. Stommelen, who'd been leading the race, was badly injured. The Spanish Grand Prix ended there and then, giving Jochen Mass in the McLaren his only GP win from Ickx in the Type 72 (his best GP result for Lotus).

The knock-on effect of Stommelen's Montjuich accident was to force the Automobile Club de Monaco to install a third layer of Armco, and restrict the GP entry to 18 cars. Trying as hard as ever, Ronnie qualified the Lotus 72 fourth quickest after Lauda's Ferrari and the two Shadows of Jarier and Pryce. Jacky was on the sixth row of the staggered grid, less than a second behind. Then the weather played its hand. Heavy rain meant everyone lined up on wet tyres, and the order was Lauda, Jarier, Peterson, until the Frenchman had a monumental accident going along the harbour section, moving the Lotus into second place. Ronnie led briefly as Lauda pitted for dry tyres on lap 24, and then he too came in for slicks. Always a lottery, Ronnie was badly placed as he returned to the fray, and was unable to get back on terms with Lauda, having been passed by Pace and Fittipaldi while in the pits. So he took fourth place, while Ickx came eighth. Ronnie later mused that the Lotus 72 was so old it knew the way round Monaco on its own.

Both Lotuses retired from the Belgian Grand Prix at Zolder with brake failure. On the 37th lap, Ronnie found he had no brakes in the esses behind the pits and ploughed into the catch fencing, while Jacky's left front brake shaft snapped on lap 53. It was an issue that Ronnie's manager took up with Lotus in a bid to extricate him from his contract. *'It was just horrible, said Staffan. 'The cars were very, very fragile, and just weren't safe. We even tried to break the contract in 1974 because of that.'* Staffan referred to a letter sent to Chapman in June 1975. *'It cites eleven brake failures in '74 and '75, as well as suspension, brake shaft and drive shaft failures,'* he said. *'We asked for an explanation as to why this was happening and what steps they had taken to address the issues. We said that it was no longer acceptable to subject Peterson to this kind of danger, and that the contract was to be terminated. However, Colin never answered in writing, and he refused to terminate the contract.'* The purpose of the letter was not merely to state the obvious, but to lay down a marker in case anything cataclysmic happened.

Svenby was also firing a warning shot. *'Everyone from Ferrari to Hesketh wanted Ronnie in 1975, if we could just get a release from Lotus. But they were not interested in getting into a legal fight with Colin.'*

Meanwhile, Ronnie was having fun in another branch of the sport. He drove in a couple of rallycross events on his home turf at Gelleråsen, Karlskoga. The first one was on 9th March 1975, followed by a round of the European Rallycross Championship at the same track on 10th August. At this event, Ronnie overturned his VW Beetle in the third heat, and then borrowed a 2.2-litre VW for the ERC race. He was 6/10ths of a second away from making it into the elusive B-final. *'But it was a lot of fun,'* he said, *'and I've never rolled at such a slow pace – ever!'*

The Swedish Grand Pix at Anderstorp was sponsored by Polar caravans, and to mark the F1 debut of Ronnie's old F3 rival Torsten Palm his Hesketh 308/3 also carried Polar logos. He qualified towards the back of the grid, albeit only three seconds off the pole time set, remarkably, by Brambilla in the works' March 751. This was partly down to the fact that most other teams

Chapter 08: The Bottom of the Barrel 134 | 135

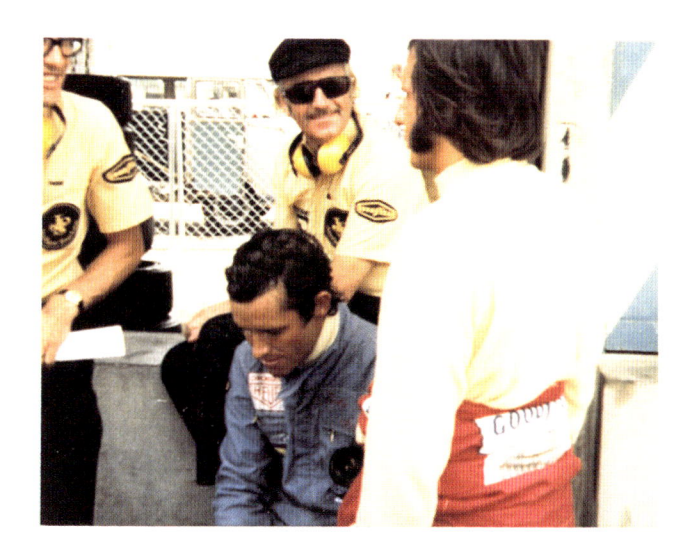

Opposite: Ronnie qualified fourth fastest at Monaco, and led the race until a tyre stop dropped him back to fourth again. He took a keen interest in the erection of taller barriers around the Monte Carlo circuit.

Ronnie Peterson: Super Swede

Above & Opposite: A fraught '75 Dutch Grand Prix came to an end for Ronnie when the Lotus's tanks ran dry while he was running fourth. By now he was growing ever despondent and lacked his usual fire.

had got themselves muddled over settings, and Ronnie lacked his customary fire on the track. He came in an unremarkable ninth, followed by Torsten, whose engine died on the last lap with fuel starvation. Apart from the anticipated win by Lauda, with Reutemann's Brabham second and Regazzoni third, the sight of Andretti in a Parnelli and Donohue in a Penske, and then Brise in a Hill, made for an unusual cocktail of cars in the top six at the finish.

Rex Hart revealed that the Parnelli team might have provided another avenue for Ronnie to consider. *'In 1975, I'd left Lotus and worked at Parnelli with Andretti. In the middle of the year Parnelli Jones got me to go and chat to Ronnie, knowing that he was fed up at Lotus. There was a certain amount of logic in the idea because their car was a natural progression from a Lotus 72. Maurice Phillippe (the designer) adapted it the way that he thought the 72 would have gone. Parnelli might have been able to tempt Ronnie because they had a lot of Firestone money, and were going to go into it even bigger the following year. The unfortunate thing was that Mr Firestone and his right hand man were both killed in a plane crash, and the contract was lost.'*

The Ferraris of Lauda and Regazzoni looked set for a walkover at Zandvoort. Although Ronnie's lap record from 1973 still stood – as it would at the end of the 1975 race – he was well off the pace, slipping into the second half of the grid, his team-mate even on the penultimate row. By mid-day on the Sunday it was pouring with rain, so wets were the order of the day. Eleven laps into the race it had stopped and the track was drying fast. Ronnie came into the busy pit lane for a change to slicks, but on the way out he collected the Ferrari team co-ordinator who was tossed in the air and had a leg broken. Ronnie's car was undamaged, so he carried on. He was up to fourth in the closing stages when his Cosworth engine died from fuel starvation, the implication being that his tanks were dry. The Ferraris didn't get their walkover. James Hunt's Hesketh 308 took the honours instead.

It just gets worse and worse

By now, Peterson's incredible will to win was being eroded and, on 12th June, Staffan Svenby wrote to Chapman on his behalf, complaining that there was still no sign of the new car: *'When I signed the extension for 1975-1976 of my August 1972 contract with Team Lotus, you told me that the new car to replace the 72/76 was under construction and that this new model would be ready fox me to test by October 1974 at the latest, thereby giving the Team plenty of time to prepare and test the car for the 1975 season. Had the full picture been put to me at the time of signing the extended contract there would be no question of this contract being signed by me.'* Part of the problem was, Chapman was embroiled with his Moonraker motor yachts and his road car business, while Warr was still on crutches from his accident.

Ronnie excelled on tracks that he liked and where he'd had a good result in the past. Monza was one, Monaco too, and Paul Ricard another. But the signs of a repeat performance of his first win in the 1975 French GP two years earlier looked slim. His spare car, 72/8, had helper coil springs added to the front suspension to aid the torsion bars, and the engine was moved backwards by a radical five inches from the chassis' rear bulkhead. The oil tank, previously mounted over the gearbox now occupied this space. Ickx's 72/R5 had the engine and oil tank modification but not the suspension detail. Having tried both cars, Ronnie settled for the shorter-wheelbase 72/R9, but had the coil spring mods transferred to that. Jacky had no choice but to drive what he was given. The major climatic factor at Le Castellet was the fickle wind, one minute blowing off the Alps, the next backing to the west. This affected both stability and top speed along the straights, playing havoc with gear ratios and aerodynamic settings, and most teams were in a muddle. Dave Brodie commented: *'In the 72 at Ricard he was 14th fastest, and Ickx was 17th or 18th, and Ronnie had bloodshot eyes. I said to him, Ron, you're going to kill yourself, you can't drive like this, what's the difference between 14th and 15th? He just looked at me. He wanted to win everything. It didn't matter what state his car was in, he utterly believed he was invincible.'* Come the race, Lauda won as he pleased, while Ronnie's drive could best be described as indifferent, although he appeared to respond when passed by

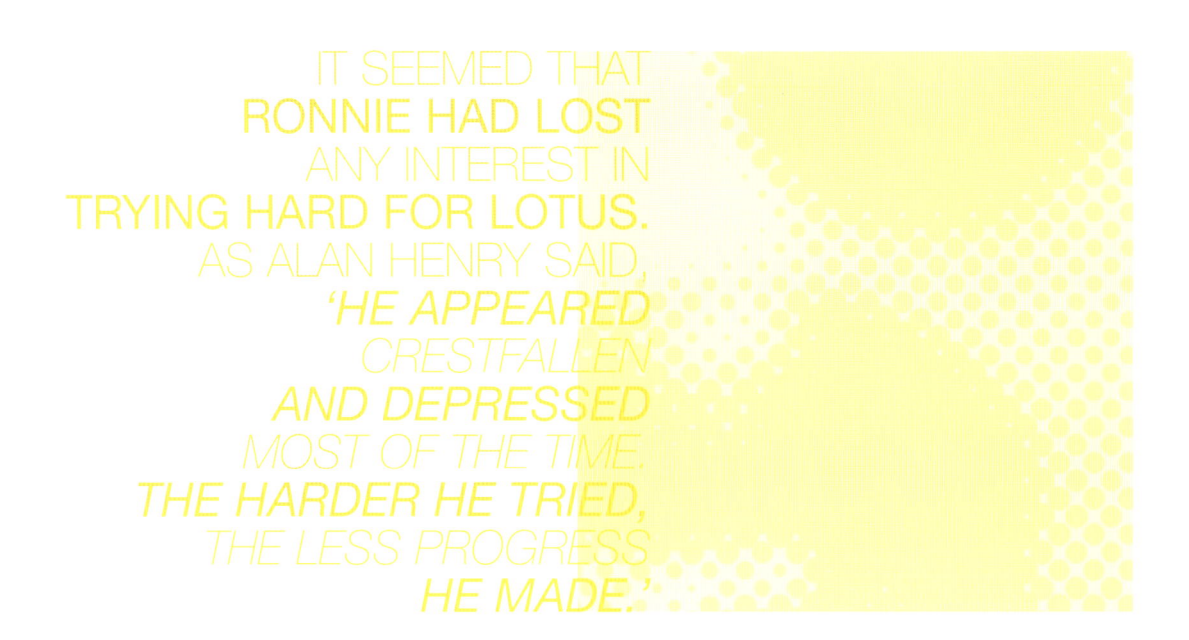

> IT SEEMED THAT RONNIE HAD LOST ANY INTEREST IN TRYING HARD FOR LOTUS. AS ALAN HENRY SAID, 'HE APPEARED CRESTFALLEN AND DEPRESSED MOST OF THE TIME. THE HARDER HE TRIED, THE LESS PROGRESS HE MADE.'

Laffite's Williams, coming in tenth. Ickx had a drive-shaft failure early on, and neither Lotus driver was enthusiastic about their circumstances. Ronnie was impressed by the Ligier. 'Laffite broke Niki's qualifying time at Ricard after only four laps,' he said. 'He was flat out through the fast kinks on the pit straight. I have never been through there flat, it may look a strange car, but it does handle.'

By the time of the British Grand Prix jamboree, Ickx had walked out of his Lotus contract. Not a cross word was uttered in public, but both Ickx and Chapman were probably happy to see the back of each other. There was a minor spat over the launch of Ronnie's Alan Henry biography at the British Grand Prix, after which Ronnie received a letter from Peter Warr reminding him of the priorities at race meetings. Ronnie's written riposte to Chapman was equally robust: 'I am well aware of my priorities and I take exception to being told what I can and cannot do with regard to my non Race driving activities by you or Team Lotus personnel. I have always acted in the best interests of our sponsors and will continue to do so. The launch of my book not clashing with any John Player activities, I obviously felt no objection would be raised.'

A bewildered Ronnie was joined by Jim Crawford and Brian Henton, also a leading F-Atlantic and F3 star. These two had their T72s' rear suspension put back to coil spring and long wheelbase format, while Ronnie's car retained its torsion bar rear end. The black-and-gold JPS cars grid positions were an embarrassment to their sponsors. The conditions on race day were so appalling that no fewer than 17 cars crashed out of the Grand Prix. Most of those went out on laps 53, 54 and 55, with just Emerson completing 56 laps and thus being declared the winner as most other people were entangled in the catch fencing. Ronnie was not amongst them, his engine having failed on the seventh lap. But the other two JPS cars were, though.

Ronnie had another axe to grind, feeling his position compromised by the emergence of Henton. Prior to Silverstone, Henton had a three-day test session with the 72 and was offered a year's contract. Ronnie wrote to Chapman: 'I would like an explanation from you why Peter Warr found it necessary to lie to me about Brian Henton. I have irrefutable evidence that Lotus had signed Brian Henton to an exclusive contract. As number one driver with Team Lotus I take great exception to being lied to. If you feel the Team's activities should be kept secret from me then please write to me confirming this and giving me the reason why, with regard to Brian Henton, I was told a direct lie.'

For the German Grand Prix, John Watson was excused his Surtees commitment and drafted into Team Lotus, with the intention of giving Ronnie a wake-up call. In fact the Ulsterman qualified 72/R8 midway down the grid, two rows ahead of SuperSwede. The prospect of any challenge came to nought however, as Ronnie's clutch began slipping irrevocably the moment the race got under way, and he retired almost immediately. A link on Watson's front suspension failed on lap 3 and he slid to a halt. It seemed that Ronnie had lost any interest in trying hard for Lotus. As Alan Henry said, 'he appeared crestfallen and depressed most of the time. The harder he tried, the less progress he made.' With Barbro heavily pregnant, he would also have been feeling pressures at home and the Peterson's daughter Nina was born on 4th November that year.

Storm and tempest

During practice for the Austrian Grand Prix, Ronnie was cut up by a slower car he was attempting to pass on the inside, and had nowhere to go but into the barriers. An all-nighter by the mechanics had the car running by the following morning, and Ronnie tried team-mate Henton's long-wheelbase car in the meantime. He reverted back to 72/R9, and then Henton crashed 72/R8, putting paid to any chance of a race as all the spare suspension parts had gone into rebuilding Ronnie's car. On the Sunday morning warm up, the versatile American Mark Donohue got a puncture on his Penske and went into the catch fencing at the fast right-hander at the top of the hill after the pit straight. This coiled up under the car and contrived to launch him over the

Above: The fastest man in Formula 1.

Ronnie Peterson: Super Swede

Above: The hard-worked team Lotus mechanics put in an all-nighter at the Osterreichring to give Ronnie a car to race after he'd been forced into the barriers during the previous day's practice.

Armco, taking out a couple of marshals. Apparently unhurt at first, Donohue died of his head injuries two days later. This crash, and heavy rain, delayed proceedings to the extent that the crowd became distinctly restless, feeling it wasn't getting its money's worth. Ronnie, a midfield runner alongside Jarier's Shadow, soon elevated himself to fourth. The rainstorm worsened, accompanied by thunder and lightening, which only served to encourage Ronnie to greater and greater efforts in his pursuit of Regazzoni. He's stopped to change visors, and was up to fifth when, on lap 29, the organisers called it a day. They'd been under pressure to do this for a few laps from the GPDA and FOCA, but Colin Chapman had mixed feelings, since Peterson looked to be capable of a podium finish, and by the time everyone was back in the pits the rain had stopped. An astonished Vittorio Brambilla was given the win, and promptly spun off whilst waving to the March pit crew.

Dijon-Prenois was another circuit that Ronnie had won on, and it was the venue for the non-championship Swiss Grand Prix at the end of August. Jarier's Shadow led from pole position for 34 of the 60 laps until his transmission failed, while Ronnie finished fourth behind Regazzoni's Ferrari, Depailler's Tyrrell and Mass's McLaren, but ahead of Watson's Surtees.

A mêlée at Monza's first chicane right after the start as Scheckter missed his braking point saw Peterson and Andretti out on the spot, with Mass, Brise, Stommelen and Crawford in 72/8 all requiring remedial pit work.

Late in September, Team Lotus announced its new car for 1976, the Type 77. Designed by Geoff Aldridge and Martin Ogilvie, it was unveiled in the car park of a Heathrow hotel, and, curiously, Ickx was present at the launch to inspect the car. The main thrust of the Type 77 was to provide an infinitely variable car, in which the wheelbase, track, centre of gravity, fuel loads, suspension movements, spring rates, downforce, tyre compounds and wheel-rim offsets were all adjustable. The designers had looked at the attributes of winning cars on all circuits, and tried to incorporate these into the new car's specification. Peter Warr was critical. *'Colin designed a car that was every which way adjustable, which was hopeless, and in the end we did something that we'd never done in our history, which was to farm out the redesign of the front end to Len Terry and he put it right.'*

Because of a disagreement between the organisers at Mosport Park and the Formula One Constructors Association, there was just one Grand Prix left on the World Championship calendar, at Watkins Glen on 5th October. Ronnie wanted to drive the Type 77 there, but Chapman vetoed the idea since no testing had been possible. By that stage in the season it was better for Team Lotus to keep its powder dry. A measure of where Ronnie might have been had he still been driving a March can be judged by the presence alongside him on the seventh row of Hans-Joachim Stuck, as hard a charger as you'd find in F2 and touring cars. On the other hand, Brambilla's March 751 was on row four, and the Shadows were higher up than that. As it turned out, Ronnie came home fifth, higher than the Marches and Shadows. He'd been engaged in a hard-fought tussle all race involving Mass, Hunt and Scheckter, and if he hadn't flat-spotted a tyre during an energetic out-braking manoeuvre on Hunt he'd have got fourth. Race winner was Lauda, who also collected the 1975 World Championship into the bargain. The pupil won the title before the teacher. Ronnie doubted if Lauda could be Champion if he wasn't driving for Ferrari. *'He's as good as all the top people, but not head and shoulders better,'* he told Autosport.

Denis Jenkinson believed that the Type 76 was never given a fair crack of the whip by its drivers. He said, critically, *'Peterson tried but couldn't convince himself of the merits of left-foot braking, and as both drivers were more interested in earning World Championship points for themselves than in any long term technical progress, they steadfastly avowed that the old Lotus 72 was better than the new Lotus 76 and they dragged on with the obsolete car in a completely misguided attitude that took Lotus fortunes downwards instead of upwards.'* DSJ went on to comment on how the Type 72 was 'generally messed around with', becoming overweight and over-complicated, with no design philosophy in evidence other than to appease the drivers. Peterson, he said, *'became a shadow of his former self, so muddled and*

LATE IN SEPTEMBER, TEAM LOTUS ANNOUNCED ITS NEW CAR FOR 1976 THE TYPE 77. DESIGNED BY GEOFF ALDRIDGE AND MARTIN OGILVIE, IT WAS UNVEILED IN THE CAR PARK OF A HEATHROW HOTEL, AND CURIOUSLY, ICKX WAS PRESENT TO INSPECT THE CAR.

confused that he had a Lotus 72 assembled to a three-year-old specification, thinking that some nostalgic magic would make it a winner again.' Ronnie may well have had the right idea though, since the car was almost undrivable in its current state. Whilst Watson was relatively polite about it, Henton said he didn't know how Ronnie drove it as quickly as he did, considering how terribly it handled. Robin Herd's view was that, had Chapman changed the weight distribution of the Type 72 to comply with the needs of the tyres that Goodyear were supplying, it might still have been competitive. A sad footnote to 1975 was the demise of the Hill team in an air crash on the way back from a test session at Paul Ricard. Graham Hill had apparently made an error with his altimeter settings, and he, Tony Brise and the designer and chief mechanic were killed. Team Lotus had been testing the Type 77 in the same session and as the teams were packing up to leave Ricard, Hill had offered Ronnie a lift in his plane. Fortunately he discovered that Ronnie's Swedish passport meant clearing customs at Luton or Biggin Hill, and so he couldn't take him as they were in a hurry to get back to the Elstree landing strip. Ronnie went in Chapman's plane instead.

Above: Colin Chapman reveals the Type 77 in the car park of a Heathrow hotel, as Peterson and Ickx absorb the philosophy behind its fully adjustable suspension.

Chapter 08: The Bottom of the Barrel

Ronnie Peterson: Super Swede

CHAPTER 09

Back with the Old Firm

The signals coming from Chapman and Peterson during the winter lay off were at odds with one another. On the one hand, Chapman was suggesting in Motoring News that Ronnie was *'unfit, a ninety-percenter, not giving as much of his effort as he might,'* who *'won't work at it,'* while a more upbeat Ronnie stated in Autosport that, *'the team can come back strongly,'* and *'I hope I can win the World Championship in 1976.'*

He thought the Type 77 was *'a very competitive car. But,'* he said *'I do wish we had done more than three test sessions – two at Silverstone and one at Ricard.'* Other changes were afoot. Ronnie's mechanic Keith Leighton left Lotus to set up his own fabrication business, being replaced by Åke Strandberg and Bob Torrie from March. A close personal friend of Ronnie and Barbro, Åke had been at Team Lotus in 1975, then returned to March in 1976. When Ronnie went to Tyrrell, Åke stayed at March, but in 1977 Lotus competitions manager Peter Warr changed horses to set up Walter Wolf Racing, and asked Åke to join him.

Interlagos was one of the more complex circuits visited by the F1 circus, an up-and-downhill mixture of hairpin bends, flat out curves and long straights. Ronnie liked it because it was difficult. In 1976, Team Lotus elected to run the new Type 77s there in their narrow-track, short-wheelbase configuration, one of many permutations available with the new chassis. Over the winter they had fitted stronger, stiffer brake calipers, and the Cosworth DFV breathed through ducts that ran either side of the cockpit surround. Its slim appearance was in marked contrast to the new Ligier JS5 that sported a colossal air scoop, like a giant teapot over the engine. With Ickx out of the picture, getting a ride in Frank Williams newly acquired Hesketh 308C, Chapman engaged Mario Andretti on a one-race deal to drive 77/1, while Ronnie took 77/2.

Almost straight away, Ronnie was in problems. A nut securing the temperature gauge bulb came undone, allowing water to spray onto a back tyre, and he slid off into the catch fencing. It took an all-nighter to make good the damage, and then a joint failed on the bottom of the car's steering column. Ronnie missed the unofficial practice on the Saturday morning and spent the official afternoon session setting the car up again. Andretti's car bucked and pitched alarmingly, and he did well to better Peterson's practice time by a second, though they were right down in the back half of the grid. It was a race to forget. On the fifth lap, the two Lotuses collided, forcing the American-

Opposite: Ronnie gives the Lotus 77 a thorough workout at Silverstone during the winter lay-off.

Italian into immediate retirement with deranged rear suspension. Ronnie pitted to have minor repairs carried out, but gave up six laps later with failing fuel pressure. The incident provided a strange echo of the debut of the Type 76 in 1974, when both cars were eliminated on the first lap at Kyalami. The debacle was enough to cause the growing rift between Chapman and Peterson to become a total split. Ronnie re-joined his old friends at March, and fellow Swede Gunnar Nilsson, an impressive performer in Formulae 2, 3 and F-Atlantic, was released from his F2 contract with March and took his place at Team Lotus.

One of the levers used to extract Ronnie from the Lotus contract was the issue of brake failures. An extract from his letter to Chapman showed how they were getting to him: *'I would like you to know that these recurring brake failures are having a very detrimental effect with my confidence in driving the John Player Specials and these failures are also having a traumatic effect on my immediate friends and family. The time is fast approaching when I feel I can no longer put my life at risk, especially in view of the fact that the answer to these brake problems seems insoluble to you or the Team.'* Staffan Svenby commented, *'We forced the issue by claiming Lotus did not honour the contract, and sent strong letters to Colin about the brake problems and the delayed new car. We suggested the switch with Gunnar with the help of Count Zanon.'*

Why did Ronnie hang on for so long at Lotus, demoralised by the lack of success and a new car so long in the making? John Watson gave his view: *'Colin was a consummate salesman, whose ability to motivate people was second to none, and he would have had Ronnie believing that his next car was going to be the best and win the World Championship. When you're in a team, there's a sort of comfort factor, which is not necessarily a healthy thing. You build a nucleus of people around you and you've got respect from those people, and it's then quite difficult to leave and go to a new team and re-establish yourself.'*

Late in 1975, a new figure emerged in Ronnie's life, who would have a powerful influence on his career. This was the Italian F1 enthusiast Count Giuseppe 'Ghughie' Zanon, a discrete philanthropist, who assisted teams who couldn't afford engines – or drivers A scion of the Lavazza coffee family, Count Zanon sponsored Ronnie directly, in effect *'giving'* March a driver for free. According to Svenby, Count Zanon's dream was to place Ronnie with Ferrari in '77 or '78. He had previously helped Frank Williams, and he subsequently sponsored Eddie Cheever and Michele Alboreto, also a noted Ronnie fan whose own helmet design was based on Ronnie's.

Ghughie Zanon explained how he came to *'sponsor'* Ronnie. *'I was a very close friend of Emerson,'* he said, *'but I had a weak spot for Ronnie. One day in '73, I rang up Emerson's hotel and asked to speak to him. But instead of Emerson I got Peterson. And during the conversation I told him, "you can be better than Emerson." I was proved right when, at last, he won the French Grand Prix that year. That was the kind of Formula 1 racing I liked – for 30 laps there were four cars, one behind the other – very exciting. The worst thing about helping Ronnie in '76 was that there had first to be a sacrifice. And that was Lella Lombardi, whom I also helped. I had to tell her that she must make way in the March team for Ronnie and, of course this was not very easy to say to her.'* Lella's F1 career was effectively finished at that moment, but she remains the only woman to score a point in a World Championship Grand Prix, coming sixth in the Lavazza-March 751 at Montjuich Park in 1975.

'As far as Ghughie was concerned, it was a love affair,' said Peter Warr. *'Like many of us, Ghughie thought Ronnie could do no wrong. Ronnie was polite and always had time for him, so he made it his life's work to support Ronnie wherever he could. The evolution of finances in Formula 1 meant that, if you couldn't get a sponsor, maybe you could get a financier who could pay some of your bills. The situation in 1976 was complicated by the fact that the whole of Formula 1 was not in very good shape. Everybody was tight. It was at that point that we decided, enough of the black arts, and set up the R & D department that resulted in the ground-effect cars.'*

The discussions about Ronnie's return to March rumbled on all through the Brazilian GP. A meeting in Peterson's room at the Sao Paolo Hilton between him and Robin Herd slipped into pure farce. *'We were discussing what might be done for Lella,'* said Herd, *'when there was a knock on the door. It was Colin.*

Opposite: Peterson and Chapman at the launch of the Lotus 77. A parting of the ways was not far off **Above:** Back with the under financed March team, Ronnie had a pretty futile season with the 761, retiring at Zandvoort with engine failure.

Ronnie Peterson: Super Swede

> FIRST TIME OUT WITH IT RONNIE DISCOVERED THE TURBO BOOST KNOB. WHEN HE CAME BACK IN HE WAS ANYTHING. "IT WAS THE TURBO!" HE SAID. "ON THE BACK STRAIGHT THE WHEELS STARTED SPINNING WHEN I TURNED IT!"

Above & Opposite: The March 761 was a simple design based on the team's five-year-old F2 chassis, adapted to take an F1 powertrain. It should have been ideal for Ronnie, but he was dogged by engine and transmission failures. The Spanish GP at Jarama being no exception.

Here was an interesting situation – why should I, of all people, be in Ronnie's room? Before Ronnie let him in, I went and lay behind the bed, and Ronnie sat on it. Chunkie was going on at him, giving March the most almighty rubbishing, urging him not to go back with us. It lasted about an hour-and-a-half, and all this time I was hidden, bursting for a pee.' The March contract was signed on 8th February 1976. Count Zanon sponsored each car to the tune of £25,000 for the whole season. He also paid for the DFV engines, but not the rebuilds. And there was another £5,000 from Beta tools. Ronnie's debut in the works' March 761 at Kyalami failed to inspire, since during practice he was half a second or so slower than Brambilla in the similarly-specced, orange-liveried Beta Utensili March. Robin Herd explained: *'At the first race, Interlagos, we had Lella and Vittorio driving. Lella came in and Max asked her how the car was, and she said "the car doesn't feel right," and Max, appearing to ooze confidence, asked her to describe the symptoms. She told him "into the corner it feels OK, then coming out it seems to jump sideways." Tongue in cheek, Max said this was a characteristic of the car, that driven on the pace, it was fine, but a couple of seconds off the pace, it behaved as she found it. So we sent Vitt out in it, and he never did a timed lap, but we asked him how it felt, and he said it was "perfect." At Kyalami, Ronnie was driving Lella's car, and we were fully expecting him to be as quick, if not quicker than Vittorio, at least. Clearly he wasn't, and we asked him what was wrong with the car. "Oh, it's very good going into corners, but on the way out it wants to jump sideways," he said. Now, we never had the money to build new cars so they were essentially the ones from '75. Basically, they were Formula 2 cars – 712 chassis.'* Three races later, Ronnie's March was written off and a new chassis built for him. When they took the old monocoque apart, March found a bulkhead was cracked, accounting for the tendency for it to want to hop sideways under power, which had caused both Lella and Ronnie so much consternation.

On lap 16 of the South African Grand Prix, Ronnie was unlucky to have Depailler spin right in front of him and nowhere to go. Next race was the US Grand Prix West, staged around the streets of Long Beach, California. Comparisons with Monte Carlo were inevitable, the Californian seaside track defined by unyielding concrete blocks rather than Armco. Ronnie put the March 761 on the third row of the staggered two-by-two grid alongside Tom Pryce's Shadow. By contrast, his new team-mate Hans Stuck was way down the back of the grid, while Merzario arrived with armfuls of lira for a rent-a-drive but didn't qualify. March appeared to be going back to their original scheme of providing cars for as many drivers as possible. This meant that resources were apt to be spread too thinly, but without a major sponsor like STP there was little alternative. At this event, the two works cars were painted white and carried Chinese lettering as they were sponsored by Teddy Yip's Hong-Kong-based Theodore Racing. Ronnie repaid them by running sixth until a leaking brake master-cylinder obliged him to pit for a fluid top up.

The other opening that Ronnie now had restored to him with his new March contract was the chance to do Formula 2 again. In April he and Stuck handled the works 762s at Hockenheim where opposition came from Tambay's Martini, Jabouille and Lecléres Elf-Renaults and Hoffman's March. In his only F2 appearance of the year though, Ronnie little success, retiring in the race with engine problems.

A straightforward car

The March operation began to come unstuck at Jarama in practice for the Spanish GP. They hadn't the funds to test in the week before the race, as the competition had, so were at a disadvantage over set-up. Still, the 761 was a straightforward, uncomplicated car, fast in a straight line but with poor brakes. It should have suited Ronnie admirably. However, the DFV engine died on its opening lap, and he had to coax it back to the pits for the electrics to be sorted. Stuck's airbox came adrift, but he carried on without noticing it. Both Nilsson and Andretti in their Lotuses were in the front half of the grid, while the March coterie languished towards the rear. It looked like Ronnie was in the right team at the wrong time again. His former Team Lotus mechanic Rex Hart observed *'there was probably no other option for him than to go back to March, because everyone else was sorted out for the season. Ronnie was not a particularly commercial pushy person, he just tended to cruise along.'* For 12 laps, Ronnie ran with the leading bunch, and then the transmission failed. Nilsson finished third.

If Ronnie was dejected about the lack of success his move had brought him, he can't have felt half as bad as his former team-mates at Zolder, for neither Ickx in the Hesketh-Williams nor Fittipaldi in his eponymous FD04 even managed to qualify. And that other potential haven for Peterson, the Shadow entourage, was not as perky or polished as it had been. The Marches on the other hand were quite well placed, grid-wise, although Stuck was in the lower half. There was now a March 'A' team comprised of Peterson (761/3) and Brambilla (761/1), and a 'B' team consisting of Stuck (761/2) and Merzario (761/4). There was also a complete car (761/5) as a source of spares. But 1976 was already panning out as the year of Lauda and Hunt, and the World Championship battle lines were drawn between Ferrari and McLaren. Hunt had won from Lauda at Jarama, only to be disqualified, as his McLaren was wider than the new regs allowed. The Austrian, whose career began in Peterson's shadow, took the laurels in Belgium and Ronnie's March now painted blue and yellow, ended it's race ignominiously in the Zolder catch fencing, that pre-gravel trap folly. Its driver having taking avoiding action when Reutemann's Brabham-Alfa lost all its oil pressure and slowed abruptly.

On Ronnie's car setting-up abilities, Max Mosley had this to say: *'He wasn't as bad as he's sometimes been painted. There was an interesting phenomenon when we had him back at March in '76. To begin with, because he was the star and Brambilla was less well known, Robin used to set up or engineer Ronnie's car and I used to do the best I could with Brambilla's. In spite of his reputation (as the Monza Gorilla), Brambilla was actually quite a good test driver, and could give you a lot of feedback. Before long we swapped, because Ronnie could actually tell what the thing was doing, and you could do something to improve it. But at a certain point, say 20 minutes before the end of practice, you'd say to Ronnie, "well that's it, I know it's understeering into this corner, oversteering out of this one (and the various things he would complain of) but that's as far as we can go, we can't get it any better and you'll just have to do the best you can." And he would then go out and do a Banzai lap. He did that at Monaco in '76. We were having a lot of trouble getting the car right, and at a certain point we just said to him just do it, and he was well up the grid.'* Indeed, right at the end of practice, Ronnie clocked third fastest time, quickest of the non-Ferraris. On the first lap he was right up with Lauda but the March was no match for the Ferrari and Lauda pulled out an eight-second lead. On lap 28 he ended his race on the harbour front with a spin at the Tabac corner, on oil laid from Hunt's McLaren that had expired a couple of laps earlier. The Monaco Grand Prix provided a pointer to the way Ronnie's thinking would go: the two Tyrrell six-wheeler P34s of Scheckter and Depailler finished second and third. Meanwhile, Stuck proved that the March could do the business by finishing fourth.

Senior team member

'Ronnie would have liked to have continued driving in the World Championship for Makes', said Staffan, *'but he drove for BMW in touring cars instead.'* The Munich firm ran a senior team, comprised of Stuck, Peterson and Redman, and a junior team with Marc Surer, Manfred Winkelhock and Eddie Cheever. *'The senior team used up more cars than all the others,'* laughed Sveneric. Ronnie had a very good relationship with BMW. *'I really enjoy driving the car, and the team is right – everything from the jackets to the machinery,'* he told Autosport. From 1972 a battle had been raging in Germany between Ford and BMW, who brought in their associated Grand Prix stars, so BMW got Ronnie and Hans Stuck and Jackie Stewart and Jochen Mass drove for Ford. By '76 both Nilsson and Peterson were allowed to drive the BMW 3.5 turbocharged CSLs. They took part in the Silverstone 6-Hours, starting from the front row, lined up against the 590bhp Martini Porsche turbo of Ickx/Mass. *'Ronnie was thrilled that he could spin the wheels in fifth gear on the straight,'* said Sveneric. *'But those cars only lasted 20 or 30 laps. As did the 2.0-litre turbocharged one with the McLaren built engine that they used at Daytona. First time out with it Ronnie discovered the*

Opposite: Ronnie liked driving for BMW and, partnered by Gunnar Nilsson, he ran the 3.2-litre turbocharged CSL with Frank Stella livery at Dijon ahead of the Ickx/Mass Porsche 935. **Top:** Meanwhile, the saga of March's mechanical woes included electrical problems in practice at Zandvoort. **Above:** After a Banzai practice lap, Ronnie was lying a strong second at Monaco until he spun out on oil at the Tabac.

Ronnie Peterson: Super Swede

Above: for 1976, Ronnie was financed by Count Ghughie Zanon, while his 761 was sponsored by a variety of firms, ranging from Beta Tools and Duckhams Oils to First National City Bank, John Day Model Cars and, at Brands Hatch, the Macconnal-Mason Art Gallery.

turbo boost knob. When he came back in he was smiling like anything. "It was the turbo!" he said. "On the back straight the wheels started spinning when I turned it!" After one hour they were just ahead, but you can only get 720bhp from a 2.0-litre engine for so long.'

Varied endorsements

Sponsorship on Ronnie's March had been erratic, heralding the charms of Monaco Fine Arts galley at the previous race. Now in Sweden he was endorsing First National City Bank Travellers Cheques. Then Duckhams was written large on the nosecone, and later in the season it would be John Day Models. March sought to address the requirements of Anderstorp circuit by lengthening the wheelbase of Ronnie's car. They did this – as had Lotus with the T72 – by inserting a spacer between engine and gearbox. This device was none other than the casing for the Alfa Romeo central gearbox from the 721X, although it was empty apart from the shaft linking the flywheel to the Hewland input shaft. Unfortunately the turbulence ahead of the rear wheels that previously cooled the radiators was no longer close enough to perform this function and the car overheated, so the idea was forgotten and the car reverted to its original set-up. Much to Ronnie's chagrin, Andretti had put the Type 77 on pole, and Nilsson was on row three. Mario was penalised for allegedly jumping the start, while Nilsson crashed out, and Ronnie played safe, circulating undramatically in eighth place. Eventually he was challenging Hunt for fifth but Regazzoni got his Ferrari between them and he had to settle for seventh, best of the March squad. Surprise winners were those extraordinary six-wheeler Tyrrells of Scheckter and Depailler.

Although it was searing hot, March fortunes looked decidedly overcast before the French Grand Prix at Paul Ricard. Ronnie's engine blew up immediately practice got under way, Brambilla's gearbox broke, Merzario skated off and damaged the nosecone, and Stuck's niggling mechanical problems went from bad to worse with each successive session. Nevertheless, they all qualified well, an on-form Ronnie posting fastest time of day on the Saturday afternoon, good enough for the third row, while Brambilla was also well up. In the early laps, a battle raged for third place between Peterson's March, Watson's Penske and Scheckter's Tyrrell, joined later by Pace's Brabham-Alfa. But a podium finish was not to be for Ronnie. Three laps from the chequered flag, his fuel injection pump malfunctioned and the intake trumpets filled with petrol. He had done enough laps to be classified 19th, while Hunt took the win.

The two favourites for the World title, Lauda and Hunt lined up together on the front row of the Brands Hatch grid for the British Grand Prix. Behind them, Andretti had put the Lotus 77 on the second row, while Ronnie was in among the six-wheeler Tyrrells and, unusually, Amon in the Ensign. In the unofficial warm-up on race morning, Ronnie's engine died of an electrical glitch and, rather than check it out, the mechanics swapped the whole engine.

As the field poured into Paddock Bend, the two Ferraris touched, ripping the side out of Regazzoni's car. Hunt ran into it and the McLaren was launched skywards, luckily not rolling, while everyone else took drastic evasive action. The only other casualty was Laffite, whose Ligier-Matra was buried in the bank on the outside of the bend. The race was stopped, and an argument ensued when the organisers declared that Laffite, Regazzoni and Hunt wouldn't be allowed to take the restart. The crowd booed, catcalled and slow-hand-clapped, making their feelings known in no uncertain terms. Not surprising, when 50,000 or so were rooting for Hunt. While the debate raged, the McLaren T-car was installed on the grid, then replaced by Hunt's hastily repaired race car. Th organisers had little alternative but to start the race again. Another fracas at Paddock Bend saw Stuck and Depailler out, while Lauda led Hunt, Regazzoni, Scheckter, Peterson and Brambilla. When Lauda's gearshift began to balk, Hunt closed up, passing the Austrian at half distance to the delight of his fans around the circuit. The two quickest Marches were wearing out left front tyres, and had to pit to change them, dropping them down the order. Ronnie's race ended when the 761/3 packed up on lap 61 with electrical gremlins. The protests about Hunt's win were thrown out, despite gross distortion in interpreting the rules.

Ronnie Peterson: Super Swede

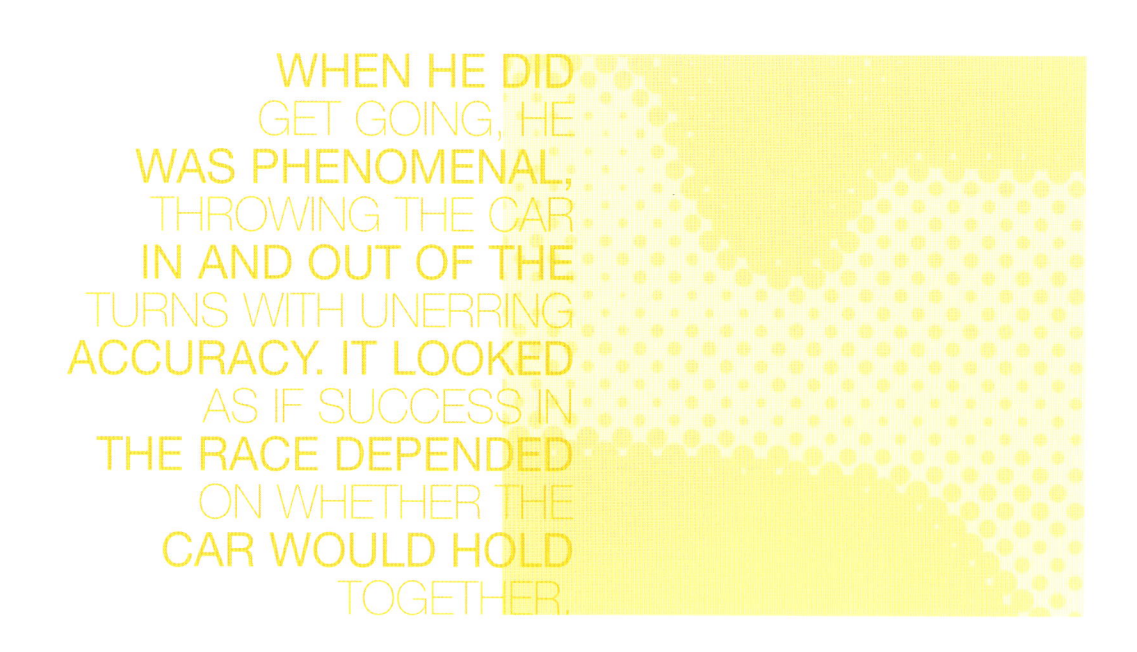

> WHEN HE DID GET GOING, HE WAS PHENOMENAL, THROWING THE CAR IN AND OUT OF THE TURNS WITH UNERRING ACCURACY. IT LOOKED AS IF SUCCESS IN THE RACE DEPENDED ON WHETHER THE CAR WOULD HOLD TOGETHER.

Switchback circuit

By the mid-'70s the old Nürburgring presented a unique challenge, relished by the best drivers and feared by the also-rans. Those who revelled in the switchback included Peterson, Hunt, Regazzoni, Mass, Stuck, Pace and Laffite. When practice began for the German Grand Prix, Peterson's March was already in trouble as the engine misfired. When he did get going, he was phenomenal, throwing the car in and out of the turns with unerring accuracy. It looked as if success in the race depended on whether the car would hold together. The trouble was, it was wet, and most peoples' grid placings were based on Friday morning's times when the Peterson March wasn't running. On the Saturday afternoon, Ronnie was quickest of all, his 7 min 27.3 sec, better than a lot of drivers had managed in the dry. It was such a long lap that the official Porsche 914/6 had to drive round to inspect the weather conditions on the far side of the circuit prior to the race, and it was judged to be wet. So treaded tyres were the order of the day. On the first lap, Hunt led from Peterson, the Swede taking the lead as Hunt stopped for slick tyres. On the second lap, Mass grabbed the lead, as Peterson pitted for a tyre swap, exiting the pits at 100mph. Then came the news that Lauda had crashed heavily at Adenau Bridge. He'd bounced off the barrier and, car ablaze, was hit by Lunger's Surtees and Ertl's Hesketh. The track was blocked and the race stopped, while the Austrian was air lifted to hospital with terrible burns and near fatal injuries. The race was restarted, with Amon walking away from his Ensign drive. Ronnie got as far as the Flugplatz on the first lap, and had a colossal accident, destroying the March but escaping unscathed himself. Hunt led from start to finish, though the win meant little under the gloom of Lauda's accident.

Wet and dry

The depression spread into the Austrian Grand Prix a fortnight later, Lauda's future was still uncertain and Regazzoni's Ferrari team entry withdrawn. With its national hero out of the picture, there were doubts that the race would even go ahead, but the Formula One Constructors Association pressured the national bank that supported the event to see that it did. After initial practice on the high-speed Österreichring, Ronnie was third fastest after Hunt and Watson. Friday afternoons times were slow because of rain, and when Ronnie tried the newest March chassis, 761/6, on Saturday afternoon he was quickest of all. March had to build two new tubs after the accidents at the Nürburgring, and chassis 761/4 was sold to an amateur Austrian driver who was mercifully blocked from getting an entry by the GPDA. The heavy rain finally abated, and race morning was sunny, the track dry. Then just before the start it began to rain again and there was widespread indecision about whether it was a 'wet' race or a 'dry' race. After delays it was pronounced 'dry', and Watson's Penske grabbed the lead at the first corner, shutting the door on Hunt, who was expecting he'd give way. Peterson also squeezed by the McLaren. It was enthralling stuff and, as they crossed the line to start lap three, the March and the Penske were side by side. On lap five, Ronnie snatched the lead, losing it five laps later to Scheckter's Tyrrell. Next time around, now lapping slower cars, Ronnie had the lead back, followed by Watson, Nilsson, Hunt and Scheckter. Then Watson led again, both first and second-placed cars in the red white and blue livery of National City Bank. As Ronnie's brakes deteriorated, Watson pulled away slightly. Ondff lap 19, Nilsson overtook his countryman, and Hunt and Laffite also closed in on him. Nine laps from the end, Andretti too had passed the brake-less March, demoting Ronnie to sixth. Watson crossed the line to win his first Grand Prix, the Penske having run faultlessly throughout. Breaking his duck prompted Wattie to shave off the beard that had characterised him for so long.

Back on form

Ronnie's sweat-soaked overalls after practice at Zandvoort indicated how hard he was trying. Deep breathing was another pointer to an on-the-limit Peterson. The reward was pole position, although at 1 min 21.31 sec, it was some way off his lap record of 1 min 20.31 sec set in 1973. Later on he had an altercation with Larry Perkins, who failed to defer to the dashing Swede as they dived into the Tarzan hairpin. The March had to be brought back to the pits on a tow truck.

Above: Revelling in the undulating switchback of the Nurburgring, Ronnie went quickest in wet practice and led briefly on the first lap. After pitting for slicks on lap 2 he crashed at the Flugplatz.

Ronnie Peterson: Super Swede

Above: Another of motor racing's most memorable sights was Peterson powersliding the March 761 out of Zandvoort's Hunzerug corner.
Pole position in Holland showed Ronnie was in-form and the fire still burned. Unfortunately he overworked the front tyres and finally the engine failed.

Ronnie had the use of two chassis, 761/3-3 and 761/6, and preferred the newer car. At the sharp end of the grid, he was joined by Hunt, Watson and Pryce. The March engine sounded rough on the pre-race warm up, so its ignition unit was replaced, curing the misfire. Ronnie led Watson, Hunt and Andretti for the first four laps, then Watson made a move at Tarzan, leaving his braking too late and having to tiptoe around the outside of the bend. Ronnie kept the lead, and Hunt dipped past the Ulsterman. But by lap 12, SuperSwede's tenure of first place was over. The front tyres were overheating, the brakes were fading and the handling was suffering as a result. He kept it going, falling back all the while, and finally the engine gave up on lap 53. During practice and for the first few laps, at least, Peterson had proved without doubt that he was back on form. The doyen of motor racing photographers, David Phipps, remembered that *"The sight of Ronnie coming out of the Hunzerug, powersliding the oversteering March, was something to behold from the outside of the bend"*, Phipps reckoned the March 711 and 712 and the Tyrrell P34 provided similarly sensational views of Peterson practising his opposite-locking craft. The Lotus 72, on the other hand, held the road too well!

Freed from the litany of failures at Lotus, yet still with a win eluding him, Ronnie was philosophical. He knew only too well how badly and for how long things could go wrong, and how to cope with the monotony of waiting for them to come right. There's the sense that he was treading water, although he was in a position to relax in the more relaxed surroundings of March. That was all very well, but fundamentally, March was too cash-strapped and spread its resources too wide to give Ronnie a serious crack at the title.

On top of the podium

Monza '76 was remarkable for two things. Firstly, Lauda made a startling comeback, having been at death's door, and was cheered around the circuit. And secondly, it was the setting for Ronnie's one victory of the year – and the third (and final) GP win for a March. More modifications had been made to the track layout, so that instead of an abrupt chicane just after the pits complex, there was now a left-right, a short straight and another left-right further along the pit straight leading into the Curva Grande. In other words, just a bigger chicane. The same was done around the back of the circuit at the Lesmo chicane.

Yet another wet practice day was endured, with just Brambilla, Stommelen and Perkins venturing out on the Friday morning. Stuck and Peterson were fastest in the afternoon, Ronnie using 761/3-3 for the official sessions and 761/6 for the untimed ones. Scheckter's P34 Tyrrell had pole, with Laffite's V12 Ligier-Matra alongside, and Pace and Depailler behind. Stuck and Lauda were next up, the Austrian making an amazing showing, and then came Peterson and Reutemann, making his Ferrari debut. The revived Ickx had his Ensign on the next row along with Regazzoni's Ferrari. Hunt was on the back row. This was because samples of fuel were taken at random from Watson's Penske and the McLarens on the Saturday and their octane ratings found to be too high. Their Saturday times were annulled and they had to resort to times logged on Friday's wet sessions, which placed Mass and Watson at the back as well. It was suggested that this was simply a contrivance to remove any opposition to Lauda's World Championship aspirations, since they were only using regular pump fuel. They were analysed and rated at over 100 octane, but the FIA rulebook didn't mention a cut-off point of 100 octane. With Watson potentially out of a race (only the sporting withdrawal of Guy Edwards' Hesketh allowed him onto the grid), the contingent of VIPs from First National City Bank who sponsored Penske were not going to have anyone to cheer on. Fortuitously, Ronnie's spare car still had the relevant advertising from Austria, covered over with masking tape. Max Mosley was induced to have the tape removed and, what do you know, there was a First National sponsored car way up the front end of the grid.

After a hectic first lap when drivers sought to regain places lost through officialdom or mis-reading the new red-green light starting procedure, Ronnie emerged fourth. On lap three he was second behind Scheckter, with Depailler, Laffite and Regazzoni in hot pursuit, just four seconds covering the lot of them. On lap ten Ronnie was sizing up the leading Tyrrell, and next time round he passed it. It began to drizzle around 25 laps, and Ronnie was still out in front with Depailler hanging on. A mix up in race control resulted in the spectacle of the clerk of the course appearing on the start finish line armed with a black flag and a blackboard bearing a large white cross. No-one knew what this meant – it was actually an indication that the red flag would soon be shown to end the race – and certainly neither Peterson nor Depailler had any intention of slowing down. One or two were caught out, Regazzoni put the brakes on, and Laffite lost a place to Scheckter. A few tail-enders – Jones, Fittipaldi and Lunger – pitted in the expectation that the race had ended, but rejoined when advised that it hadn't. The drizzle that had caused the panic didn't develop, and the race settled down again. On lap 31 Depailler got his front wheels ahead of the March, but that was as close as he came to wresting the lead. The March held together, which the Tyrrell did not and, with Regazzoni and Laffite just a couple of seconds behind him, Ronnie swept past the chequered flag to take the victory. He'd also set a new lap record two laps from the end, and it was a hugely popular win with the tifosi as it was now his third time on top of the Monza podium for the former Ferrari sportscar driver. Max Mosley recalled some last minute adjustments to Ronnie's set-up prior to the race. 'We were eighth on the grid, and we even fiddled with the set up at the end of the warming-up lap, which in those days was a cardinal sin, you just didn't do that. We changed the front wing slightly. The problem with that car was that because of the shape of the nose the front tyres overheated and at a certain point in the race you had trouble. The shower half way through the race cooled the front tyres down and Ronnie's talent overcame the slippery conditions.

By this time, it was common knowledge that Ronnie would replace Jody Scheckter at Tyrrell the following season. He had a drive in the P34 at a wet Silverstone later in the season. It was easy to see why Ronnie was impressed with the six-wheeler, having sat behind both of them for several races in 1976. As Jackie Stewart observed: *'I wasn't surprised to see him in the six-wheeler. It was a natural thing for Ken Tyrrell to take him on, and Ken was then very much someone you wanted to go and drive for.'* According to Staffan, Ronnie received *'a good fee'*, and also got personal sponsorship from First National City Bank as part of the Tyrrell deal.

John Watson revealed the prospect of another drive that came to nothing. *'At the end of '76 there was the possibility that Penske might run two cars, and Ronnie could have been my team-mate, or Roger might even have replaced me with Ronnie. The common link with Penske was First National City Bank. But the bank pulled out, Penske pulled out and that was that.'*

Right car, wrong time?

The Canadian Grand Prix was back on at Mosport Park, where a determined James Hunt sought to claw back the points he'd been disallowed from a magnificent win at Brands Hatch which he lost after an appeal by Ferrari. Lauda having been sidelined for a couple of races, it was understandable that they'd try and level the playing field one way or another. Hunt set the pace on the first day of practice, and although Brambilla ousted him from pole on the Friday afternoon, the Englishman was quickest on Saturday morning. Next up came Ronnie, with Depailler and Brambilla on the second row. Lauda and Andretti were on row three, followed by Stuck and Scheckter. This demonstrated that, although the Tyrrells were well to the fore, the three quickest Marches were also at the front end of the grid. Was Ronnie making another mistake by changing horses?

Both Hunt and Peterson made fantastic starts, and it was the Swede that led through the first complex of bends. Hunt continued to harass him for seven laps, passing him on the inside at the hairpin as the March's handling began to steadily deteriorate. Not one to give in easily, Peterson clawed his way back as Hunt ran wide. But it was to no avail, as the McLaren was the superior car under the circumstances. Ronnie faded to tenth place, with Watson a thwarted eleventh. Hunt won, Ronnie's prospective employers, Team Tyrrell, finished second (Depailler) and fourth (Scheckter), his old firm Lotus being represented by Andretti in third place.

Only two days separated the Canadian race from the opening of Watkins Glen for unofficial testing, so mechanics and truckies had their work cut out

Opposite: Ken Tyrrell offered the kind of family environment Ronnie could thrive in, plus reliable cars that didn't break. **Above:** Bearing armfuls of silverware, Ronnie shares the Monza podium plaudits with Jacques Laffite. The March 761 held together for the Italian GP, and Ronnie saw off Regazzoni and both Tyrrells to win.

Ronnie Peterson: Super Swede

Above: While running 4th in the US GP, his March had a serious front suspension failure. **Opposite:** Ronnie leads Laffite and Pace at Watkins Glen.

moving the F1 circus across the border to the Finger Lakes region of New York State for the US Grand Prix East. Hunt was just eight points behind Lauda in the World Championship, and needed a win to retain a chance at the title. Fridays' first practice was wet, and Pryce in a Shadow and Stuck in a March made the best of it. Once the track dried for the afternoon session, Hunt laid down a marker, with Scheckter next and the two Marches of Peterson and Brambilla followed by Lauda and Stuck. Saturday's session was cancelled by rain so severe that the organisers feared part of the track might subside. So Friday afternoon's times were what counted. The March directors were overjoyed, having all three 761s at the top end of the grid. But they nearly had the smiles wiped off their faces when Brambilla and Peterson ventured out in the late afternoon to see what the conditions were like – and while the Italian did only one lap before coming back in, Ronnie went for a flyer. He spun on the straight in second gear, knocking the nosecone off the car.

It was dry and cold for the start of the race and Scheckter got the jump on Hunt to lead from Brambilla, Peterson, Lauda, Depailler, Watson and Andretti. Brambilla, who'd had to have a new tyre fitted after the warming up lap but no time to check the pressure, found his handling awry, while Peterson's car began to act up after two laps. After 12 laps he came into the March pit with one front wheel leaning crazily inwards, and it was discovered that the front crossbeam onto which the tops of the dampers were located had cracked. Shades of the problem experienced earlier in the year with the hopping phenomenon, only up the front this time. It spelt instant retirement for Ronnie, while Hunt ran away with the win. Later in the race, Ickx's Ensign plunged into the barriers, breaking off the front suspension in a way reminiscent of the Rindt crash at Monza. The rest of the car spun back into the middle of the track ablaze, and Ickx did well to scrambled out of it with badly broken foot and ankle. Scheckter nearly collided with the fire engine and, reminded of the Cevert accident three years before, found it difficult to concentrate thereafter because he believed Ickx was still in the burning car. In a psychological show of strength, he brought the Tyrrell home second.

Halt to the March

The World title fight that year went down to the wire at Japan's Fuji International Speedway, with the backdrop to Japan's first World Championship round provided by the eponymous Mount Fuji volcano. It was a dismal end to Ronnie's 1976 season. In practice, local man Masahiro Hasemi made the running to begin with in his Dunlop shod Kojima KE007, until Goodyear produced some sticky qualifiers for Hunt and Lauda. Hasemi's performance was still good enough to make him fourth quickest at the end of the first session, although he crashed heavily in Saturday morning's qualifying. In this session Ronnie just managed to beat Hasemi's time and they were thus on the fifth row together. Up at the front, Andretti had pole in the improved Lotus 77/R1, Hunt next him in the M23/8, and Lauda and Watson occupying row two. It was Team Lotus's first pole for more than two years, and Andretti's first in F1 since his Watkins Glen debut in a Lotus 49 back in 1968.

After two day of sunshine, slanting rain and low cloud, obscuring the conical Mount Fuji provoked arguments as to whether or not the race should be postponed, dogged race day. The two opposing camps included the racers like Peterson, Pryce, Brambilla and Suck, and the more cautious souls such as Lauda, Fittipaldi and Hunt, who of course had most at stake. After a couple of exploratory warm-up sessions, the drivers voted by a large margin not to race. But by then the organisers had decided to go for it and the start time was given. Conditions were diabolical, but Hunt got away well and led the ball of spray down to the first corner with Watson and Andretti in pursuit. Halfway round the first lap, Peterson's March came to a standstill, its electrics drowned. Hunt, meanwhile, opened up a substantial lead over Andretti and Brambilla. But the dire weather was too much for Lauda, and in a courageous and understandable act of self-preservation, he came in to retire at the end of the second lap. As Hunt pressed ahead, leading Andretti by eight seconds, another Japanese driver, Kazuyoshi Hoshino came into third place driving an old Tyrrell 007, overtaking Regazzoni and Scheckter in the process. The natural order sorted itself out, with the racers – Brambilla, Mass and Pryce –

> RONNIE MUST HAVE VIEWED ANDRETTI'S WELL-JUDGED VICTORY WITH SOME IRONY, SINCE IT WAS IN A CAR THAT HE MIGHT HAVE BEEN DRIVING. BUT AT LEAST HE COULD CONTENT HIMSELF THAT HE'D MADE THE RIGHT CHOICE IN GOING TO TYRRELL

challenging Hunt at the front, but tyre wear on a drying track now brought a wave of attrition. The canny Andretti was busy conserving his rubber and, while Hunt hung on out in front waiting for a signal to pit for tyres, his team waited for him to make that decision for himself. At the end of lap 68, Hunt's left front tyre deflated, and he had the luck and presence of mind to dart into the pitlane. With a mechanic holding one corner of the car up so as to get the jack underneath, a new set of tyres was fitted. Hunt was now fifth with just five laps left, and he surged past Regazzoni and Jones to take third place behind Andretti and Depailler. After the race he was furious with McLaren boss Teddy Mayer, not realising that he had just scored enough points to secure the World crown. Ronnie must have viewed Andretti's well-judged victory with some irony, since it was in a car that he might have been driving. But at least he could content himself that he'd made the right choice in going to Tyrrell since Depailler and Scheckter had acquitted themselves well. Over in the Shadow camp, things didn't look rosy. The UOP sponsorship had gone and designer Tony Southgate had decamped to Lotus, so it was perhaps just as well he hadn't gone there.

John Watson defined his motivation: 'The difference between Lotus and Tyrrell was that there was something solid and dependable about Tyrrell. Lotuses may have been fast but they were fragile, and Ronnie was still smarting from an abundance of brake failures. Tyrrell made good strong cars that rarely failed mechanically, and therefore a good place for Ronnie to go, especially as far as Barbro was concerned.

While Max Mosley tried to persuade Ronnie not to go to Tyrrell because he believed the P34 to be over-complicated, Robin Herd had already produced an experimental six-wheeler March for 1977. The difference on the March was that its four small wheels were at the back, and all driven by a complicated double gearbox arrangement. *'Max fought very hard to hang on to Ronnie, but the problem at March was that they just didn't have the resources,'* said Staffan. *'It wasn't even a one-year contract, more an agreement that we would co-operate, because the funding was mostly down to Ghughie Zanon. But it was all pretty amicable between the personalities involved. Everyone knew it was a stop-gap. Ronnie liked the idea of the technical innovation of the Tyrrell six-wheeler. It looked potentially fantastic, and Ken's team was friendly and secure. If Goodyear had followed through what was agreed, history could have been different.'*

Above: Ronnie would replace Jody Scheckter at Tyrrell in 1977, and had a late season test in the P34 six-wheeler at Silverstone.

Ronnie Peterson: Super Swede

CHAPTER 10

The Six-Wheeler

Mediocre practice times on account of a bad bout of 'flu threatened Ronnie's chances in the 1977 Argentine Grand Prix, though he showed his rapid reflexes in qualifying when, as Rex Hart remembers, *'He came round the first corner, which was a left-hander onto the start-finish straight. His hand touched the ignition switch, which cut the engine, and he flicked the six-wheeler into the pit road, realised what he'd done, switched the ignition back on, and just howled through the pits at full speed back onto the track.'*

Opposite: Early in 1977 Ronnie sports the latest Nomex pin-stripe overalls and two safety innovations – flame-proof scarf and air pipe.

Ronnie's Tyrrell team-mate Patrick Depailler fared better, starting the race from the second row of the grid. But both P34 six-wheelers handled erratically, and both of them spun off in separate incidents when the race was about a third of the way through. The man Ronnie replaced at Tyrrell, Jody Scheckter, took a fortuitous win with the new Wolf WR1, while the Brabham BT45s of Watson and Pace set the pace after Hunt's McLaren went off. The race was also the debut of the new Lotus 78, harbinger of the ground-effect generation.

Originally seen as a curiosity, the advantage of Derek Gardner's Project 34 Tyrrell six-wheeler was the smaller frontal area presented by the diminutive 10in diameter front wheels, reduced frontal lift, greater braking area with two extra discs, and the broader footprint provided by the double front tyres in cornering. The concept worked impressively in 1976, when Goodyear went all-out to provide suitable compounds for the smaller tyres but that support was lacking in 1977, when the compounds suited only the conventional-sized rear tyres. The P34s had been worked over during the winter break, with new, all-enveloping bodywork, wider front track and a longer wheelbase achieved by the spacer-between-engine-and-chassis method, ominously putting on weight in the process.

Their fortunes improved only slightly at Interlagos at the Brazilian GP on 23rd January, where the six-wheelers were extremely fast in a straight line, but prone to vicious terminal understeer. Their drivers resorted to throwing the cars sideways at the entrance to corners, powering their way round in a huge tyre-damaging slide. Ronnie was no stranger to this technique, but it was not by any means the quickest route. In fact, Depailler proved a second a lap faster in practice. Nevertheless, they were both ahead of Lauda, the Scheckters (Jody and Ian), and Depailler was only half a second off Hunt's pole time. Early in the race, a series of accidents and offs occurred at the double left-hander at the bottom of the hill after the pit straight on the newly resurfaced track. In a concertina pile-up on lap 11, Mass's McLaren knocked down the catch fencing, which collapsed onto the circuit, enmeshing

Regazzoni's Ensign and causing Depailler to spin in avoidance and Ronnie to dive straight into yet more catch fencing. Lauda later described it as *'like driving on black ice.'*

At Kyalami, Hunt's McLaren and Lauda's Ferrari looked both smooth and effortless through the fast 150mph section following Crowthorne Corner and the uphill left-hander that followed. In contrast the Tyrrell P34s of Peterson and Depailler were equally quick, but extremely twitchy, and hard work as a consequence. In order to take this section flat out with confidence, the front and rear aerodynamic settings and rear anti-roll bar stiffness had to be exactly right but producing enough downforce for twisty sections made the car slower on the straight. On the first lap Ronnie was running eighth, but after only six laps his brand-new P34/5 expired with no fuel pressure, the legacy of a faulty fuel injection metering unit. Depailler's car kept going and he finished third. Tragically, the South African GP witnessed a fatal and avoidable accident. Tom Pryce was amongst a gaggle of cars moving swiftly up the rise onto the pit straight, when a couple of fire marshals sprinted across the track to tackle a blaze on Zorzi's Shadow which had pulled up opposite the pits. Pryce had no chance to miss one of the marshals, who was flung into the air, while his fire extinguisher caught the Welshman in the face. The impact, at 160mph, was probably fatal, and Pryce's wayward Shadow carried on at unabated speed, veering off the track at Crowthorne and taking Laffite's Ligier with it through the catch fencing and into the safety wall. The Frenchman was fortunate to escape with bruises, but Pryce and the marshal were beyond help. Ironically just four years earlier, fire marshals had been castigated for not rushing to the aid of Roger Williamson. Ronnie had a high opinion of Pryce, suggesting that of the current crop of British drivers, he was the most likely to go the furthest.

With half the F1 circus gathered at Brands Hatch for the race of Champions – only one car per team was permitted – the news broke that the Brabham team's Carlos Pace had been killed in a private plane crash in Brazil. Against such a backdrop, the stars continued to ply their trade, and the deaths of two of their number somehow exalted their heroic status. For Ronnie it was not a good race as the Tyrrell's rear-most front wheels blistered their tyres through overheating and then the engine note changed ominously prior to going bang on Top Straight.

Darting cars

The US Grand Prix West at Long Beach was no better. Both Ronnie and Patrick were midfield runners, well off the pace of Lauda's 312T2 and Andretti's Lotus 78. No amount of fine-tuning of roll-bars and spring-rates made the P34s behave themselves, as they hopped and darted over the bumps. Having broken an upright against one of the unyielding retaining walls, Patrick tried the spare P34/6, but its cockpit surround was designed for Ronnie and was too tall for him. In the race it was the Frenchman's turn to get lucky again, coming in fourth while Peterson abandoned his car at the trackside with a broken fuel line on lap 63.

There were signs that Ronnie was trying too hard with the Tyrrell at Jarama, and he was going slower as a result. Two seconds off Andretti's pole time in the Lotus 78, Ronnie was way back on the grid, with newcomer Rupert Keegan's Hesketh 308 alongside him. Once James Hunt had retired, the race degenerated into a mere procession, led by Andretti, with Ronnie eighth in the queue. The main excitement centred on a scrap between Ronnie and Alan Jones' Shadow DN8, which resulted in a certain amount of dramatic wheel-to-wheel banging.

Tin tops

One of Ronnie's best results of the year came in a BMW touring car. In the Kosset Six Hours at Silverstone, the works Porsche 935 turbo of Mass/Ickx was dominant in the first half of the race, challenged by the similar Kremer-run 935 of Wollek/Fitzpatrick. A brilliant drive by Ronnie in the Faltz team's Jägermeister orange BMW 320 turbo saw him and Helmut Kelleners take fourth overall and win the 2.0-litre class. It was the only non-Porsche in the first 14 finishers. Ronnie's next foray in a Group 5 BMW was in the McLaren prepared 320 Turbo at the Watkins Glen 6 hour Group 5 race. This car was used regularly by David Hobbs in IMSA events, but it was pressed into service for the newly production-

Opposite: Ronnie and team-mate Patrick Depailler share a joke with Ken Tyrrell in the pits. **Top:** the P34 had side windows in the cockpit so drivers could observe the front wheels at work – Ronnie's was designed specially for him. In typical oversteer mode at Druids hairpin, Brands Hatch. **Above:** Pre-race parade at Jarama.

Ronnie Peterson: Super Swede

Top & Opposite: Relaxing at the Petersons' Monte Carlo flat. The six-wheeler P34 was quick but exceedingly hard work, and Ronnie often appeared to be trying too hard. Fellow Swedes Peterson and Nilsson enjoyed a good rapport; Ronnie would later take Gunnar's place at Lotus for 1978. **Above:** Ronnie and Helmut Kelleners brought their BMW 320 Turbo home 4th in the Silverstone 6-Hours.

car-based World Championship for Makes (as distinct from the World Championship for Sportscars). Porsche Carrera Turbos and 935s ruled the roost, but the 3.2-litre turbocharged BMW could still do well – as at Zandvoort – while Broadspeed fielded the Jaguar XJ12 coupe with little success apart from several pole positions. Unfortunately Peterson's BMW crashed out on lap 17 at Watkins Glen whilst doing well, when a bleed valve fell out of its braking system.

Round seven of the World Championship for Makes series was staged at Brands Hatch, ostensibly a six-hour race, which again developed into a battle between old team mates Peterson and Ickx for pole position. The verdict went to the Belgian and his Porsche 2.9-litre 935 Turbo from the Swede's 320 Turbo by 0.12 sec – a close run thing. Almost the only other non-Porsche was the Walkinshaw/Winkelhock BMW 320. Ronnie's efforts in practice came to nought when team-mate Stuck put the BMW into the catch fencing whilst challenging Ickx. Because of heavy rain the race was stopped, and re-started as a completely new race, but the Peterson/Stuck car was literally that, stuck in the catch fencing and couldn't make the restart.

Losing the plot

For Monaco, the Tyrrell squad appeared to be going backwards, reverting to a set up as identical as possible with the 1976 round-the-houses race in a quest to find out why their promising form had evaporated. By this time Ronnie, Barbro and Nina spent much of their time in their Monte Carlo flat, so he could walk to work. Fourth fastest in qualifying was Ronnie's reward for hurling the six-wheeler around the tight turns with gusto. In the race Ronnie had the Tyrrell P34/5 mostly sideways in the corners, so there wasn't much room for anyone to come by him but it mattered little. By lap ten, Ronnie was in the pits with failing brakes, the first retirement of the afternoon. Monaco is one place where brakes are a priority and Ronnie had predicted as much to Lars Berntson. '"That car will be lucky to last five laps so I'll see you for tea in the afternoon. Before I cross the line six times the brakes will have gone."' His estimate wasn't far out. 'That night we finished up drinking Ronnie's champagne in Jimmie's nightclub with the Swedish King, Karl Gustav, and his wife, who was seven months pregnant with the future queen, Victoria. Staffan was the only one of the entourage not in black tie, and he took that as a complement – he alone could get into Jimmie's in jeans.'

At Zolder the potential of the Lotus 78 with its ground-effect skirts was obvious, and Andretti's pole time was a second-and-a-half quicker than Watson's Brabham-Alfa BT45 alongside on the front row, an astonishing margin. Ronnie, on row four was just 0.8 sec slower than Watson. The Tyrrell P34s varied with one another in terms of wheelbase, front track, brake balance and rear wheel geometry, a reflection on the confusion within the team and the differing requirements of the drivers.

When the race got under way, everyone on wet tyres, Watson and Andretti went off at the first chicane, leaving Scheckter, Lauda, Mass and Nilsson to scrap for the lead. The two Tyrrells were in amongst the second bunch, Ronnie fighting it out with Regazzoni and Jones, running three abreast down the pit straight. On the 13th lap Ronnie pitted for slicks, despite the incessant showers. Most people followed suit. Through a mixture of attrition as others spun or broke down, the gaggle of Nilsson, Brambilla, Jones and Peterson worked its way to the front, although Lauda by this time had a clear lead. As the track dried further, Nilsson's ground-effect Lotus came into its own and he sailed past Lauda on lap 50 for the lead. By now Ronnie was up to third, even lapping his team-mate who latched on for a tow. That was how they finished, Nilsson winning his first (and only) Grand Prix, with Lauda second and Ronnie third, six seconds behind him.

The same two cars fronted the Anderstorp grid – Andretti on pole and Watson beside him, but this time it was Depailler who'd made the P34 work around the multi-curve Scandinavian Raceway. Ronnie started from row five, but it was a short-lived event for him, the Tyrrell's ignition giving up on lap eight. His team-mate finished fourth, once again suggesting that, short of mechanical problems, the six-wheeler could do reasonably well. Damned by faint praise!

A fairly radical solution was tried at Dijon, where Derek Gardner, on the point of leaving Tyrrell, introduced a wide-track front suspension system for P34/7. This meant the wheels projected some 5in beyond the neat bodywork, a reversal

WITH THE PROSPECT OF A LOTUS DRIVE IN THE BAG, RONNIE PROCEEDED TO HURL THE SIX-WHEELER AROUND WITH EVEN GREATER ABANDON THAN EVER

of the original concept, which was to conceal the front wheels from the airstream. A new full-width nose containing the oil radiators was fitted, requiring relocation of other ancillaries. In the race, Depailler drove this new configuration while Ronnie stuck with P34/5. Although Patrick had logged a faster practice time, there was nothing to choose between them in the first 20 laps, at which point, Peterson came in to have the left-front tyres changed. While this was going on, Depailler was shunted off by Stuck, leaving Ronnie to soldier on, three laps in arrears by the finish, in a lowly 12th place.

There was more of the same at a Silverstone, with Ronnie lined up on the fifth row, seven-tenths slower than Hunt's pole-setting time. His P34/5 had the wide track front end of P34/7 grafted onto it, while Depailler's car received a slightly wider still front suspension and nose. It sported a lighter bodyshell, the widest possible rear track, and nylon brushes around the nose and leading edges of the sponsons to prevent air going underneath the car. This was the exact opposite of the Lotus 78, where the air was encouraged to go under the car and channelled through venturii so it induced downforce. This time though, Peterson's Tyrrell lasted just three laps before its Cosworth DFV expired and Depailler's suffered brake failure causing an accident on lap 17.

The catalogue of failures extended to Germany, where this year the Grand Prix was to be held at Hockenheim. The Tyrrells were both in the second half of the grid, and it was clear they were no longer in the running, with Scheckter, Watson, Hunt and Lauda still in the ascendant. In the race both succumbed to engine failure, Depailler on lap 23 and Peterson on lap 43.

For the Austrian GP at the Osterreichring, Ronnie and Gunnar Nilsson shared the eighth row, halfway down the grid. In the final practice session the Swede's Tyrrell had been clouted from behind by Ribeiro's March 761 and its right rear suspension deranged. Just before the start it had been raining but with everyone was on wets the rain started to ease. There was much indecision but then the teams' nerves started to break and, one by one, cars were fitted with slicks. Several teams gambled by leaving one car on wets and putting the other on drys but Tyrrell opted for slicks for both cars. To start with, those on wets had the advantage and even quick drivers like Ronnie were passed by lesser lights in the early laps. The need to switch to dry tyres confounded the race order and the battle for the lead was between Hunt, Jones and Scheckter, while Nilsson produced a meteoric drive through the field after his tyre change. As others fell by the wayside, Ronnie was gradually elevated up the race order, and to his astonishment, the Tyrrell kept going and he came in fifth. Those ahead of him were first-time winner Jones, Lauda, Stuck and Reutemann.

The Lotus 78 of Andretti was uncatchable at Zandvoort, a good half second faster than second quickest man Laffite in the V12 Ligier-Matra, who headed the braver drivers including Hunt, Lauda, Nilsson, Peterson, Regazzoni, Reutemann and Watson. Once the race had settled down, Ronnie was running fourth and leading the second bunch, getting the six-wheeler sideways at every turn, but on lap 19 he pitted with the DFV running rough and a terminal ignition problem was diagnosed. A dozen laps later his team-mate's engine expired too.

Marking time

Respectable times only a few tenths off Hunt's pole at Monza were viewed by the Tyrrell drivers with indifference, even though they were in the front half of the grid. The team was simply marking time until a new car – and at least one new driver – was in place for the 1978 season. Twelfth and thirteenth on the opening lap, the Tyrrell twosome didn't figure in the frontline action, and Depailler's engine blew at 25 laps. Monza punishes mechanical deficiencies, but Ronnie's P34/6 kept going and he finished a lonely sixth, the last driver not to be lapped. Even so, he had to work hard for it, applying bags of opposite lock through the Parabolica. Meanwhile, it had been a runaway victory for Andretti in the Lotus 78, the Team's fifth win of the season. Small wonder, then, that the prospect of a return to the Hethel-based squad looked particularly appealing to someone who'd had a dearth of luck for a whole year. Yet again Ronnie was chasing established success.

Team Lotus had been enjoying a complete renaissance during 1977, thanks to the phenomenal handling qualities of the ground-effect Type 78, coupled with

Chapter 10: The Six-Wheeler

Opposite: Publicity shot for Goodyear, despite the fact that in 1977, the six-wheeler's Achilles Heel was its unsuitable front tyres. **Top:** The Tyrrell's engine lasted just three laps at Silverstone. **Above:** as the season progressed, Tyrrell tried every which way to make the P34s competitive – and always in vain.

Ronnie Peterson: Super Swede

Above: At the Italian GP the wide track configuration of the P34 in its later guise negated the original aerodynamic advantage of the small front wheels. Nevertheless, Peterson flung the car around with even greater abandon, setting fastest lap at Watkins Glen. **Opposite:** At the Dutch GP Ronnie retired with ignition problems.

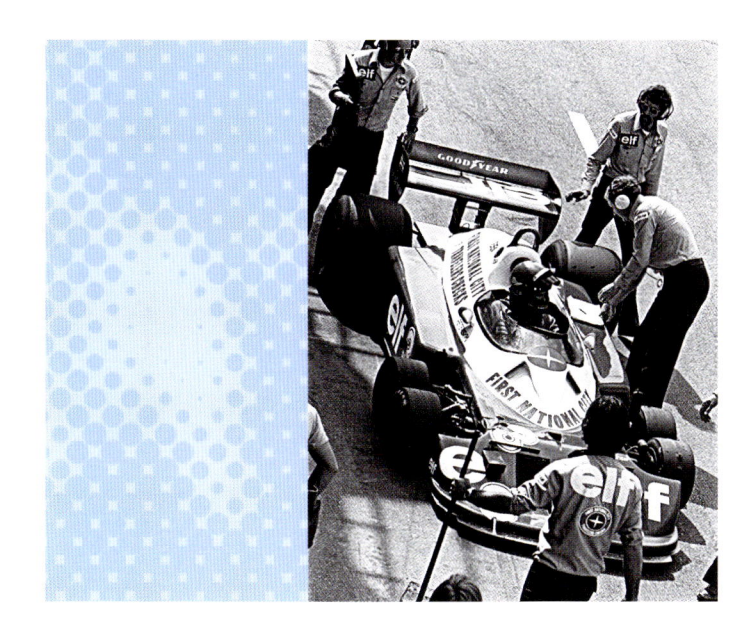

Andretti's fighting spirit and Nilsson's raw passion. At Watkins Glen the vibe within the team was not good, however. Having turned down a Ferrari contract to stick with Chapman, Mario was less than delighted to discover that Ronnie was likely to be joining him for the 1978 season, while Gunnar was off to the nascent Arrows squad. With the prospect of a Lotus drive in the bag, Ronnie proceeded to hurl the six-wheeler around with even greater abandon than ever, taking his place on row three. As Stuck shot into the lead, followed by Hunt, Andretti, Reutemann and Peterson, and it was soon obvious that SuperSwede wasn't going to give anybody an easy time trying to wrest fourth place from him. First to experience this was Jones on lap three, and then Nilsson who on lap 18 found the door shut on him and off he went. Then Laffite was edged onto the grass a few times as he tried to find a way past the six-wheeler. By now it was raining enough for a tyre change, and Ronnie took on a set of wets. He came in for a set of drys on lap 34, but was sent out with another set of wets as Ken Tyrrell thought it wasn't time for drys yet. Five laps later, Ronnie was back for his drys, but by now he was struggling down in 16th place. While Hunt won from Andretti and Scheckter, Ronnie had the amazing distinction of setting fastest lap. In spite of his lowly finishing position, Ronnie was not exactly bereft. He told Lars Berntson: *'I can't believe it! Just for coming 16th I get a sack-full of money!'* *'There were all sorts of bonuses flying around'* said Lars, *'and one was supposedly from Elf, gauged on the amount of TV exposure.'*

Against a backdrop of anxiety over the installation of Armco barriers and the lack of a permanent landing facility for the helicopter ambulance, the Tyrrells conjured up some unexpected speed for the Canadian GP at Mosport Park. Spurred on by this, Ronnie got onto the second row alongside Nilsson, although they were more than a second adrift of Andretti's pole time. Depailler was on the row behind, along with Mass in the second McLaren. The Peterson car had a puncture in its rearmost left front tyre in practice, with flailing rubber wrecking that corner's suspension. Team Lotus chief mechanic Bob Dance recalled the incident: *'Ronnie said he'd had a front tyre come off, and he didn't even notice it had gone! Which he thought was quite a good feature of the car – it didn't create a huge drama for him as it still had another wheel on that corner.'* During the race he was running with the leaders, but spun back down among the midfield runners on lap 12 as he grappled with appalling understeer at every turn. A fuel leak on lap 35 put him out for good, but Depailler went on to finish second to Scheckter's Wolf.

Ronnie finished the season with a bang. Literally. Starting the Japanese GP from a lowly grid position, he was rammed by Villeneuve's Ferrari on the sixth lap when the French Canadian missed his braking point. The Ferrari rode up over the back of the six-wheeler, and was launched into a sickening series of end-over-end flips, ending up over the barrier and in amongst a group of spectators in a prohibited area, killing a marshal and a photographer. Tucked inside the Ferrari cockpit, Villeneuve was unhurt. Depailler, who was third, had the curious distinction of occupying the podium entirely alone with his champagne, as winner Hunt and second-place man Reutemann had left for the airport straight after the race in their haste to catch the first flight home.

Gardner's question time

The six-wheeler P34 had achieved a relatively high number of successes during 1976 in the hands of Scheckter and Depailler, and there was no reason to suppose that level of attainment wouldn't be sustained or surpassed in 1977. Plainly that didn't happen, and it was a disastrous season for Ronnie. Tyrrell designer Derek Gardner cast some light on the reasons. *'At that point in F1 we were having the same sort of trouble as they have today – trying to introduce ways of making the cars slow down. The rule makers are the same people today. We were told that the overall height of the cars was going to have to be reduced to make the rear wings less effective, and that the towering air boxes would be banned.'* Derek went on to describe the battle with Goodyear who supplied the tyres. *'The problem was an imbalance between front and rear. The smaller front tyres had a much higher rotational speed, and it was necessary to contain the profile of the tyre so it maintained itself at high speed. Originally the front tyres actually lifted off the rims, but they cured that. The compounds were the same,*

> LOTUS WAS ON A WINNING STREAK, AND DESPITE THE ROWS BETWEEN CHAPMAN AND PETERSON TWO SEASONS EARLIER, LOTUS WAS FAMILY FOR RONNIE. THE CARS MIGHT BE FRAGILE, BUT WHEN THEY HELD TOGETHER, THEY WON RACES.

front and rear, but construction of the front tyres left a lot to be desired.' To be fair to Goodyear, they supplied all the teams, so in theory everyone was in the same boat, although in practice whoever shouted loudest got the tyres they wanted. Tyrrell needed special tyres for the P34's front wheels, but Goodyear was too stretched to satisfy all the F1 teams, let alone develop and manufacture a relatively small number to special order.

Derek Gardner had no choice but to introduce a number of compromising features into the P34. *'I elected to go for a smaller car, making it lower with no airbox, and fed the engine via a pair of NACA ducts running in the upper body section either side of the cockpit. Basically there were question marks over the engines, tyres and aerodynamics. There were just too many variables in there for Ronnie and although I thought we would have a reasonably successful season, it never happened. We just didn't get the tyres. Simple as that. The way forward was to go to Michelin, who wanted to supply their radials and were amenable to doing what we wanted. But it came down to sponsorship.'* Tyrrell was not alone in experiencing tyre problems. At the Austrian Grand Prix, Colin Chapman argued with Goodyear about the hard, puncture-proof compounds that its top brass insisted everyone use, and Enzo Ferrari had been making similar complaints all season, centred on the lack of development in racing tyres.

Fast-forward to the Thoroughbred Grand Prix series of the 1990s, and there's a postscript to the P34 saga. Now owed by Simon Bull and driven by Martin Stretton, Derek Gardner was able to supply Ronnie's settings data for P34/6 and, shod with Avon tyres, it proved to be the pace-setter in the TGP series.

Quality environment

Although Ken Tyrrell is reputed to have compared Ronnie to a bungalow – nothing up top – he'd always been a fan. Ronnie was a driver at the peak of his career, and Tyrell could offer him a quality team environment. Ronnie told Watson that he had an excellent financial package, but as Watson recognised, the car was very quickly sidelined because ground-effect was coming in and also because the small front tyres dictated that the compounds were always going to be different to the rear. So there was always this front-to-rear imbalance. The biggest issue of all was that it was too heavy, mainly because it had four sets of wishbones up front, four hubs, four wheels, four tyres, plus the structure. It was a bit of an engineer's fantasy. That seasons Wolf on the other hand was a very simple car, which disproved the need to go down a very complex route. It was basically an updated Hesketh, a simple, light, well-balanced car in the hands of a good racing driver and Scheckter won three races.'

Keith Leighton was blunt: *'He was the senior driver at Tyrrell, but the problem there was that the year before, Goodyear had a good exclusive with Tyrrell and they didn't in 1976. So when Ronnie was there they didn't have the tyres and they lost the plot.'*

By now at Walter Wolf Racing, Peter Warr agreed. *'It was probably another case of Ronnie waking up in the night thinking, "Wow, that car's quick, I want to drive it!" Goodyear were having a lean time, yet here they were, being asked to supply special tyres to one team. Leo Mehl was one of the most even handed people in Formula 1, and he didn't like a situation where one team was getting a special deal. In addition the costs of producing moulds in those days were astronomical.'*

Derek Gardner believed that one of the reasons Ronnie left Tyrrell for Lotus was that he, Gardner, had quit, not just the team but motor racing as a whole. Maurice Phillippe, who he worked with back in 1967 on the Lotus 56 gas turbine Indianapolis cars, took his place. But it wasn't just that. Lotus was on a winning streak, and despite the rows between Chapman and Peterson two seasons earlier, Lotus was family for Ronnie. The cars might be fragile, but when they held together, they won races.

Count Ghughie Zanon was once more in the wings, having been closely in touch with Ronnie during the year at Tyrrell. Brokered by Staffan Svenby, Chapman and Count Zanon made a deal. Lotus didn't pay Ronnie anything. The Count paid Ronnie's salary, and helped Chapman with some DFV engines on loan. Ghughie recalled: 'At Lotus, Andretti was developing the car with its skirts,

and the results were there. When he knew Ronnie would be joining, Mario said to me, *"Ghughie, why should we have two stars in the team?" And I said to him that we have a very strict contract and we respect that contract. Ronnie was always to keep his distance from Mario. But an Italian gentleman had already said to Ronnie, "you can beat Mario, especially if the track conditions are not favourable."'* Team Lotus had employed two number ones in the past – Graham Hill joined established star and Chapman's soul-mate Jim Clark in 1967. Chapman had a special relationship with Andretti, which seemed to echo his partnership with Jim Clark, so Peterson was always going to be the second among equals, just as Hill had been. Bob Dance observed: *'Jimmy was a nice guy, and all the mechanics thought the sun shone out of his backside. I'm not saying Graham wasn't a nice guy, but he came into a team which revolved around Jimmy and the Old Man. Chapman felt that having Mario in the team was like having Jimmy again. He said that before Mario got pole at Watkins Glen for the US Grand Prix in 1969. Mario had actually said to him, "when do you want me to put the car on pole?" and he went and did it. So Chapman had great respect for his abilities. He said, "it's just like having Jimmy all over again." That was in his mind, and it never went away.'*

Ronnie had already had a stint with two top line drivers in Emerson and Jacky. Temperamentally as well as in driving style, Ronnie was as different from these two as Hill had been from Clark. Sveneric summed them up: Ronnie and Mario were more like Schumacher and Montoya. They were virtually as quick as one another, but had different mentalities and driving styles.'

His career in the doldrums, Ronnie desperately wanted a competitive drive again, but Chapman stressed that Andretti took precedence in the team as he'd earned it. After all, Andretti had dragged Lotus back from the depths of despair, and Chapman appreciated that. He had galvanised the team around him and, with Nilsson's support, had made the Type 78 a winner, taking more Grands Prix wins than anyone else in 1977. Only a lack of reliability cost him the World Championship. So there was a strong feeling that 1978 should be Andretti's year, and that was made clear to Ronnie, Count Zanon and Staffan Svenby before the Lotus deal was fixed. *'Ronnie felt, quite rightly, that he was the fastest driver out there, and, given the right car he could win the Championship,'* commented Peter Warr. *'The only way he could get to drive the best car was to agree to play second fiddle to Mario, and he accepted it willingly.'* As Chapman increasingly raced in order to sell cars, rather than as he had in the past, sold cars in order to go racing, Andretti's vital attraction was his nationality. An American World Champion driving a Lotus could only help sell cars in the US.

The driver swap took place and Gunnar signed to the new Arrows team, made up of key people from the Shadow squad. What convinced Gunnar to move was that the new Arrows car was going to be built around him, and he was ready to be in that position. He could see that he was destined to be number two to Andretti, and whilst he was good friends with him, he saw the Arrows opportunity as his big chance. *'In spite of the fights that we had with Colin, he always held Ronnie in very high esteem as a racing driver,'* said Staffan. *'In 1978 he knew he had a very good car and he wanted to be absolutely sure he had the best driver line-up. Gunnar wasn't unhappy about the prospect of going to Arrows because he liked Tony Southgate. You went from one meeting to another, and the team managers were all very good at convincing you that it was their car that was going to be the next winner, and in this case it was Jackie Oliver convincing Gunnar.'* As it turned out, poor Gunnar never raced the Arrows. He became ill with cancer and died the following October. Staffan also said that, attractive as the Ferrari and Brabham camps might have looked at the time, there was no chance of Ronnie driving for Bernie. And, *'although a lot of talk did go on with Ferrari, Lotus came with a firm contract.'* Was Ronnie disappointed to leave Tyrrell? *'Absolutely not,'* said Staffan. *'When Goodyear did not get behind the six-wheeler we did not believe it would work.'*

When their relationship was at its lowest ebb, Colin Chapman had said in the press that Ronnie was not as fit as some other drivers. Ronnie didn't understand this, and suggested that the Lotus boss must have been watching a Superstars TV competition which featured Mass and Scheckter doing very well. Ronnie believed that the best training for racing was to drive racing cars as much as possible. He told Autosport that, *'when I was at March I drove every weekend, F1, F2 or sports cars with Ferrari. Then I was always strong enough to drive wherever I went. At Lotus I expected to drive F1 and F2, but the F2 programme faded out, so I have only been driving 15 or 16 races a year with not much testing. This perhaps isn't enough to keep at a peak.'*

In 1974 he went on a fitness-training course with BMW, learning various exercises, particularly for the arms, and this stood him in good stead in F1. Now though, he needed something more. Taller than the average racing driver, he was apt to put on weight now and again, and had become noticeably chubbier as the decade wore on. Dave Brodie came up with a regime. *'I used to do a lot of running and generally kept myself fit. In the winter months I used to run round to Ronnie's house, Grey Thatch, which was up on a hill at Cookham and take him out for an hour's work out on the roads. He was hard work to train though, he didn't like it and because he'd never done anything as physical as that I had to really push him.'*

Above: At Monaco in 1977, Tyrrell reverted to their previous year's set-up in a bid to recover their form. But Ronnie predicted the brakes wouldn't last and, sure enough, he was out by lap 10.

Ronnie Peterson: Super Swede

CHAPTER 11

Ground Effect

Although Team Lotus hit rock-bottom in 1976, behind the scenes its aerodynamicist Peter Wright and designers Ralph Bellamy and Martin Ogilvie were beavering away on the Type 78, the car that would revolutionise motor racing. By trial and error in the Imperial College wind tunnel they harnessed the phenomenon known as ground-effect, where the air passing under the car was channelled via skirts into venturii to create a low-pressure area under the car that sucked it down onto the track.

This massive *'something for nothing'* downforce gave the cars a huge advantage on most circuits, demonstrated by Andretti and Nilsson on several occasions in 1977. This quantum leap helped lure Ronnie back to Lotus for 1978. The significance of the Lotus 78 and the Type 79 that evolved from it early in the 1978 season cannot be stressed too highly, since they caused a revolution in single-seater racing car design. By 1979, the rest of the grid had caught up and the *'ground-effect'* generation was in full swing. Although relatively short-lived in Formula 1 – outlawed from 1983 – its legacy endured in CART and IRL single-seaters in the USA, which feature controlled ground-effect aerodynamics into the 21st century.

Staggering ability

Ronnie revelled in his instant competitiveness in the Parc Almirante Brown Autodrome at Buenos Aires, logging third-fastest practice time in chassis 78/2 for the 1978 Argentine Grand prix, held on 15th January. He had no difficulty adjusting to his new car. Team Lotus had three Type 78s present, and Mario Andretti was initially slowest, the Cosworth engine in his 78/3 having a problem with its injection system. Soon enough, Andretti set second fastest time, with Reutemann's flat-12 Ferrari running on new Michelin radials the quickest. Now threatened by a rival tyre maker, Goodyear produced a batch of qualifying tyres available only to the top teams, who received two sets each, so they had to be used sparingly. Ronnie's set de-laminated on the splice, (the point where the rubber overlaps like a Swiss roll), but Andretti made his work to good effect. A key facet of Andretti's arsenal was his ability to play with the *'stagger'* of the tyres, an art he'd learned over years of racing all kinds of machinery in the USA. Team Lotus tyre man Clive Hicks had to measure the circumference of every tyre to ascertain which ones were slightly larger. In conjunction with tyre pressures, these would then be selected to give better turn-in and grip on particular corners. When the tyres had been fitted by Goodyear, Hicks would inflate and measure them, decide on the rotation and

Opposite: Ronnie put the Lotus 78's ground-effect induced downforce to good use to claim pole at Jacarepagua. However a collision with Villeneuve in the race eliminated him.

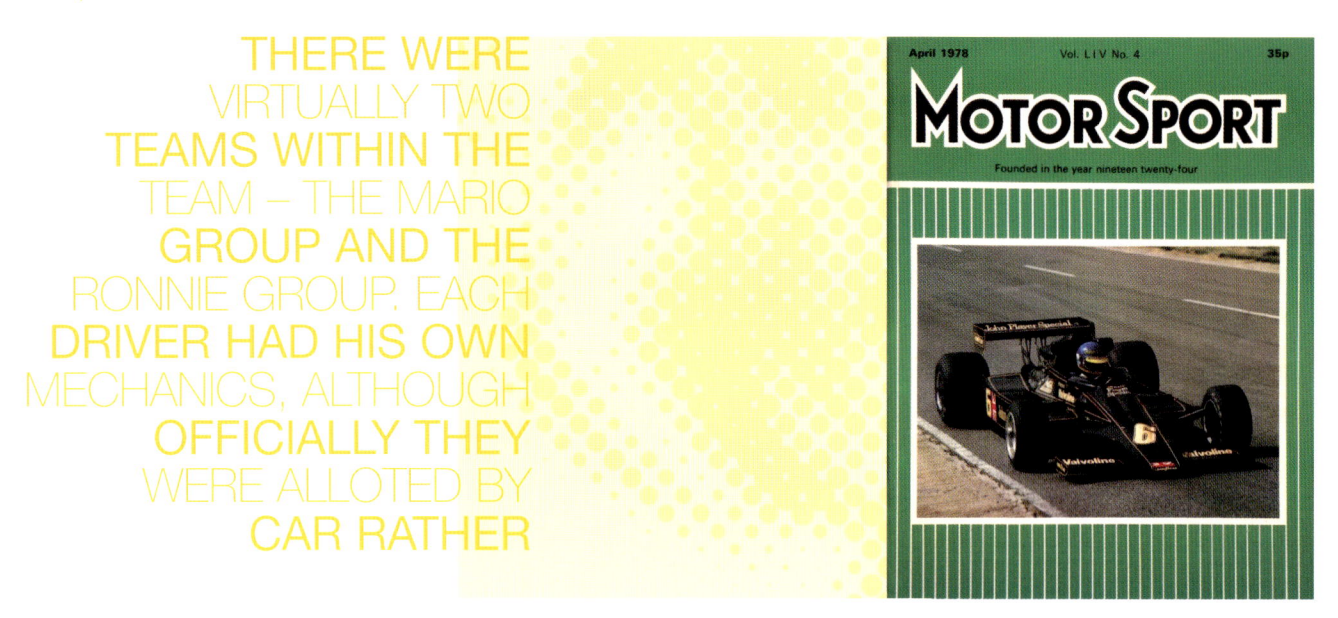

> THERE WERE VIRTUALLY TWO TEAMS WITHIN THE TEAM – THE MARIO GROUP AND THE RONNIE GROUP. EACH DRIVER HAD HIS OWN MECHANICS, ALTHOUGH OFFICIALLY THEY WERE ALLOTED BY CAR RATHER

put the big one on the outside, so the car pulled into the corner, rather than away from it. Ronnie's tyres were automatically put on in a similar fashion to help the stagger, although *'he wasn't into the stagger of the tyres to the extent that Andretti was,'* said Rex Hart. Ronnie had more input into suspension and aerodynamic settings, working with race engineer Nigel Bennett, chief mechanic Bob Dance and his mechanics. 'Both cars started off the same, for instance with 2 degrees of front wing, and 6 degrees of rear wing, unless they'd both been tested somewhere and finished up with a different setting.

There were virtually two teams within the team – the Mario group and the Ronnie group. Each driver had his own mechanics, although officially they were allotted by car rather than driver. For the 1978 season, Mario's mechanics were Glenn Waters and Phil Denney, while Ronnie's were Rex Hart and Bobby Clarke. Also on hand were Clive Hicks (the tyre man), Arthur Burchill who looked after gearboxes and John Moses who drove the truck. Tony van Dongen and Trevor Weston worked on the spare car, and Reg Underhill and Gilbert Sills were seconded from the factory on occasion. Bob Dance had to be impartial about the attention paid to each driver, according to a job list from the engineer following Chapman's instructions, though Rex Hart believed that Ronnie's popularity with the Hethel workers meant he got preferential treatment when parts had to be hastily replaced.

Many teams were running with rudimentary nylon brush skirts, the first phase of the ground-effect era, though the Lotus 78's set up was by far the most effective. Team Lotus also tried out its new Getrag gearbox in Argentina, but Ronnie had selection problems with this, so a Hewland six-speed box was installed for Saturday's practice. Team Lotus designer Martin Ogilvie recalled Ronnie circulating for lap after lap testing the Lotus-Getrag gearbox. His lap times were consistent, until suddenly he speeded up. *'When he came in, we said to him, "so, you've sorted the selection problem out, then." He just smiled, "no, I just stopped using the clutch!" He was so confident of the Hewland box that he predicted he'd soon be winning races again. But in the final hour of Saturday's practice, Andretti got pole, with Peterson third quickest overall.'*

It was boiling hot on race day, with the concrete reflecting the light so that the tarmac was almost too hot to walk on. Bob Dance was in the garages, which were separate from the pits, along with Trevor Weston and Barbro. Trevor was wearing flip-flops, not acceptable for the track. Bob took action; *'I said to Trevor, "We'll have to spray your feet black so it looks as if you've got shoes on." So I got the aerosol and started spraying his feet. Trevor didn't mind, but Barbro could not believe what we were doing. I said' "what's the matter? Don't you think he looks better like that?" She was in stitches; she thought we'd gone completely mad.'* It was still a family affair for Ronnie, Barbro and Lotus.

Come the start, Andretti made a lightning getaway to lead Reutemann. Ronnie nearly got past him as well, but just three laps into the race the Italian-American was some seven seconds ahead. Ronnie then fell into the clutches of Watson, Lauda and Depailler, who was driving the new four-wheeled Tyrrell 008. Maintaining a ten second gap between himself and Watson, Andretti led from start to finish. Ronnie came fifth, although actually he received the chequered flag first, waved by no lesser figure than Juan-Manuel Fangio, who mistook him for Andretti. Ronnie was nursing an understeering car, not having had the set-up adjusted to allow for the heavier Hewland gearbox installed after first practice. He was also afflicted by another problem: the heat within the cockpit made the accelerator pedal so hot that it blistered his foot. From time-to-time he had to lift off, just to let it cool down. Significantly, Depailler had come third in the conventional new Tyrrell 008. Had Ronnie made his move too soon?

The Brazilian Grand Prix took place on 29th January at Rio's Jacarepagua circuit. Ronnie was quickest in the Saturday practice session with a 1m 40.45 sec, while Andretti's 1m 40.62 placed him on the inside of the second row. At the start of the race Ronnie got bogged down and was passed by Reutemann and Hunt, and in just a couple of laps, Reutemann's Ferrari was six seconds ahead of Hunt's McLaren. Not long after the Lotus's right front tyre blistered and he dropped back behind Andretti. Such were the high temperatures that both their gearboxes started overheating. Then on lap 15, Ronnie came under attack from Villeneuve's Ferrari, and they collided at the end of the back straight. The

French-Canadian ace always held Ronnie in high regard, having first seen him in action overtaking Stewart in the wet at Mosport in 1971. Now, the rising star battled with the old hand and, rear tyre punctured, Ronnie limped back to the pits, but the suspension was damaged and he spun off shortly after rejoining the race. With five laps to go, Andretti lost his safe second place to Emerson's improved Fittipaldi F5, partly because he was having severe gear selection problems. By the end of the race he was pushed back to fourth.

A long overdue win

In practice at Kyalami, Ronnie put some more miles on the Lotus-Getrag gearbox, but a crownwheel-and-pinion broke, so he had to sit out the rest of the session while it was replaced. The spare chassis 78/4 was reserved for Andretti, and he needed it for Thursday morning's untimed session as a track rod end had sheared off on his race car, 78/3. Then the fuel-injection metering unit on the Cosworth development engine failed in the afternoon session just as Andretti went out in his repaired car. Already Ronnie was experiencing the frustration of being Number Two.

At the green light, Lauda rocketed away, only to miss a shift and let Andretti through to a lead he held for 20 laps. The Lotus's tyres began to overheat and first Scheckter and Patrese in the Arrows FA/1 stole the lead. The Italian newcomer was drafted in to cover for Nilsson who was already unwell. As car after car fell by the wayside, Depailler's Tyrrell took the lead. Behind him was Andretti with Ronnie obediently settled in third place. He'd had the inner shoulder of his left-hand front tyre hand-cut for better cooling, and it paid off around the corners, although the car wasn't so swift on the straights. Then the Tyrrell began to smoke, and the possibility of a Team Lotus one-two finish looked to be on the cards but, astonishingly, Andretti ran out of fuel with three full laps to go. On the last lap Ronnie drew alongside Depailler and they were side-by-side for the entire final half lap, neither former team-mate giving an inch. Sitting it out, Ronnie had the racing line out of the last corner and took the chequered flag by less than half-a-second. It was vintage Peterson, his first win since Monza 1976. Now he could declare that the Lotus 78 was *'The best car I've ever driven.'* Ghughie Zanon remembered: *'That was a very happy day. They looked at each other at the chicane and Depailler understood that if he didn't back off, neither of them would make it to the finish.'* Rex Hart provided a different angle. *'It was a constant headache for the Old Man that Ronnie was as quick as he was. He put a brave face on it, but you should have seen the look on the Old Man's face at South Africa when Ronnie won because Andretti ran out of petrol. The Old Man made a big scene about it because the journalists were all around, but there was a black thundercloud over his face, that's for sure.'* Perhaps Chapman's anger was partially self directed, because he had done the fuel calculations himself, driven by his obsession with using the bare minimum of fuel to complete the race distance. Fuelling the cars before a race, the mechanics always erred on the side of caution and poured in *'the mechanic's gallon'*. They could get away with it when Chapman wasn't around to see what they were up to. On this occasion he was. *'I was responsible for that,'* confessed Bob Dance. *'One of the reasons I fell out with him in 1968 was because he didn't want mechanics putting their extra gallon in.'*

The new weapon

Team Lotus's new weapon was the Type 79, which refined the Type 78's chassis dynamics to generate yet more ground-effect downforce. Clearly Ronnie excelled in anything he drove, but how radical was the shift from non ground-effect to ground-effect, in terms of a change in driving style? *'He simply adapted to it,'* said Max Mosley. *'And he would have been very good when they had those weird active suspensions. For example, Mansell could cope with it, but Patrese just didn't trust it and couldn't. The Type 79 prototype had been tested during the winter, and 79/2 made its race debut at Silverstone in the rain-sodden 40-lap Daily Express International Trophy on 19th March. A total debacle ensued, with Ronnie crashing his Type 78 on the warm-up lap and Andretti skating off at Abbey Curve in the Type 79 on the third lap, colliding with Regazzoni's beached Shadow DN9. Conditions were so bad that of the 15 starters, only four finished,*

Opposite: Now at the wheel of a winning car, the Peterson smile returned. **Above:** At Monaco, the Lotus 78's gearbox failed at 56 laps while he was lying fifth. Ronnie crashed out on the first rain-drenched lap at Silverstone in the Daily Express International Trophy.

the leading pair, Rosberg and Fittipaldi, being three laps ahead of Trimmer and Lunger.'

Long Beach street circuit was the venue for the US GP West, the North American counterpart to Monte Carlo, only with much wider streets that enabled overtaking and precluded too much baulking. Team Lotus arrived with three cars: 78/2 for Peterson, 78/3 for Andretti, and 78/4 as the spare. All had the normal Hewland 'box instead of the Lotus/Getrag transmission, though there was a degree of variety in the cars' specification. Three versions of the 3.0-litre Cosworth-Ford DFV engine were available to the top teams – Cosworth's own development motor, the so-called *'super-screamer'*, plus the Nicholson-McLaren built unit, and the standard-issue Cosworth-assembled version. Goodyear provided five different front and three different rear tyre constructions for Lotus, Brabham and McLaren and Andretti was able to capitalise on the tyre situation by use of the *'stagger'*. He also knew that hand-cut tyres built up more temperature through increased tyre movement, and thus gave better grip, and Goodyear duly obliged. The new Ferrari 312T3s of Reutemann and Villeneuve proved quickest in practice, with Lauda's Brabham-Alfa BT46 next up. Watson's similar car separated Andretti and Ronnie, with Hunt following in the M26. At the green light, Gilles Villeneuve led his more experienced rivals, while Alan Jones made an excellent start to get the better of Ronnie and then Andretti. As Villeneuve was coming up to lap Regazzoni on lap 40, the cars touched and the Ferrari spun into the barriers. Jones then challenged Reutemann for the lead, but the Aussie fell back with fuel pick-up problems and was passed by Andretti, Depailler and Peterson in succession. Ronnie had to stop to have his flat-spotted front tyres changed, so fourth was not a bad result under the circumstances. Ahead of him was Depailler in that Tyrrell once more. Now, Andretti and Reutemann led the World Championship table with 18 points apiece, Ronnie and Patrick were joint second on 14 points.

For Monaco, Ronnie had 78/2 and Andretti had 78/3, with the rebuilt 79/2 chassis on hand as the spare car. The paddock gossip focussed on aerodynamics, notably Brabham's V-shaped skirt under the nose of the car to deflect air sideways, its skirts designed to prevent air going under the car, to achieve downforce from above rather than by ground-effect generated suction. Other teams had begun to catch on, notably Arrows, Shadow, and Wolf. But while the Lotus 79 still used flexible skirts, the Wolf had sliding skirts that moved up and down or rock fore-and-aft within narrow boxes along the bottoms of the side-pods. They were protected from abrasion against the track surface by metal skids, and were retained within the boxes by locking pins when the car was being moved around in the paddock. The sliding skirt was the key to the next phase of ground-effect aerodynamics. When Team Lotus saw that the Wolf passed scrutineering, they too implemented sliding skirts.

During first practice on the Thursday morning, Ronnie went quickly but crashed towards the end, so was forced to sit out the afternoon session. Meanwhile, Andretti abandoned the Type 79 and carried on with 78/3. This car used a Nicholson-built engine, while Ronnie used a standard-issue Cosworth-built unit. As the race got under way, Watson led from Depailler, Lauda and Andretti, while Hunt and Reutemann came together at Ste Dévote. Ronnie lay seventh behind Scheckter and Jones. Soon enough, the battle for fourth place developed into one of the race highlights, involving Andretti, Scheckter, Peterson and Villeneuve. By lap 45, Depailler's Tyrrell led, but on lap 56, Ronnie's gearbox packed up when he was running fifth. It was Patrick Depailler's well-deserved first Grand Prix victory, but the outside observer could be forgiven for wondering whether it might have been Ronnie being fêted by the Rainiers had he stayed at Tyrrell.

Before the Belgian Grand Prix, Ronnie tested 79/2 at Anderstorp, lapping a startling two seconds faster than the existing record. Unfortunately for Ronnie though, number One driver Andretti had sole access to the car for Zolder, so a new seat was installed and the pedals reset accordingly. His pole position time was almost a full second quicker than Reutemann's Ferrari, an incredible gap. In the 78/2, Ronnie was seventh quickest. Rex Hart recalled: *'The 79 never got used in anger until we took it to Monaco. Immediately after that it went to Sweden, and since Andretti didn't want to go, Ronnie took it there. Andretti hadn't shown a lot of interest in the 79 at that time, but then Ronnie was suddenly two seconds a lap quicker round Anderstorp than anybody expected. They rushed another one through, and we raced it with virtually no spares for quite a few races. The 79 totally suited Ronnie; he just eased into it.'*

Immediately after the start at Zolder there was a huge coming-together when Reutemann missed a gear and was enveloped by the rest of the field. Lauda and Hunt were out, but Andretti motored blithely away. The Lotus 79 had so much grip he could venture onto parts of the track where no-one else felt comfortable, brake much later and re-define apexes. In second place was Villeneuve's Ferrari, while Ronnie moved up to third. When the French-Canadian's Ferrari got a puncture at 40 laps, Ronnie was second. There was a mini-drama on lap 56 when he dashed in for a new left-hand front tyre, leaving the pit-lane at some 100mph, after which it took him just eleven laps to catch and pass Laffite and then Reutemann, with a magnificent outbraking manoeuvre to recover second place. The Lotus one-two finish was a dream 50th birthday present for Colin Chapman. Andretti now led the title chase with 27 points to Depailler's 23, Reutemann's 22 and Peterson's 20.

When a second Lotus 79 was unloaded from the transporter in the paddock at Jarama, as well as a pair of Type 78s as back-up cars, the rest of the Grand Prix circus could only shiver in anticipation. What chance had anyone else now? It was the perfect package, the *'racer's racer'* as Andretti was known, and SuperSwede, the 'fastest man on four wheels', were both equipped with the quickest cars, at least on their Zolder showing. Ronnie had 79/2 at his disposal and Andretti had the brand-new 79/3. Practice went according to the form book, Andretti taking pole position on the twisty Madrid circuit with 1m 16.39 sec, and Ronnie close behind on 1m 16.68 seconds. Carlos Reutemann's Ferrari 312T3 was third fastest on 1m 17.40 sec, and James Hunt's McLaren M26 was alongside on 1m 17.66 sec – each almost a second slower than the corresponding Lotus. Even running with full fuel tanks and race tyres their times were faster than most others could manage on qualifiers and near-empty tanks. When the race started, Ronnie was hindered by a policeman standing on the track and Hunt blasted through to get the lead at the first corner. For five laps Andretti held fire, then moved ahead when the Englishman missed a gear, leaving him to fend off Reutemann. Next came a gaggle consisting of Watson, Villeneuve, Patrese and Laffite, with another gap to Scheckter, Peterson and Lauda. As the race sorted itself out, Andretti began lapping the tail-enders, having a 12-second cushion over Hunt. Ronnie extracted himself from fifth place as the back-markers were lapped, drawing the bunch on in his pursuit of Hunt. At the beginning of lap 53, Ronnie was past the McLaren for second place, which he held to the finish, some 20 seconds behind Andretti for another Lotus one-two. Getting back to the control tower from parc fermé for the presentations by King Juan-Carlos, Ronnie, Mario and third-placed Laffite had to fight their way through the fans who'd invaded the track en masse.

On the way back from Spain Ronnie went straight to Brands Hatch for a test session, and was exceptionally quick, *'He was flying,'* said Rex Hart. *'He just staggered everybody.'*

Thank you, fans

Anderstorp often produced surprise results, and 1978 was no exception, as the Brabham-Alfa BT46B had a sting in its tail. It presented the first real challenge to the Lotus 79, achieved by a large 18in-diameter fan driven off the gearbox main shaft to draw cooling air down over the radiator. Having extracted hot air from around the engine and gearbox, the fan also drew air from underneath the skirted sides of the car and effectively sucked it to the ground – a reprise of the system used in the Chaparral 2J CanAm car of 1970 that used a pair of fans driven by two constant-speed Snowmobile engines. FOCA, the Formula One Constructors' Association, was divided, and five official protests were submitted on the grounds that the Brabhams contravened CSI rules on movable aerodynamic devices, which, if fitted, had to be firmly fixed while the car was in motion. Andretti told Chapman they'd have to get them banned as, for one thing, the fans threw grit at following cars. For another, they were very effective. While the FOCA chiefs debated in the Marlboro motor home, the Brabhams weren't so

Opposite and above: Ronnie's regular mechanics during 1978 were Rex Hart and Bobby Clarke, with Bob Dance as chief mechanic. Here he discusses set-up with engineer Nigel Bennett.

Ronnie Peterson: Super Swede

Above: Super Swede in the Lotus 79 on home ground at Anderstorp, where he finished third behind Lauda's Brabham fan car and Patrese's Arrows.

> **HIS HOME CROWD WAS TREATED TO A SCINTILLATING DISPLAY OF PETERSON MAGIC AS, CAR BY CAR, HE CLIMBED BACK TO THIRD PLACE. ONLY PATRESE'S BLOCKING AND WHEEL-BANGING TACTICS PREVENTED HIM FROM COMING SECOND.**

quick. But they'd been sandbagging. In the final 30 minutes of qualifying, they found another two seconds a lap and were up alongside the Lotus 79s at the front of the grid.

Andretti told Ghughie Zanon he would have liked to help Ronnie win on his home turf, but since they were so close in the points chase, he felt he couldn't do it. At the start of the race, Watson got bogged down, while Lauda took advantage of Andretti's clean getaway to follow him into second place. Patrese's Arrows FA1 made a good start as well, putting Ronnie behind him. Watson spun off, instantly exposing the major problem with the fan-car as it sucked dirt into the engine. Andretti managed to hold off Lauda, but they were closely matched. When Andretti was obliged to tiptoe over the oil and debris from Pironi's wrecked Tyrrell, by sticking to the customary line, Lauda saw it coming and was able to force the Brabham-Alfa past the American. Just 7 laps later the Lotus's DFV holed a piston, ending his race on the spot. Meanwhile, Ronnie picked up a puncture and had to stop for a new tyre, relegating him to 17th place. His home crowd was treated to a scintillating display of Peterson magic as, car by car, he climbed back to third place. Only Patrese's blocking and wheel-banging tactics prevented him from coming second. On the podium afterwards, Ronnie reminded the Italian that he was competing in Formula 1 now, not Formula 3; Patrese's behaviour would come back to haunt him at Monza.

Lauda's Anderstorp victory was allowed to stand, but the Brabham fan cars were subsequently declared illegal by the CSI and they were restored to their original format, just an interesting glitch on the record books.

For the French Grand Prix at Paul Ricard, Team Lotus was confident enough to regard the Type 78s as little more than museum pieces. The two driver's engines differed though, with Andretti using a Cosworth development engine – like Depailler's Tyrrell, Scheckter's Wolf and Patrick Tambay's McLaren – while Ronnie's 79/2 was fitted with a less extreme Nicholson-built DFV unit, like Hunt's McLaren. By 1978, Cosworth had made 12 of these 500bhp *'development'* engines, and the fact that Mario had one but Ronnie didn't, helped account for the American's superior performance. Even so, the fastest cars along Paul Ricard's back straight were the Alfa Romeo flat 12-powered Brabham BT46s, at 177.7mph. By comparison, Tambay's McLaren M26 was timed at 170.9mph, and Laffite's Ligier JS9-Matra V12 struggled at 167.8mph. Andretti again experimented with tyre combinations including some ultra-sticky qualifiers that only lasted a single lap qualifying just 500ths of a second slower than Watson's pole-winning Brabham. Behind them were Hunt and Lauda, with Tambay and Peterson another row back. Jackie Stewart headed the field for the warm-up lap in the spare Renault RS01/03 equipped with a camera for the occasion while, perversely, the V6 turbo engine in Jabouille's RS01/02 began to smoke. It lasted a couple of laps, to the consternation of the Renault chiefs present, who until that moment had been basking in the reflected glory of Pironi/Jaussaud's recent Le Mans victory in the A442. Although Watson made the best getaway, Andretti forced his Lotus into the lead before they had reached the end of the long back straight. Tambay was third, Lauda fourth and Ronnie fifth, the Lotus driver having already bent his right-hand front wing in a vain attempt to pass the Austrian's Brabham. Tambay was soon demoted to fifth and Peterson set about tackling Watson, who'd been overtaken by his team-mate. Having passed the Ulsterman, Ronnie was gifted second place when Lauda's Alfa Romeo engine blew up, his mission having been to hold Hunt at bay. Peterson hung relentlessly onto Andretti's gearbox, although team orders precluded him overtaking. Late in the race, Hunt made a bid to challenge Ronnie but the Lotus 79's traction and grip was such that he never got close enough to make a serious move. Andretti crossed the line three seconds ahead of Peterson, reasserting the supremacy of the ground-effect Type 79.

After the French Grand Prix, Ronnie's car was used by Andretti for tyre testing at the Österreichring, and it was then taken via Hethel to Brands Hatch for Ronnie to use in the Friday morning practice session for the British Grand Prix. Andretti's own car had gone straight back to Norfolk from Le Castellet for its chassis to be fitted with a new front bulkhead and have the rippled scuttle panel straightened, although its Cosworth development engine remained in place. Having lapped Brands Hatch fastest in the recent tyre testing, Ronnie was in fine form for Grand Prix practice. He was quickly down to 1m 17.16 sec, while everyone else struggled to break 1m 20 sec, although Andretti soon managed 1m 17.83 sec after judicious adjustments to the handling set-up. Ronnie's mechanics Rex Hart and Bobby Clarke then set about dismantling 79/2 to fit a new oil tank between engine and gearbox, so he took over 78/2 for the afternoon session. Meanwhile Andretti's Hewland gearbox began playing up and the internals were replaced, but then the engine refused to start due to fuel vaporization. A push start down the pits access road got him going, only to rip one of its side skirts on a manhole cover. No-one came close to matching their morning times. Another 79 was present for the second day of practice, the refettled 79/1 prototype, and Ronnie shone, getting swiftly down to 1m 16.80 sec, and calling it a day at that.'

Deliberately slowed

Nothing was said officially about *'the agreement'* between Chapman, Andretti and Peterson and, by implication, team manager Andrew Ferguson, race engineer Nigel Bennett and chief mechanic Bob Dance, until Brands Hatch, where Andretti decided to go public. Chapman was not too happy, but Andretti felt it needed airing, such was the paddock gossip. But it was one thing to settle for second place in the races, and another to be restricted in practice, when it was difficult to gauge how one's team-mate or rivals were performing.

Ronnie knew he was being hampered in practice, because he asked to try the other car and was refused. Staffan believed that, it was not a matter of being treated unfairly, because it was in the contract that Andretti had the use of the spare car whenever he wanted it.' When Ronnie went faster than Andretti it didn't click into Chapman's plan – Ronnie didn't follow the script. He knew what his position should be in the races, but he thought that in practising he could go as fast as he liked. So they tried to slow him down. He also thought he could be ahead of Andretti in the races and then let him through. But Colin wanted the American winner. So, Ronnie was the willing dupe of a policy designed to promote Lotus Cars in the USA, though it is painful now to think of his exuberant talent being deliberately suppressed. *'Colin was no shrinking violet when it came to his own interests,'* said John Watson.

'It's a shame Peterson was slowed up,' said former chief mechanic Eddie Dennis. *'They talk about Schumacher and Barrichello today, but Peterson and Andretti was just as much a deliberate slowing down of the number two driver. I know they regularly put 20 gallons of fuel in Peterson's car for qualifying and maybe 5 gallons in Andretti's. Plus they'd ballast Ronnie's car to slow him down a bit. Criminal really.'*

At Brands Hatch, Mario had 16 sets of qualifying tyres while Ronnie had his old race tyres from the previous outing. Sent out on full tanks he still qualified a second ahead of his team-mate. Though he accepted the situation publicly, and made the best of it, privately he suffered. Keith Leighton said *'I'd talk to him on the phone and he would basically be crying to me. I said, "you signed that at the beginning of the year Ronnie;" what could he do? He was definitely the number two. Ultimately Chapman stitched him up because of money.'*

There was more to it than met the eye. Ghughie Zanon revealed that he wasn't merely paying Chapman to have Ronnie drive at Team Lotus. *'I had a personal contract with Ronnie,'* he explained, *'and every pole position and every first place he scored, he would get a bonus from me. Chapman didn't know about that, until Ronnie told him. Ronnie was very genuine, but not very bright! Chapman was not happy about it at first. He said, "that goes against my plans," and I told him, "that's up to you, but you're a sportsman, you should be able to accept it." But getting pole position was not in the Lotus contract, only deferring to Mario in the race. Ronnie was kept in second position by the Team, and finally he got upset by that. Anyway, I said to Colin, "I do what I like with my money," and it gave me great pleasure to see him on pole at Brands Hatch.'* Ronnie fought back in practice, insisting on qualifiers and empty tanks Within three laps he'd destroyed the opposition, his frustrated aggression making this success one of the few times he was heard to be triumphal, telling both Brodie and Count Zanon, *'now I would like to see someone do it better!'* One of the benefits of *winning pole position at Brands Hatch was the 100 bottles of champagne that*

Opposite: Type 79 minus cockpit surround in the Brands Hatch pitlane. Ronnie also practiced a Type 78 at Brands Hatch. **Above:** Thanks to its full-on ground effect aerodynamics, the Lotus 79 was far and away the quickest F1 car in 1978, and looked the best, running here at Brands Hatch without John Player branding.

> 'BY 1978, MARIO WAS VERY EXPERIENCED, BUT RONNIE HAD A VERY NATURAL TECHNIQUE, VERY RESPONSIVE CAR CONTROL AND WAS A VERY, VERY GOOD RACING DRIVER.'

went with it. But that didn't go far once Chapman had taken his cut. Ronnie bought some more bottles himself to make sure everyone in the team got their share. It was a moment to celebrate.'

The pole-winner at Brands Hatch could also elect which side of the track to go for, and Ronnie chose to start on the higher left-hand side of the grid to avoid the steep camber affecting the inside line. It was to no avail, as Andretti led out of Paddock Bend, and inexorably the Lotus pair in their 79s built up a commanding lead over Scheckter, Jones, Lauda, Patrese, Reutemann, Depailler Watson and Hunt. All too soon the demonstration run was over. On lap 6, Ronnie stopped on the exit of Druids with his fuel pump defunct. By lap 19 Andretti had a puncture, and after a pitstop resumed in 12th place, only to retire ten laps on with a blown engine. Reutemann won for Ferrari with the Brabhams of Lauda and Watson in pursuit.

Should I stay or should I go?

When the circus arrived at Hockenheim for the German Grand Prix on 30th July, there was already speculation amongst the F1 fraternity that Ronnie would switch teams the following season. If Andretti stayed at Team Lotus for 1979, Ronnie would only be able to beat him through better reliability, since Andretti would insist on his continuing number one status, and Ronnie would be just as disadvantaged as he was in 1978. Qualifying was virtually a repeat of the Brands Hatch scenario, as Ronnie set provisional pole running full tanks and harder race tyres. Andretti broke down while warming up his car because the fuel system malfunctioned. He tried 79/1, but to no avail. Then, having played with the set-up of 79/3, Andretti went out and eclipsed Ronnie's time by just 100th of a second. So was Mario quicker than Ronnie? A fresh engine may have helped, giving him another 600rpm down the long straights. Jackie Stewart was ambivalent. *'I don't know if Ronnie was quicker than Mario. By 1978, Mario was very experienced, but Ronnie had a very natural technique, very responsive car control, and was a very, very good racing driver.'*

Robin Herd acknowledged that, while *'Mario was very good, Ronnie was quicker. If it had been an open fight, Ronnie would have won the Championship.'* Rex Hart was brutally forthright: *'Andretti wasn't that chuffed about Ronnie coming back to Lotus, because Ronnie blew him off everywhere. He was far quicker than Andretti, simple as that. If Andretti was quicker, then why did we run Ronnie in practice on race tyres with extra fuel all the time? At Hockenheim, within five laps of the start of first day's qualifying he got pole position, and it took Andretti till five minutes before the end of qualifying Saturday afternoon to beat him by 100th of a second. It was embarrassing. That night, Ronnie came back to the garage fairly late, saying, "nobody wants to bloody speak to me."*

Chief mechanic Bob Dance pointed out that, *'as we got towards the end of the season, Chapman was seriously concerned that Ronnie shouldn't have any more wins as it would jeopardise Mario's World Championship chances. If the Old Man had let them race against each other, maybe neither of them would have won it, as happened in 1973. Perhaps he'd learned a lesson from that.'*

Bob Dance admired Andretti. *'I enjoyed working with Mario very much,'* he said. *'He was easy to get on with as a person; he knew what he wanted to do, but he had to have the attention and he needed to be going well. You have to remember that he and Chapman went back a long way. The Old Man saw him at Indianapolis in the mid-'60s as a young, charging driver. Mario was an outgoing person and they got on well.'* Technically, Andretti and Chapman hit it off. They would discuss things even if they didn't agree on set-up. Mario would do things to the car that would show improvements, like fiddle about with corner weights, and could discuss how they made it go better. Chapman didn't always agree – he was not that keen on the tyre stagger issue – but if something worked, he was happy to let the driver get on with it. *'Mario was mechanically minded, but Ronnie wasn't in at that depth. He wasn't the same engineering type as Mario,'* said Bob. *'But if you said to him, "this is the best possible set-up for the car," that gave him the confidence to really go out and push it. His speed came from natural ability. Of the two of them, Mario was the one who knew what he was doing, mechanically. Eventually, he did became disenchanted with us and went to Alfa Romeo in 1981.'*

Top: In several races, Peterson dutifully shadowed Andretti, as here at Brands Hatch, but grew less enamoured of the situation as the season progressed. **Above:** Having proved he could still win, Ronnie needed a number one seat to stand a chance of winning the Championship, but Mario wouldn't let that happen at Lotus.

Ronnie Peterson: Super Swede

Above: Outraged to discover that his 79 was deliberately being slowed with full tanks and race tyres in qualfying, Ronnie insisted on equal settings with Andretti at Brands Hatch, and promptly went a second quicker to secure pole. **Opposite:** Ronnie and Jackie Stewart discuss form.

Andretti had galvanised the team around him, dragging Lotus from the depths of despondency in 1975 to the threshold of the World title in 1977 and 1978. A firm Mario supporter, his biographer Nigel Roebuck said, *'Ronnie freely acknowledged that the Lotus 79 wouldn't have been the car it became without Mario's supreme skills as a test driver. There's no doubt in my mind that he deserved the World Championship in 1978. Chapman is on record as saying, "Mario's efforts made the Lotus 79 the car it was, and Ronnie benefited from that." They were both very honourable men, and the atmosphere within the team that year was the happiest I can remember.'* Just as with Emerson Fittipaldi, there was a world of difference in the approach to car set-up between the two Lotus team-mates. Andretti's Team Lotus mechanic Glenn Waters summed up the difference between the two drivers: *'in the same car on the same day, with the same settings and the same set of tyres, there would be no question – Andretti will tell you – Ronnie was the quicker of the two drivers. But Ronnie couldn't bring it all together, incrementally improving the car. He couldn't engineer himself out of a problem, whereas Andretti could.'*

Though firmly in the Ronnie camp, Rex Hart agreed: *'Andretti knew what he wanted and was able to achieve it. He fiddled around a lot more. At the time we had an adjustable roll bar which he would adjust between corners. He'd say, "that left hander has to be five notches on the front and three on the rear," and the next corner was four on the front and two on the rear.'*

Meanwhile, Ronnie became the first driver to lap Hockenheim in under 1m 52 sec, posting 1m 51.99 sec during final practice, before spinning on the pit straight when a top-link in his rear suspension broke. Just at the end, Andretti took pole with 1m 51.90 sec. Scheckter's 1977 pole-winning time of 1m 53.07 underlined the superiority of the Lotus 79s. As the race got under way, Andretti braked too late at the first chicane allowing Ronnie to pass and lead away onto the forest-lined 180mph straights. The two Lotuses fenced with one another through the chicanes, kicking up the dirt as their wheels trespassed the track's edges. The Swede had thrown down the gauntlet. They circulated nose to tail, Peterson making a race of it, but at the end of the fifth lap as they entered the stadium, Andretti out-braked him on the inside to take the lead. But Ronnie didn't let up, and the Lotuses were side by side down the straights. Knowing that cooling is crucial in a car that's following closely behind another one, both drivers had a vested interest in staying in front. *'Those cars always had problems with their rear brakes fading away, and if you're following somebody it's always a bit easier if you run alongside them,'* said Bob Dance. Ronnie's engine was misfiring due to fuel vaporisation, so he planned to overtake Andretti, put enough distance between them to make his point and then pit for a splash-and-dash, emerging behind the Lotus number one with both drivers' honour intact. It never happened, as Ronnie's challenge crumbled along with his crownwheel and pinion. He managed a few more laps with just fourth gear, clocking 11,000rpm along the straights before pitting for good. It was a clear win for Andretti, with Scheckter coming in second and Laffite third.

Rain master

The practice scenario at the magnificent Österreichring was a familiar story, Ronnie setting the early pace while Andretti bided his time, making careful adjustments to all the variables like tyres, roll-bars and aerodynamic settings. His car 79/3 was fitted with new elliptical-section lower wishbones front and back, while Ronnie's car retained its round-section ones. At first, Andretti was unable to match Ronnie's best time, and Reutemann was second fastest. It was thought that the aerodynamics of Andretti's car could have been affected by the elliptical wishbones upsetting the vortices under the car. So they were covered with split plastic hose pipe to give a circular profile. Andretti's times suddenly came close to matching his team-mate, who was unable to respond as his Nicholson DFV engine had broken a conrod. Saturday afternoon's timed qualifying session was halted by a mis-timed parachuting display, and then a rainstorm put paid to any further running. That meant Ronnie's Friday morning best of 1m 37.71 sec was good enough for pole, and Andretti sat alongside him with 1m 37.76 from Friday afternoon. Reutemann's Ferrari and Jabouille's Renault RS01 V6 turbo lined up behind them, and a steady drizzle on the morning of the race ensured that all cars were shod with wet-weather tyres.

Ronnie got a good start, but Andretti was passed by Reutemann. When he attempted to go round the outside of the Ferrari at the third corner, Reutemann gave him no space, being more intent on Scheckter on the inside, and Andretti spun off into the barriers. Crucially, in the light of Ronnie's death, that accident changed the line up of cars available to Team Lotus at Monza in two race's time. The bottom of the chassis was damaged as it passed over a tree stump, and an errant Scheckter cannoned into it next time round. Meanwhile, Ronnie was building up a massive lead on that first lap, rooster tails fountaining from his tyres as he left the rest of the field to skate round in the gloom and spray. At seven laps the officials decided it was too wet to carry on, since six cars had crashed, and the red and black flags were held out to signify the race being stopped. Good timing for Ronnie, since he spun off on the slowing down lap. When the rain abated the race restarted, competitors forming up in the order that they'd completed the first seven laps. Those that had gone off or whose cars were undriveable, like Andretti's, were excluded. Fortunately, once the marshals had extricated Ronnie's car, he was able to drive back to the pits. He now had Depailler's Tyrrell alongside him for the re-start. As the green light came on, Watson's Brabham stalled, causing confusion on his side of the grid, and Ronnie simply repeated his original performance, gaining a substantial lead over Depailler on the opening lap. After eleven laps the track had dried sufficiently to go for dry tyres and the Lotus pitted. This dropped Ronnie to sixth, but he quickly moved back to the front as, first Depailler, then Fittipaldi and Pironi also came in for slicks. Villeneuve kept going as long as he dared on wets, but at 21 laps he too had no alternative but to go in and with Reutemann having spun off, Ronnie regained the lead. Driving clinically, he set fastest lap just before the finish, and only Depailler and Villeneuve remained on the same lap as him. From the pits, Ghughie Zanon (whose engine Peterson was using) asked the mechanics to put out the 'Slow' sign. *'He had so much in hand, he could have relaxed his pace a little. But afterwards he told me, "If I slow down I loose my rhythm, and if I back off, the engine can give up."'* It was undoubtedly one of Ronnie's best ever races, bearing in mind he'd set pole and controlled a wet Grand Prix in the absence of his team-mate.

Chapter 11: Ground Effect

Opposite: With BMW Motorsport division competitions manager Jochen Neerpasch and engine specialist Paul Rosche at Hockenheim in August 1978 for the launch of the M1 ProCar series that would support European Grands Prix in '79 and '80. **Above:** In atrocious conditions, Ronnie led the Austrian GP by a country mile, taking the win when the race was stopped.

Above: That distinctive Swedish blue and yellow helmet was a well-known symbol in F1 circles. **Opposite:** Ronnie's friend since their Formula 2 days, John Watson picked up his McLaren drive in 1979. The beard went after he won his first GP.

> HE TOLD ME OVER A CUP OF TEA THAT HE COULD DRIVE ROUND ANDRETTI WITH ONE HAND ON THE WHEEL AND THE OTHER UNDER HIS BUM. HE SAID THAT WHEN HE GOT TO NORTH AMERICA HE WAS GOING TO BLOW HIM INTO THE WEEDS.

Duet in the dunes

Ronnie had 79/2 and 78/3 as his spare car for the Dutch Grand Prix at Zandvoort on 28th August, while Andretti had 79/4 and 79/1 as back up. Predictably, Ronnie was fastest of all on the Friday morning session, and then, with new rear springs fitted, Andretti improved on that by 100th of a second in the afternoon. Ronnie's car had a stuck fuel-pressure relief valve, so couldn't respond. In Saturday's session his left-front brake was grabbing, and the water radiator had a slight leak. There was an element of compromise about Andretti's strategy to hone the car's pitch and ride set-up for certain corners, which he could then commit to absolutely flat-out and gain a significant advantage at the expense of other corners where he would be giving away less. One such was the crucial hill after Hunze Rug and the following corner onto the main straight. Setting the Type 79 up for this element of the circuit enabled a cracking 1m 16.36 sec pole time for Andretti. Yet again, the Lotus duo were almost a full second a lap quicker than the third quickest car, which was Lauda's Brabham-Alfa, followed by Reutemann's Ferrari.

At the start, the red changed to green in short order, and Andretti had the lead from Ronnie with Lauda, Laffite and Reutemann in pursuit. Confusion reigned behind them as, first, Stuck hit Pironi who cannoned into Patrese, while Daly, Jones, Scheckter and Rosberg were entangled in a separate brawl. The next bunch included Watson, Fittipaldi, Villeneuve, Hunt and Depailler, but the Lotuses were heading off into the distance, enjoying a four-second lead after only ten laps. When it seemed that Lauda was closing, Ronnie began to pressure Andretti, pursuing him through seemingly impossible gaps as they lapped the slower cars. Chapman instructed that Ronnie be shown pit signals to back off, but Lauda closed to within three seconds of Ronnie, who made fresh efforts to give Andretti a hurry-up call. Side by side on the pit straight, he gave Andretti the signal: lets have a go. But Andretti couldn't respond and by now Ronnie's rear brakes were going off. With 19 laps to go, Andretti's 79 broke an exhaust manifold, with accompanying loss of power, and suddenly the prospect of another win for Ronnie looked possible. Andretti wasn't about to give up though, and on lap 67 when the Brabham-Alfa's transmission began vibrating, Lauda backed off. Although by the time he'd decided that it wasn't terminal, the Lotuses were out of reach. The black-and-gold pair came first and second to team orders, with Lauda third, Watson fourth and Fittipaldi fifth.

Zandvoort's Bouwes Hotel was a hotbed of inter-team machinations and political manoeuvring. It was that time of year when team managers tried to consolidate their driver line-up for the following season, and it was make-your-mind-up time for those after the best seats. Ronnie's contract with McLaren for 1979 was signed there on 26th August, before the race.

John Watson, who drove for McLaren in 1979, said, *'James Hunt was becoming something of a monster in the team, and the results weren't coming, while all the hassle and aggravation was increasing. Marlboro could see what Ronnie was doing over at Lotus, and were pressing McLaren to embrace ground-effect technology and reassert themselves as a World Championship team.'* The decision as to who drove for McLaren was largely down to Marlboro rather than team principal Teddy Mayer. McLaren's technical director at the time was Alistair Caldwell. *'Ronnie was a great admirer of McLaren,'* he said. *'We knew the ones that wanted to drive for us because they'd hang around, sit in the cars and make engine noises Ronnie was one of those. Rindt was too. Ronnie found the Lotuses fragile, whereas McLarens were rough and tough and bits didn't fall off them. So they were attractive to drivers for that reason and they were also pretty competitive. Trouble was, the M29 was a technical low point, although of course they did eventually come good.'*

Dave Brodie remembered the last time he saw Ronnie. *'He was cutting his grass, and I'd bought a bag of doughnuts – he just loved jam doughnuts. We sat in the long grass; it used to get very long between races. He'd got a little tractor for mowing it. And he told me over a cup of tea that he could drive round Andretti with one hand on the wheel and the other under his bum. He said that when he got to North America he was going to blow him into the weeds. Of course, he never had the opportunity to do it. Next race on the calendar was Monza.'*

Ronnie Peterson: Super Swede

CHAPTER 12

The Tragedy Unfolds

The manner of Ronnie Peterson's death is still distressing and still controversial, 25 years on. He'd survived several major accidents, and initial indications were that he'd survive this one too. It was the kind of pile-up that modern-day drivers walk away from, ironically thanks in part to the quest for torsional rigidity in the ground-effect chassis. They became stronger in order to resist the downforce, to the point where they could absorb high-speed impacts. Monza was tensely exciting that year because it could be the Championship decider.

Opposite: His Lotus 79 not raceworthy, Ronnie was obliged to take the spare 78 at Monza. He started the race from a lower grid position than might have been the case had there been more time to practice the newer model.

But for Ronnie, the Italian Grand Prix of 1978 was jinxed, a catalogue of mishaps, culminating in the hideous tragedy of his death in the small hours of Monday morning. *'It was in the wind'* said Sveneric Eriksson. *'The whole meeting had that feeling about it.'* It hadn't started off that way. The weather was warm and sunny, and Ronnie was relaxed. Barbro had stayed at home in Monaco, fuelling rumours that the couple weren't getting on too well. On the Saturday morning, Ronnie asked Åke Strandberg, *'can you take my race overalls and stuff back to Maidenhead instead of Monte Carlo?'* In the Travco motor home before the race, he and Mario were in boisterous mood. Typically, the boy racer was in action on the public highway after practice. The Italian Rolls-Royce concessionaires had lent Mario and Ronnie a car each as transport between Monza and the Villa d'Este at Como where they were staying with other senior Team personnel. Staffan Svenby was in the front passenger seat of Ronnie's Rolls: *'After Friday's practice, Colin asked for a lift back to the hotel, and he got in the back of Ronnie's car. The two drivers looked at each other through their windscreens, and it was like a signal. They raced back to Villa d'Este, neck and neck, Colin screaming at Ronnie to slow down. When we got back there they parked the cars – Mario won – and I went to my room. I could smell burning rubber so looked out of the window and there were these two Rolls-Royces, one white, one silver, and the tyres and the brakes were still smoking! They drove them back to the circuit on the Saturday and the Rolls-Royce people asked, "Are the cars all right?" "Oh yes," they said, "we drove them very carefully just like Mr Chapman wanted, hardly used the brakes at all!" That was how it was with Ronnie. Every time you went with him it was racing. That was part of the game.'* Despite the intense rivalry between them, off the track the two professionals were good friends.

Ronnie was looking forward to the prospect of his number one status at McLaren in 1979, his moral obligation to honour his deal with Chapman was over, and, with a 12 point gap between him and Championship leader

> RONNIE WAS LOOKING FORWARD TO THE PROSPECT OF HIS NUMBER ONE STATUS AT MCLAREN IN 1979, HIS MORAL OBLIGATION TO HONOUR HIS DEAL WITH CHAPMAN WAS OVER, AND, WITH A TWELVE POINT GAP BETWEEN HIM AND ANDRETTI, THERE WAS EVEN A CHANCE OF HIM TAKING THE 1978 F1 TITLE

Andretti and three rounds to go, there was even a chance of him taking the '78 F1 title. Both drivers were acutely aware of the position. Throughout the season, Ronnie had smouldered in the number two role while Andretti racked up the wins. No car was that reliable in 1978, and Ronnie picked up victories as and when Mario retired, all the while knotching up second places to put himself within reach of the F1 crown. *'It was a pretty fraught weekend,'* recalled Bob Dance. *'Chapman was anxious that Mario should win the race and was very concerned that if he didn't win, his chances of the Championship would take a severe knock. If Ronnie had won, it would have been a difficult scenario to contemplate.'*

'For some time Ronnie had been tired of sitting on Andretti's gearbox,' said Staffan. *'The signs were there, like at Hockenheim and Zandvoort, where he would come alongside Andretti and give him a hurry-up call. At Monza, Ronnie decided he'd ignore team orders to make a race of it with Andretti. That was before the car situation got out of hand during practice. Colin knew that Ronnie was leaving him, and we were worried that he wouldn't let Ronnie have a car in America. So we hoped that Andretti would not be successful at Monza, so that Ronnie would have a car in America.'*

Mechanical failures

Then the problems started. The engine of Ronnie's Lotus 79 blew after a few laps of first practice on the Friday morning. Andretti, meanwhile, was setting the pace. Ronnie was obliged to use his spare Type 78 for the afternoon's hour-long session as a new DFV was still being installed in his race car.

The allocation of chassis within Team Lotus had been complicated by Mario's off at the recent Austrian Grand Prix, which ripped the bottom out of the tub of 79/3. So he was thus using 79/4, with 79/1 as his spare. Ronnie's race car was 79/2, but because 79/3 was still being repaired back at Ketteringham Hall, his spare car was 78/3 in which earlier in the season he had won the South African GP. Number One driver Mario could choose which car he wanted as back-up and Ronnie's partisan mechanics felt Andretti was exercising an unfair advantage, although this was standard practice. Although still current in terms of its ground-effect aerodynamics, the Type 78 was regarded as last-year's thing. Its chassis construction was quite different from the 79, being made of aluminium honeycomb, and broader, with fuel tanks in the side extensions, as opposed to just behind the cockpit in the case of its narrow, single-sheet aluminium successor. The Type 78 suffered from fuel pick-up problems, which were solved by the installation of a catch tank in the cockpit footwell, an ad hoc solution that played its part in Peterson's accident. Fully expecting to be back in his Type 79 for race day, Ronnie didn't spend much time setting up the old 78, and was two seconds off the pace set by his team-mate. During the untimed session on the Saturday morning, Mario briefly drove 79/1, while Ronnie, reunited with 79/2, was in trouble with overheating rear brakes. To make things worse, his clutch began to slip as oil leaked from the main gearbox oil seal along the primary shaft. As a result, Ronnie couldn't improve on his Friday morning practice times. That put him on the third row of the grid, alongside Alan Jones and behind the slow-starting Renault turbo of Jean-Pierre Jabouille. Turbo technology was in its infancy and, fast as it was, the Renault took a while to get up and go. Another bad sign.

The last race

On race morning there was a 30-minute test session and unfortunately at the second chicane, Ronnie's Lotus 79 darted though the catch fencing and struck the barrier, crumpling the front of the monocoque. Brake failure was diagnosed, but there was no time to repair the tub before the race, and all his mechanics could do was prepare the Type 78 once again.

The 24-car grid began to assemble for the 3.30pm start, and Ronnie used the warm-up to check the feel of the car, diving into the pits for a last minute tweak to the aerodynamics.

The formation lap was led away by Andretti and Gilles Villeneuve's Ferrari. As they arrived back at the start line, the starter raised the Italian flag. But before the back of the grid had negotiated the Parabolica, let alone come to a standstill, the flag fell and the race was on. Villeneuve and Lauda got away well, Andretti

Chapter 12: The Tragedy Unfolds

Above: Distant smoke and fire extinguishant cloud the site of the pile-up. The leading cars have completed the lap and come to a halt as confusion reigns.

> **WITHOUT HESITATION, HUNT WAS OUT OF HIS CAR STRUGGLING TO RELEASE RONNIE FROM HIS BELTS, HAMPERED BY THE FLAMES AND SMOKE AND THE TWISTED PEDALS TRAPPING RONNIE'S ANKLES.**

hesitated, as did Ronnie. The back markers were already doing around 50mph when the starter dropped the flag, and several of these cars passed the midfield runners. The broad starting grid at Monza funnelled abruptly into the short straight leading to the first chicane, compressing the field even more. Ronnie made such a leisurely getaway that maybe he wasn't in the right gear. As the cars funnelled down to the first chicane he was engulfed by at least half the field. In a video of the event, we see Scheckter's Wolf coming up from behind Ronnie, moving much faster, darting from left to right across the track to pass the Lotus and Hunt's McLaren, which is coming up along Ronnie's right hand side. The Swede appears to drift slightly to the right at the same time. Now Patrese's Arrows hurtles down the extreme right of the track, cutting in behind Scheckter, and Hunt is left with nowhere to go. We see the back of the McLaren jump into the air as it collides with the Lotus, and next thing a fireball erupts as the Lotus is pitched into the barriers, where it was struck by Brambilla's Surtees, bouncing it back into the opposite side. Seven other cars were caught up in the chaos. It all happened in the twinkling of an eye. A huge fireball erupted from the Lotus's punctured footwell fuel tank. Without hesitation, Hunt was out of his car struggling to release Ronnie from his belts, hampered by the flames and smoke and the twisted pedals trapping Ronnie's ankles. In his Autosport column Hunt wrote, *'I tried to pull Ronnie clear but found one of his legs trapped between the steering wheel and what remained of the chassis. Flames and smoke enveloped the whole car again but the marshal flattened them and, with additional assistance now on hand (Shadow driver Clay Regazzoni) we managed to wrench the steering wheel clear. I picked up Ronnie by the epaulettes of his uniform and dragged him clear of the car. I knew that Ronnie's injuries must be pretty severe, as there was nothing left to the front end of the car.'*

Medical facilities

Emergency facilities at Monza were as good as anywhere in the late 1970s. The medical centre was small and basic, located at the back of the paddock, containing essential pharmaceutical equipment and run by six doctors trained in anaesthesia and trauma care. Seven ambulances, including two mobile intensive care units, were strategically placed around the circuit and staffed by doctors and nurses. Although it was before the days of dedicated medical vehicles, there had been fast course cars since the early 1970s such as the VW-Porsche 914/6s at the Nürburgring. At Monza, these Alfa Romeos were manned by doctors and stationed at the end of the pit lane, at the bridge before the second chicane, and at the Variante Ascari curve. There was a helicopter pad with a large, specially-equipped helicopter in attendance by the medical centre. In theory, pretty well covered. The designated hospital for Monza casualties was the Ospedale Maggiore at Niguardia, ten minutes by air.

Professor Sid Watkins provides a chilling account of events following the accident in his book Life at the Limit – Triumph and Tragedy in Formula 1. Professor of neurosurgery at the London Hospital since 1970, he took on the role of GP surgeon in 1978. He was stationed at Race Control for the race, a five-minute walk from the medical centre. As soon as the accident happened he made his way towards the scene, but was prevented from getting there by police and carabinieri who had formed a barrier across the track. They were in no mood to negotiate, and Pete Briggs from Team Surtees was coshed with a truncheon when he tried to establish what had happened to Vittorio Brambilla.

Professor Watkins reached the medical centre at the same time as the ambulance containing Ronnie. So much for the on-track medical presence; 18 minutes passed between Hunt's extraction of Peterson from his burning Lotus to the arrival of the ambulance at the crash scene. Ronnie was *'conscious and rational, but both his legs and feet were badly smashed, and he had some superficial burns on the shoulder and chest.'* Rex Hart reported, *'We had his gloves and helmet back immediately after they'd taken him away. There were virtually no burn marks on them.'*

'He was still in his race overalls,' said Åke Strandberg, *'and you could tell one leg was crushed. He said, 'it really hurts,' and that was the last thing he said to me.'*

At the medical centre they got drips into the arm veins, and his blood pressure was normal. As the medical team splinted the leg fractures, the medical centre filled up with people, including paparazzi. Professor Watkins said, *'Ronnie was talking sensibly. He was very anxious that I should come to the hospital as soon as I could, and I promised to do so. In fact he said, "Please don't leave me, Prof."'*

In Gerald Donaldson's biography of Hunt, James is quoted by girlfriend Jane Birbeck as being *'very, very shaken when he pulled Ronnie out of the car. When James looked into his face he said it was filled with fear. He saw that Ronnie knew he was in trouble and was terribly frightened.'* For his part, Hunt went to the Wolf motorhome before the restart and talked with Warr and Postlethwaite. He was given a cup of tea to try and calm him down. *'His hands shook, his face was pale, his voice was trembling with emotion, and he talked about stopping racing there and then,'* said Donaldson. Other drivers, like Depailler, had little stomach for continuing. There's a precedent for a great driver packing it all in after the death of a comrade. Back in 1954, Foilán González quit racing very soon after his friend Onofré Marimón was killed at the Nürburgring. During practice for the 1979 Monaco GP, Hunt abandoned his Wolf and walked away from F1 altogether. He was subsequently awarded the *'Golden Shield'* by the Royal Swedish Automobile Club for his part in rescuing Ronnie.

Reine Wisell managed to speak to Ronnie after the accident, and he was calm, even sanguine. *'It's shit about the legs,'* Ronnie said, *'but they fixed up Graham Hill so they must be able to fix me. I'll be ready for next year.'* He was then carried on a stretcher past gawping crowds to the helicopter. At this point Chapman arrived on the scene and Watkins told him what the situation was. The first news from the hospital was that Ronnie was in a stable condition and was being X-rayed.

Restart

Meanwhile, the re-started race was delayed again when, on the warm-up lap, Scheckter's Wolf flattened the Armco at the second Lesmo corner and the barrier had to be replaced. The crowd became aggressive, throwing bottles and baying for the race to begin. Bob Dance and Glenn Waters fired up Andretti's car in an attempt to mollify them. Almost two hours later the shortened 40-lap race got under way, ending in twilight with another farcical situation – Andretti and Villeneuve who'd come first and second on the road, were penalised for jumping the start. It mattered not that much, since Mario's single point for sixth place effectively clinched the Championship.

Post race, Team Lotus mechanics set to work. *'There was a major panic loading up immediately after the race because we had to get the truck out of Italy,'* recalled Rex Hart, *'so that the truck and the cars weren't confiscated. Two guys went off with the truck – no time to wash or anything like that. Just cross the border and then you can stop. Which is what they did.'* Chapman was simply playing safe. He'd had cars impounded and faced litigation after two fatal accidents involving his cars at Monza; in 1961 when Clark and Von Trips collided and the German and 11 spectators died, and in 1970 when Rindt was killed. In Italy, nothing changes in that respect – the Williams équipe still faces charges over Senna's death at Imola. As Peter Warr recalled, *'I know that Jochen was dead within 30 seconds of hitting the Armco. But they went through all this performance of loading him into the ambulance and taking him back to the medical centre and rushing him to hospital, just so they could say he died on his way to hospital. If it was stated that he'd died at the circuit, Italian law says there'd have to have been an inquest, which would have meant the race being cancelled. My saga with the Rindt accident went on for many years.'*

Staffan Svenby had the unenviable task of deciding how and where Ronnie should be treated. Should he go with the hospital in Milan or fly Ronnie to a hospital in Austria or Switzerland specialising in leg bone fractures? In consultation with Watkins, he decided to go with the Milan option, since a top surgeon would be present and they were used to dealing with breakages of this kind.

Before the race had ended, a hospital bulletin spoke of a threat to the blood supply in Ronnie's leg. According to Professor Watkins, the hospital sought to deal with this by *'replacing the fractured bones and securing them in the correct position with internal or external pins and nails.'* *'They called in the top surgeon to*

> HE WAS ON HIS ELBOWS TALKING TO PEOPLE. HE WASN'T UNCONSCIOUS OR ANYTHING LIKE THAT. OBVIOUSLY WE KNEW THERE WAS A FIRE BECAUSE WE'D SEEN IT FROM THE PITS. SO WE HAD A FEW BEERS AND THAT SORT OF THING. NO ONE THOUGHT THAT RONNIE WOULD DIE.

perform the operation because he was not on duty at the time,' said Staffan. *'It was about 7.00 o'clock in the evening by then.'*

There was another issue. Whether to amputate the worst of the injured limbs, or effect a repair. What turned out to be Ronnie's last words to Staffan made his mind up. *'I want to be able to drive at Watkins Glen,'* he said. *'Please make sure I can.'* That settled it. There could be no amputation.

Anarchy and confusion

Typically for Monza, there was no security in evidence once the race had ended, and anarchy reigned as the tifosi milled aimlessly about. In the face of dissatisfied and surly race fans, Professor Watkins, Andretti and Chapman set off to drive to the hospital in Mario's Rolls-Royce. The crowds were hostile to them using the access roads and, just as problematically, started mobbing the car when they realised it was being driven by their hero Andretti. He knew a short cut across the fields to the motorway, and eventually they reached the hospital where a large crowd had gathered. Ronnie was still in the operating theatre, so Professor Watkins joined the operating team. *'It all seemed to be going well,'* said the Professor. *'The surgeons were working on the last fractures to be immobilised. I talked to the anaesthetist and Ronnie's vital signs were all fine. The blood transfusion with the correct blood group was in progress. The surgeon in charge indicated that he thought all was going to plan and that they would be finished shortly.'*

The X-rays had revealed some twenty-seven fractures in both legs and feet and it was a two-and-a-half hour operation. Not so long, then. Ronnie was to be transferred to the intensive care unit, where Brambilla had already been taken. Meanwhile, the Team Lotus mechanics had gone back to their hotel. *'We saw the news that night, and there were pictures of Ronnie being stretchered away,'* said Rex Hart. *'He was on his elbows talking to people. He wasn't unconscious or anything like that. Obviously we knew there was a fire because we'd seen it from the pits. So we had a few beers and that sort of thing.'* No one thought that Ronnie would die.

At the hospital, Andretti, Chapman and Svenby waited in an ante-room, and Staffan rang Barbro in Monaco. Confident that Ronnie was going to recover, Professor Watkins reassured her and arrangements were made for her to helicopter into Milan the next morning. Close to midnight, Staffan and the Professor checked into an hotel near to the hospital while Mario and Colin returned to the Villa d'Este at Lake Como. *'At that time it didn't occur to me that anything would go wrong,'* said Staffan. *'Chapman came back from the hospital with a look of relief on his face,'* said Mike Doodson. *'We thought then it was going to be a long recovery as he'd been very badly hurt; perhaps not a David Purley or Johnny Herbert scenario, but at some point he'd be back in an F1 car.'*

Just before 4.00am, Staffan took a call from the hospital, saying that Ronnie condition was deteriorating. He woke the Professor, and they rushed to the hospital. In a bizarre and unhelpful twist, somebody claiming to be a doctor had telephoned Barbro during the night to tell her that the Italian doctors were killing her husband – no-one ever ascertained the identity of this mystery caller. Most likely it was someone who'd impersonated a doctor in order to get into the hospital.

At the intensive care unit, the neurosurgeon told the Professor that Ronnie had developed breathing difficulties and was being ventilated to keep up his blood oxygen levels. A chest X-ray revealed the presence of multiple embolisms in his lungs, obstructions caused by blood clots or fat globules. He was unconscious by then, and a neurological examination showed signs of severe brain damage. *'The outlook was pretty hopeless,'* said the Professor. *'The neurosurgeon agreed to my suggestion that we should have an electroencephalogram to get objective evidence of brain function in addition to our neurological observations.'*

They informed Colin Chapman and Bernie Ecclestone, who arrived shortly afterwards. By then though the neurologists doing the brain scan reported that the trace showed no activity and indicated brain death. It was clear that the end was near and, by dawn, Ronnie was dead. The autopsy subsequently confirmed the cause of his death as fat embolisms in the lungs, kidneys and brain.

Åke Strandberg was at the hospital until the bitter end. When he walked out into the Milanese dawn he wondered why the trams were still running. *'I couldn't understand why they hadn't stopped,'* he said. *'For me the world had suddenly come to a standstill.'*

Question marks

Ronnie Peterson's death was so shocking and unexpected that it has always been the subject of speculation. Did the surgeon or the hospital bungle the job? In his keen-ness to mend the legs of F1 hero Peterson, did the surgeon overlook something crucial? It's been suggested that there was a competition between hospitals for the glory of saving the great Ronnie Peterson's legs – and a quick operation would ensure that he stayed at the Niguardia hospital. Should they have waited to operate until he was more stable? Money no object, some say he should have been flown to Austria or Switzerland to a hospital experienced in mountaineering fractures. Would amputation have saved him – despite Ronnie's express wish to drive again? *'With hindsight, it's easy to say that his leg should have been amputated, but Ronnie wouldn't have wanted that,'* said Staffan. As Bob Dance pointed out, *'if they'd cut the leg off and he'd recovered, people would have said, "why the hell did you cut his leg off?"'*

Historically, that kind of disability hasn't precluded participation in motorsport. Alan Stacey had an artificial leg and did well in Lotus sports cars and F1 in the 1950s; Archie Scott-Brown had the full use of only one arm; Clay Regazzoni and Jason Watt still drive in spite of lower body paralysis, and we've seen Alex Zanardi recover from horrendous leg-loss. But amputation would have put an end to Ronnie's World Championship prospects, and F1 drivers really get back to form after serious fractures, viz Laffite, Jabouille and Cecotto. Graham Hill was an exception to the rule, storming back with the Rob Walker Team's Lotus 49 after breaking his legs at Watkins Glen, 1969. *'He might not have driven again, but he shouldn't have died,'* said Lars Berntson. *'It's all, "what if?" But if they'd amputated, Ronnie's life wouldn't have been worth living. Racing was his reason for living. It was all or nothing. So you could say what happened was a blessing in disguise, because I could never imagine Ronnie hopping about with crutches or prosthetic limbs.'*

More fundamentally, would Ronnie have survived if amputation had been carried out? *'Impossible to say'*, according to Professor Watkins. Would he have survived if he'd been fitter? He was healthy, though not as sharp as current Grand Prix drivers; this was not a contributory factor. Neither did his physical condition contribute to the fat embolisms that killed him – anyone can get them although medical science has advanced their prevention since 1978. Professor Watkins said: *'Colin Chapman came up with the answer when I next saw him at Montreal. He asked me what had really killed Ronnie, and I told him about the embolisms. He said "Why didn't they open him up and put in a filter to stop the embolisms getting to the heart?" And, some years later, that's precisely what the medical people started doing. In major surgery or if there's already been a blood clot, they inset a filter, a stent, like an umbrella that traps embolisms before they reach the heart. Chapman had invented it on the spot.'*

There remains a groundswell of opinion that something went wrong with Ronnie's treatment, and it is particularly strongly felt in Sweden. According to Staffan Svenby it was a rumour started by a journalist on a Swedish evening paper and people very close to Ronnie still believe it. George Johansson said, *'My neighbour at the time was a leading Swedish surgeon, and he read the reports in the papers and he said to me, "you don't operate on a guy in that condition. That's rule number one, by the book. You stabilise him first, make sure he has all the life support systems. You don't just go in there and operate. That's how these embolisms start. Any doctor in the Austrian or Italian Alps dealing with skiing accidents would have understood that, because that's what they're dealing with every day. They let the patient rest, sort out what needs to be done, and they wait.'* Reine Wisell shares his view. Mike Doodson was sports editor of Motor magazine: *'The word that got out to the press was that he'd been neglected in some way and that his treatment had not been up to the high standard that you'd expect.'* Said Peter Warr, *'Everyone's feeling was that, given the injuries Ronnie had, there's no way he should have succumbed. The*

Ronnie Peterson: Super Swede

Above: When news of Ronnie's death got out, the whole of Sweden went into mourning. **Opposite:** Ronnie lived to race, as here at Jarama in the Lotus 79 when he took 2nd place.

embolisms arose out of bone marrow getting into his blood stream, and it seems to me that that's a pretty fundamental precaution that you take when you're confronted with an injured person lying on the table with very badly smashed legs.' Indeed, as far as the drivers and mechanics were concerned, Monza was not the place to have a big accident. Bob Dance had been to the hospital on a previous occasion. 'It was a pretty basic, old world sort of place, with white tiled walls and a bit depressing. It wasn't a flash place like now.'

Ghughie Zanon's memory of events is laced with sorrow and a certain bitterness. He recalled: 'a Milanese friend of mine who saw the disaster said, "God help Ronnie – keep him out of that hospital." They tried to find the best surgeon but he was off duty, and by the time he'd arrived they'd already started operating. They tried to save the driver, not the man. It would have been better to chop the foot off. The surgeon said that, in any case, they should have waited until he was less shocked. Italian opinion is that it was a mistake to operate.'

No malpractice

However, Professor Watkins refutes this suggestion. As far as he is concerned, there was no significant delay either in the paddock medical centre or the flight to the hospital. A transfer to, say, a Swiss hospital was out of the question because of the extent of the leg injuries and, in any case, the Niguardia hospital was 'a major trauma centre level 1'. And, he asserts, it was not negligent. An emergency situation developed and they had to act there and then. 'I counted 27 fractures in his legs and feet, and they had to operate on the ones in the major bones because they were threatening his circulation as they were out of line,' he said. 'The bone-marrow or fat embolisms were evident after surgery.'

Rex Hart articulated a popular view. 'There is an injection they give you to stop your bone marrow going into your blood stream. He didn't have that injection. I went to see Count Zanon in London a week or so after the accident and was still really upset. He said that, initially, they spoke about amputating the foot. But this guy said, "no, we can repair that," meaning, "I can be a hero 'cos I can make Ronnie Peterson's leg work again." And while they were buggering about like that, someone didn't give him the injection that stops the bone marrow going into the blood stream. That was the story that we all heard at the time.' The injection that Rex Hart was referring to was probably Heperin, which prevents clots forming. But this cannot be used before major surgery or following major trauma, for the simple reason that the surgical wounds wouldn't stop bleeding. It can be used 24 hours after surgery in tiny doses called mini heperin, but that would not have been any use to Ronnie. So that rather scotches the overlooked injection theory.

Max Mosley added: 'It was important to all of us that Sid (Watkins) was there, because we would all have said that the Italians screwed up like they did with Jochen Rindt. But Sid was there and was able to say it was an act of God; Ronnie was just unlucky.'

Second opinion

Fat embolisms come from bone marrow, and they get into the blood stream and thence into the heart and lungs. They deprive the lungs of the ability to absorb oxygen, resulting in the patient's death. A broken femur, being a big bone, is the one most likely to cause fat embolisms. It also happens in hip replacements, but modern techniques involve draining the marrow from the bone before installation to prevent embolisms forming. The bone repairs itself and creates new marrow very quickly. What causes the embolisms to form – and this is true of the Peterson case – is the reaming of the bone to introduce a wire that will unite the broken sections. The reaming is carried out from end to end of the bone, displacing a certain amount of the marrow, creating a risk that it may enter the blood stream. A patient's genetic make-up, or a previous injury can make the formation of fat embolisms more likely. But it is normal to repair a broken femur as soon as possible after an accident, as the quicker it is nailed the less likely are respiratory problems to arise, and the hormones that promote the body's healing process can get on with their job. The only fractures that aren't handled straight away are ribs, where the lungs may be at risk. The alternative to reaming and nailing is plating, which doesn't interfere

> WHEN SOMEONE AS IMPORTANT AND WITH THE CHARISMA OF SENNA LOSES HIS LIFE, THAT A MAN OF HIS STATURE COULD LITERALLY BE KILLED IN YOUR LIVING ROOM AS YOU WATCH IT ON TV, IT SHAKES FORMULA 1 TO ITS CORE. AND THIS WAS ALSO THE CASE WITH RONNIE.

with the bone marrow. But the regeneration of new bone is compromised by this older technique.

Hero's funeral

I watched the race on television in Rome, and coverage of the drawn-out event and its dreadful sequel dragged on for hours. It was one of the first *'death on the screen'* accidents, and that had an enormous impact. The Italian press and TV were full of Peterson's death for days, just as they were in the UK and Sweden. There was talk of getting Monza banned from the World Championship calendar. At Malpensa and Niguardia airports on the Monday morning, race personnel were heading home. *'When the newspaper vendors started shouting "Peterson e morti" everyone's knees crumpled,'* said Sveneric. He already knew the worst, but no-body else had heard until then. *'Some very well known people were weeping openly,'* he said. *'It took me years to understand that Ronnie wasn't going to pop round the door any more. We thought of him as indestructible.'* The mechanics were shocked to hear the news. *'When we got up in the morning we heard nothing,'* said Rex Hart. *'But at the airport one or two people came up and said, "Christ, have you heard the news?" That he'd died overnight. It was more of a shock because we were over the accident part of it and expected he'd recover. I was talking to Staffan, and he'd been to the hospital with him, and they'd had a conversation. Ronnie had said to him, "bloody hell, my leg don't half hurt," and that sort of thing. On the plane it was a quiet old journey home from Italy, that's for sure.'* Ronnie's coffin was flown back to Sweden in an aircraft dispatched by Lotus, and supervised by Staffan and Åke. The funeral was two days later.

Intensely affected, Colin Chapman was hit as hard as Ronnie's other associates. Rex Hart said, *'The Old Man had a lot of good feelings for Ronnie. He was not just any old driver; he was quite close to him in many ways. They had their little problems, but he was shaken when Ronnie died. He was quite upset. I remember at the time thinking, "I didn't know he'd be like that; Ronnie was just another employee," but he knew Ronnie was quicker than all the others.'*

Sveneric said: *'When he died, Sweden went quiet, to the extent that schools closed as a mark of respect.'* An indication of Ronnie's popularity can be gauged by the massive attendance at his funeral. Something like 15 – 20,000 mourners gathered at Örebro's St Nicklas cathedral. The streets were crammed with people representing the two facets of Ronnie's life, his home town and the world of racing. Many went on to the burial at Almby church close to his family home on the edge of Örebro, overflowing from the little cemetery of the tiny suburban church. The coffin was borne by Åke Strandberg, Niki Lauda, Jody Scheckter, John Watson, Emerson and James Hunt. Andretti was conspicuous by his absence, his busy schedule governed by a prior CART commitment.

It was a very public demise. As John Watson said, *'When someone as important and with the charisma of Senna loses his life, that a man of his stature could literally be killed in your living room as you watch it on TV, it shakes Formula 1 to its core. And this was also the case with Ronnie.'*

Ronnie Peterson: Career History

Born: 14th February 1944
Died: 11th September 1978
Age: 34 years 7 months

1962: 2nd, national kart championship with Robardie, class D (200cc).
1963: National kart champion with the Robardie, class D (200cc).
1964: National kart champion with the Robardie, class A sport (100cc).
1965: 2nd, national kart championship with the Robardie, class D (200cc) Nordic challenge champion, classes C&D, 3rd, European team championship.
1966: 3rd, national kart championship with Robardie, class A international, 3rd, karting world championship, class A. 4th, European team championship.
1967: First full season in F3, driving Brabham BT18.
1968: National F3 champion with Tecno.
1969: European F3 champion with Tecno. 1st Monaco F3 race.
1970: 9 : F1 Grand Prix starts with quasi-works Antique Automobiles Racing (March 701), no points. F2 (March-Cosworth 702) 4th in European Championship with 14 points.
1971: 11 : F1 Grand Prix starts (March 711), 33 WC points, 2nd in WC. F2 European champion with (March-Cosworth 712), 54 points.
1972: 12 : F1 Grand Prix starts (March 721), 12 WC points, 9th in WC. Limited F2 programme (March 722). Sports cars: 1st at Buenos Aires and Nürburgring (Ferrari) with Schenken.
1973: 15 : F1 Grand Prix starts (Lotus 72), 52 WC points, 3rd in WC. 4 GP wins (France, Austria, Italy, USA).
1974: 15 : F1 Grand Prix starts (Lotus 72 & 76), 35 WC points, 5th in WC. 3 GP wins (Monaco, France, Italy).
1975: 14 : F1 Grand Prix starts (Lotus 72), 6 WC points, 12th in WC.
1976: 15 : F1 Grand Prix starts (1 Lotus 77, 14 March 761), 10 WC points, 11th in WC. 1 GP Win in Italy.
1977: 17 : F1 Grand Prix starts (Tyrrell P34), 7 WC points, 14th in WC.
1978: 14 : F1 Grand Prix starts (Lotus 78& 79) , 51 WC points, 2nd in WC. 2 wins (S. Africa, Austria).

Involved in first lap accident at Monza, leading to severe leg injuries. Once in hospital, complications set in. Slipped into coma and died hours later on September 11th 1978.

Formula One races from:	1970 –1978
Grands Prix started:	123
Podium places:	26
Grand Prix wins:	10
Grand Prix pole positions:	14
Grand Prix Fastest laps:	9
Total world championship points:	206

Drove Formula One races for:

March Engineering (1970-72, 1976):	47 Grands Prix starts (1 win, 1 pole position)
Lotus (1973-76, 78):	59 Grands Prix starts (9 wins, 13 pole position)
Tyrrell (1977):	17 Grands Prix starts

Best F1 World Championship placing:	2nd in 1971 and 1978
First GP win:	France 1973
GP victory, pole position & fastest lap:	Austria 1978
Number of starts in front row:	25
First pole position:	11th of February 1973 (Brazil)
Last pole position:	13th of August 1978 (Austria)

Statistics on his Grand Prix races:

Total laps driven in Grands Prix:	5,724
Total kilometres driven in Grands Prix:	26,645 km
Grand Prix start-finishes:	72 (59%)
Grand Prix retirements:	51 (41%)

In leading position:

Grands Prix:	29 (23%)
Total laps in front:	707 (12%)
Total kilometres in front:	3,310 km

Total Race Entries from 1962-78: 406

76	Kart races, 63 heat victories
1	Formula 4 race, no wins
74	Formula 3 races, 29 victories
54	Formula 2 races, 11 victories
123	Formula 1 Grands Prix, 10 victories
18	Formula 1 Non-Championship races, no wins
60	Sports car & other races, 5 victories

EC = European championship, WC = World Championship, GP = Grand Prix

Ronnie Peterson: Super Swede

CHAPTER 13

Aftermath

The aftermath of the death of a great driver like Ronnie is a story of extremes. On the one hand, like all heroes that die young, he becomes iconic, if unattainable. On the other, the recriminations are bitter. For the rest of his own life, James Hunt vilified Riccardo Patrese whenever the opportunity arose, using his platform as Grand Prix TV commentator to turn the screw. Without any shadow of doubt, James saw him as being the villain in the startline shunt.

He was among the senior F1 drivers who insisted that Patrese be excluded from the subsequent race, the US GP, as punishment for his 'reckless' driving at Monza. Patrese was portrayed as having a vendetta against Peterson since their wheel banging in Sweden earlier in the season. Patrese's main offence seems to have been his arrogance, while blame for the accident was placed at the door of the Italian starter for dropping the flag too soon.

Nigel Roebuck came to Patrese's defence. *'Riccardo was one of those young drivers who was very quick from the outset, and he frequently drove over his head in those early days. In the subsequent hysteria, other drivers judged Patrese culpable for the chain reaction disaster, which occurred within seconds of the start. It was a witch-hunt, nothing more or less.'* As for Hunt's role in the accident, Alistair Caldwell ventured, *'to my mind, James thought he'd caused the accident himself, and that's why he protested so long and loud that it was all Patrese's fault. He felt guilty that it was his car that took Ronnie off.'*

For Count Ghughie Zanon, *'The starter was responsible – he gave the start when the back rows were still moving, which was how Patrese came to be in third gear when everyone else was in first.'* Grand Prix statistician Mike Doodson had a different view: *'I was in a unique position to see the start. I did the lap charts for Ensign at the time before going to do the same thing for the BBC. There was no electronic scoreboard in those days, and they stacked up some tyres for me on the pit wall and I would watch the race from there. The starter was in my direct line of sight, and the car that was closest to me was Patrese's. The starter was watching Patrese, who was the best-placed Italian driver and Patrese intimidated the starter by keeping going instead of stopping in his box, and the starter saw this and dropped the flag. The consequence was that all the cars behind Patrese, which were still coming up to their boxes, just floored their throttles. That was what caused the bunching going up to the first chicane where the accident happened. Patrese also ignored the white line, which they'd been told they weren't allowed to cross. When you've got*

Opposite: To make a car work on the limit it had to be driven on the limit, and Ronnie did just that, his March 712 deliberately wingless at Rouen in 1971.

cars six abreast it's immaterial who touched whom. In my mind, Patrese was solely responsible for it because he threatened the starter. At the restart, Patrese tried to do exactly the same thing. But the starter knew there'd be an investigation about his handling of the original start, and he held the flag for a long time, while Patrese was rolling well past his line. The starter waited for him to stop, which he seemed inclined not to do. The consequence was that Andretti and Villeneuve on the front row were cooking their clutches, so they just went before the flag dropped. Patrese was a nice, old-fashioned sporting gentleman by the end of his career, but when he came into Formula 1, he would have you off the road as soon as look at you. So what the drivers did was to take action against Patrese, and most of the impetus for this was from Emerson and Mario to get him excluded from Watkins Glen.' Outrageous maybe, but bearing in mind the lack of any disciplinary procedure in those days, that was probably the best thing that could have happened.

Compared with the pace of events in F1, the wheels of justice roll slowly. Three years later, in autumn 1981, the Monza district attorney sued the starter, Giovanni Restelli, for manslaughter, while Patrese faced an eight months suspended sentence. They were both cleared at an official inquiry in 1983, and the blame was put on Hunt.

Recriminations

Nothing would bring Ronnie back, and now, the recriminations look like a flawed way of dealing with the shock of loosing a man who was respected and liked throughout the paddock. For Mario Andretti, *'Ronnie was the third or fourth really good friend that I had lost in my lifetime. You make a lot of friends, the ones you socialise with; you know you can't replace them, and things are never the same. In Ronnie's situation there was something even worse about that, mainly because, just after the accident, I didn't think that the injuries he received were life threatening. I thought that, yes, his legs looked terrible, but all of that would be fixable; maybe a long recuperating period, but he'd be back racing. I spoke with Dr. Watkins several times about that, and he drove home a lot of necessities to create our own F1 medical team. That obviously was useful in many countries that we were going to, where we didn't know how effectively we would be treated in the event of potential life threatening injuries.'*

As Eddie Dennis saw it, there were one or two peculiarities about Peterson's accident. *'One of the reasons why the car caught fire was because of the fuel catch tank down in the footwell of the car. Fuel pick up wasn't good on the 78, and it was done to alleviate that. It was almost certainly illegal, as you weren't supposed to have fuel going anywhere away from the fuel tanks, but that was why that car caught fire. I know that wasn't what killed him, but it didn't help get him out, poor bloke. All the chassis were difficult for Peterson to get into anyway because he was so tall. But at least the 79 didn't have the catch tank in the footwell. There was also the issue that an R-clip was left out and the brake pads fell out of Ronnie's 79, causing him to crash in practice.'*

This was a thread picked up by Rex Hart: *'In the 79 there wouldn't have been a fire for starters, because there was no petrol tank down in the footwell. Possibly he would have fared better. In any case, the aluminium chassis were not too good in that respect, and although they were strong they didn't stand that much impact. But in a 79 he might have been in a different position on the grid and in front of the accident when it all happened.'*

Team Lotus designer Martin Ogilvie, largely responsible for the Type 79 chassis, had his own take on the Monza tragedy. He's not convinced that the Type 79 chassis was stronger than the Type 78 *'It would probably have been even worse,'* said Ogilvie. *'Ronnie practised in the 79 and had a rear brake failure. A little R-clip securing the pads broke, and he lost his brakes and had a minor shunt. He then had to take to the 78 for the race. So, because the R-clip was one of my bits, it has always been on my mind. Something as small as that built up this chain of events, and he ended up being killed, and I have always felt pretty bad about that.'* Bob Dance put the accident in the context of a harsh working environment: *'You can't feel responsible for things like that; you had to put them to one side. The reason why Ronnie went off in practice on the Sunday morning was because the wire R-clip either broke or came out. Once that*

Opposite: Ronnie Peterson's career evolved from karts to F2, starting with the ex-Max Mosley Lotus 59. **Top:** Ronnie receives the winners trophy at the 1965 European Kart Championships. **Above:** Ronnie and Barbro with his proud parents Bengt and Maj-Britt in the early F3 days.

Ronnie Peterson: Super Swede

Above: Ronnie in the March 721X at the Spanish GP. **Top:** Having fun on Copacabana beach in 1973. **Opposite Left:** Ronnie and Barbro at 5 The Farthingales, Maidenhead. **Opposite Right:** In the March 722 at Mallory Park for the 1972 European Championship F2 round.

happened the pin securing the pads was able to feed back and the pad pop out; you've then suddenly got uneven braking, and the car went off. That wasn't Martin Ogilvie's design; that was the caliper manufacturer's design. No way was he responsible for that. It was a manufactured component. You could lock-wire the ends of the R-clip shut, but I don't know if that was done at the time.'

Colin Chapman was shocked at loosing another driver and took his remorse out on the fabrication shop back at Ketteringham Hall where the chassis were made. Half the staff of six, including Eddie Dennis, were sacked on the premise that, had they repaired Andretti's Österreichring wreck on time, Ronnie would have had a spare Lotus 79 at his disposal. In other words, the arguably stronger pedal box of the 79 chassis would have saved his legs. The sacking looked opportunist though, another issue being the length of the fabricators' working day, which Chapman had long wanted to extend. While Team Lotus mechanics worked all hours at circuits, the staff back at base tended to work normal 9.00-to-5.00 hours, and when union involvement was mentioned, the more vociferous fabricators got their cards.

As for Ronnie's 78/3, it was a write-off. *'I had to cut the chassis up, or what was left of it,'* said Rex Hart. *'There was nothing used from that at all. They took the engine and gearbox out and that was it. I spent two or three really cheering days just cutting it up with an air tool and ripping it apart. I was told "if anyone comes in, throw a sheet over it so no-one can see it, just get it cut up." They didn't want any part of it left around at all.'* Although a car bearing the 78/3 number was built up shortly afterwards on a spare 78 tub for Team Lotus's World Championship celebrations in nearby Norwich, Clive Chapman had the remaining fragments of the original car destroyed in 2003 to forestall mawkish souvenir hunters.

Tributes

Ronnie's death hit his fellow drivers hard. Dave Brodie spoke for many. *'He was an amazing bloke, and I still feel it. My best mates then were Hailwood, Roger Williamson and Ronnie, and they all died.'* Torsten Palm summed up the tributes:

'He was a nice guy, he was very sportsmanlike, he was interesting, and he was a clean guy, never tried to screw you up. We had a lot of fun with him, and I miss him.' And from Jackie Stewart: *'What sticks in my mind was his driving flair, so nicely controlled, so enjoyable to watch. He was a modest, quiet soul really.'*

John Watson had known Ronnie since 1970, when they did F2 and Wattie had accidentally tipped Ronnie into the unyielding railway sleepers at Crystal Palace. *'I liked him because he wasn't flashy. He was a straightforward man who enjoyed his toys. Ronnie was a contemporary, but he was also a legend, and there was admiration and respect for him which was genuine and sincere, just because he was Ronnie.'*

The hypothetical Champion

What might have been for Ronnie? Ronnie hadn't wanted to leave Team Lotus, but he had no choice. *'We knew he was going to McLaren because he'd mentioned it to us at Zandvoort,'* according to Rex Hart. *'He still wanted to drive for Lotus the following year. He talked to the Old Man for a whole day one time and came into the workshop at lunchtime and said he was struggling to make any progress on it. He was really a Lotus man, and he was looked after pretty well. He just liked the set up, and got on well with everybody. But Andretti wouldn't have him as equal number one. That's when Ronnie went to McLaren and got tied up with them.'*

'Racing drivers always want to beat their team mate,' said Lars Berntson. *'Ronnie told me in the summer of '78, "I could easily pass Andretti," but he wasn't worried about the situation as he'd "just signed a fantastic two-year contract with McLaren. My time will come," he said. He'd given his word and he wasn't about to break it. But he was so happy when he came to tell me about the McLaren deal. I think it was £700,000 over two years.'*

Would Ronnie have been World Champion with McLaren? Not in 1979, that's for sure. The M28 and M29 proved to be duds amongst the emergent ground-effect generation. Sveneric's view was: *'The McLarens were useless in 1979, and Ronnie would have got the blame. He would have been handicapped as well because he wasn't good at sorting out cars. The real problem that he would have had with full-on ground effect cars was with his neck. He still had problems with that from the Montlhéry accident (back in 1969), and that's why he often had his head tilted forwards.'* By 1981 the ground-effect cars had no suspension whatsoever. That would have hurt.

McLaren didn't come good until 1982 with the MP4. *'As it turns out, the M28 was the worst car they ever produced,'* said John Watson. *'When I think about it now, I get the shivers. Ronnie would have been expecting McLaren to build a proper ground-effect car that would be competitive, reliable and safe, and he could get in it and win the World Championship in '79. Marlboro would have been over the moon to have had Ronnie in the team, because he was legendary. So it would have been a massive disappointment for him.'*

Alistair Caldwell said, *'Maybe Ronnie would have been a better test driver than John Watson, but I somehow doubt it. McLaren's first attempt at a ground-effect car was disastrous. We tested it at Watkins Glen and it just disintegrated. The chassis had zero torsional rigidity – you could pick up a rear corner and the two front ones would stay on the ground.'* Watson was equally scathing: *'The M28 was disgraceful. A bicycle would have had more torsional rigidity. By the time of the first race in '79 in Buenos Aires, it was probably 70- or 80lb overweight, simply because they had to strengthen it. At the same time, Ligier rewrote the aerodynamic rules, and they just pushed everybody into the weeds in Buenos Aires and Interlagos, and Teddy Mayer was running round measuring the (ground-effect) tunnels and the diffusers; hell, it was like Monty Python's Flying Circus.'*

'It's futile trying to guess how he would have got on in '79, since the McLaren was totally impossible,' said Staffan. By the end of April 1979, the benchmark Williams FW07 had appeared and McLaren realised that they'd missed the plot and had to start again. So it would have been a disappointing first half of the year for Ronnie. The M29 came out at Silverstone, and that was an improvement, but McLaren were still about nine months behind Williams, with Brabham catching up quickly and Ligier holding their own. Scheckter and Villeneuve dominated the 1979 Championship for Ferrari more because of consistency rather than sheer performance.

'If you don't know what to do, then you copy what is working,' said Watson. *'McLaren copied the FW07, but they didn't fully understand the aerodynamics, and they didn't get that right until late 1980.'* To cap it all, McLaren as a team was in trouble in 1979, and it was at this point that Ron Dennis effectively took over. Robin Herd was brought in as a consultant to help develop the car, and then John Barnard came in at the end of 1980 and designed the MP4. McLaren lost two years by not grasping the essentials of ground-effect aerodynamics and how wind tunnel research would effect the performance of a car on the track. They were still working in the days of mechanical gain, tweaking roll bars, springs, dampers, a methodology that was overtaken by ground-effect. As it turned out, Ronnie would have had to stick around for at least three seasons until McLaren came up with a winner. Another case of choosing the wrong team at the wrong time.

A different hypothetical avenue would have placed Ronnie in a Williams FW07. Robin Herd proposed: *'Alan Jones and Keke Rosberg are great people and good drivers; but they're not Ronnie Petersons! Ronnie in an FW07 would have been sensational.'* It wasn't a far-fetched notion. Staffan had been in discussions with Williams on several occasions: *'Frank likes a fighter. He tried very hard to get Ronnie on board for 1979. Even at Monza we talked about it before the race. We made a mistake with hindsight, but as early as Zolder, McLaren was working on a new car, while Frank was launching a new team with an unproven designer called Patrick Head. Furthermore, we had very good contacts with Marlboro, and that made the decision easy at the time.'*

By 1977, Åke Strandberg was living with the Petersons at Grey Thatch while the garden house was done up for him. He moved into that at the beginning of 1978 and stayed there after Ronnie died, working for Wolf and Emerson Fittipaldi until he went to work for Saab's powertrain division at Trollhättan in 1981. Meanwhile, the garage was being converted to

Opposite: Emerson, Graham Hill, Barbro and Ronnie relax at Michigan Speedway during the IROC meeting when they drove Camaros. Above: Ronnie liked children and was happy to sit for ages signing autographs, here at the launch of the Sveneric Eriksson/Staffan Svenby book on the 1971 season.

accommodate an F3 team, which Ronnie anticipated would be financed by Marlboro and run in his name by Åke. The stipulation was that one driver would be Swedish, and that was Eje Elgh.

According to Åke, by mid-season 1978 Ronnie had already considered his retirement from F1. When he signed for McLaren, he told him, *'this will be my last drive in F1. When I'm finished with F1 I can always drive BMW saloons."* Åke, who was set to go to McLaren with him, reflected, *'I don't think he would have carried on driving an uncompetitive F1 car like Regazzoni and Ickx did. He was already talking about things that we could do after he'd retired from F1, like running the F3 team.'*

Ghughie Zanon confirmed Ronnie's intentions. *'He told me after he'd signed for McLaren, "I'll drive one more year, and whether I win or loose the Championship, I'll retire from F1, whatever."'*

Swedish fan club

Ronnie had a small, dedicated band of Swedish friends who followed him from circuit to circuit. Among them was photographer and journalist Kenneth Olausson, who observed almost all of Ronnie's Formula 1 career as well as his F2, F3 and karting days. When asked about Ronnie's hobbies away from the track, Kenneth was blunt in his affirmation of his friend's prowess: *'That's easy,'* he said. *'He had no other interests. The one thing that defined him was that, behind the wheel of a car, he always went flat out, whether on the road or the track. Early on in his career he kept himself to himself, isolated himself in his own personality. But as he became more confident in Formula 1, he grew out of that – he matured and was more outgoing as his fame increased. Sitting behind Andretti in 1978 must have pissed him off a great deal.'*

He wasn't coerced by anyone, not even Barbro, and wasn't particularly bothered by what others thought of him. According to journalist George Johansson, his epitaph could have been *'One strives to do one's best,'* which implies, that, fundamentally, he was trying to impress. In his account of Ronnie's career in his book Motor Blandning, Johansson alludes to Peterson's chauvinism, with Barbro playing a supporting role but never influencing his behaviour despite her nervousness of her husband's risk-laden career. There were signs that all was not well between Ronnie and Barbro in that last year. Torsten Palm hinted at the chinks that were appearing in the Peterson marriage: *'They had a bad time in their life that last summer. There was some disconnecting between Ronnie and Barbro then. That summer of 1978 when he and I took the boat out in the Baltic, he told me that things weren't good because of his womanising. When the accident happened, Barbro was still in Monaco, and that was one of the reasons why.'* She wasn't going to the races so much, and had had a miscarriage in 1978. Another friend of Ronnie's spoke of being thrown out of a shared hotel room so that Ronnie could entertain a one-night stand. Robin Herd spent much of 1971 with Ronnie, and recalled winter testing at Kyalami. *'Ronnie told me he liked the receptionist at the hotel, and asked me to find out if she'd like to go for a drink as he was a bit shy and his English wasn't so good. So I said to her, "one of our drivers would like to take you out," and she said, "which one?" So I pointed him out and she said OK. They went out three or four times, and on the fifth date she found out that he drove the racing car, not the truck.'*

Sveneric painted a broader picture: *'Being a travelling man as well as an F1 star, he was not at all slow when it came to girls. So there were affairs, but nothing really serious; more like one-night-stands. I believe Barbro was his greatest love. There were rumours about them considering splitting up. As in all marriages, things go up and down, and I believe they had one or two difficult occasions. I never asked him or Barbro about it, as I thought it was a very private area.'*

For most of Ronnie's career, Barbro was never very far away. Nevertheless, she was now a widow. Friends rallied round. Ghughie Zanon explained: *'I gave Barbro financial advice. We were her bankers, and I said to her, "you won't have any problems, such as schooling for Nina." I remember Nina as a baby swimming in my pool. Some people were saying that Barbro and Ronnie were about to divorce, but I don't think so.'*

The tragedy compounded

Some years after Ronnie's death, Barbro began a relationship with John Watson, and did a course in interior design, working for the auctioneers Sotheby's. Tragically, she became deeply depressed, and died in 1987. She is buried close to her husband in Almby churchyard. Torsten Palm could shed little light on her unhappiness: *'At Ronnie's funeral in Örebro she took some very tough medicine – she was not in good shape. She went with John Watson a couple of years later. After that, we saw each other maybe once a year. I don't understand why she killed herself. Obviously she was very unhappy. It was just before Christmas, and she went to see her parents in Örebro with her daughter. She was very close to John Watson at the time, but I think she was drinking and he said, no more. That was a bad story.'*

The view is that Barbro committed suicide. Not necessarily the case, in the opinion of Robin Herd. *'If someone is totally pissed and falls asleep in a hot bath, it's easy to see how they could simply drown. It was desperately sad, as she was such an adorable person. She was either insane or drunk.'*

If it was suicide though, one wonders how someone that's lost their partner can reach a point where they deprive their child of its surviving parent by taking their own life. But Barbro suffered from chronic grief. As a widow who had been totally identified with her husband's career, who had lost him traumatically, and who seemed to have loved only him, she was especially vulnerable. Psychiatrists say that people really do die of a broken heart. The bereaved take deliberate risks, or seek refuge in excessive consumption of alcohol or, most drastically, commit suicide.

Deep depression

'It was such a tragedy with Barbro,' said Max Mosley. *'I occasionally saw her after the accident, and always thought I should take more trouble over her because Ronnie and I were pretty close friends, but then on the other hand, what could one do?'*

Mario Andretti concurred: *'I don't think she ever dealt with it properly. I don't know what dealing with it properly is, but she certainly had a difficult time.'* One or two of Ronnie's mechanics kept in touch as well. Keith Leighton: *'That was sad what went on there. I saw her about four times after his accident, and she was never the same.'* Åke Strandberg and Eje Elgh were living above the garage at Grey Thatch at the time of Ronnie's death, and helped sort things out for Barbro on the domestic front. Rex Hart was also kept in touch after Ronnie died. *'I spoke to her quite a few times on the phone, just to have a chat,'* he said. *'A few years later I was running a Group C car at Silverstone, and John Watson was there driving a Jaguar. I bumped into Barbro as she was walking along behind the pits. She was not the same woman; she seemed totally depressed. She was hard work to speak to; not that she didn't want to speak, but she seemed as if… she couldn't care less. I was really quite surprised. She was always a pleasant, bubbly sort of person.'*

'We had a tradition of seeing Barbro for Christmas,' said Eje Elgh. *'She used to come out here every year, and my wife spoke to her on the phone only a couple of days before she was found dead, and they were discussing what we would have at the Christmas dinner in a weeks time. She was certainly not happy, but she was hiding it, for sure.'*

When Barbro died, Nina was 12. She went straightaway to live with Ronnie's parents in Örebro and, after six months, moved in with Tommy Peterson. Two years later, she went to boarding school near Stockholm, and when she was 18 she went to study interior design in London. Only then did she discover that she was doing the same course as her mother had done. Nina worked for fine art auctioneers Sotheby's for a while, then set up as an interior designer herself, working in a north London art gallery. In 2002 she married Calle-Johan Kennedy and moved near to Katrineholm in central Sweden. Their project was to renovate a large, derelict 18th century house.

Sorcerer's apprentice

Ronnie had his own understudies back in the mid-1970s. One was Eje Elgh, managed by Torsten Palm, contracted to Chevron Cars and sponsored at Ronnie's behest by Lars Berntson's Plastic Padding company. *'Eje came to see*

Opposite: Proud parents: ronnie and Barbro with Nina at Askersund in 1978 **Above:** Henri Pescarolo gives Ronnie a ride to the pits at Mosport Park for the start of the 1972 Canadian GP.

Ronnie Peterson: Super Swede

Above: Ronnie beat the Ferraris of Regazzoni and Lauda to win the 1974 French GP at Dijon driving the ageing Lotus 72. **Opposite:** Pounding down Paddock Hill Bend at Brands Hatch in the Lotus 79 during the 1978 British GP.

me,' said Lars, *'and I liked him. In fact I thought he was too nice to be racing driver because he didn't have a cutting edge. Later on Marlboro came in with a bigger £8.5K budget and changed the colour of the car from blue to red.'* He won F3 races in that Chevron B37 and graduated to F2 alongside (Stockholm born Finn) Keke Rosberg with a March 792, run by Tim Schenken and Howden Ganley.

Nowadays Eje Elgh is an F1 race commentator for Swedish TV and runs a successful Nissan and, in 2003, BMW team in the Swedish touring car championship. Eje and Ronnie went back a long way. Although a good ten years Ronnie's junior, they met in 1966 on the karting circuit. Because the keys to Karlskoga circuit were kept at Eje's father's garage on the edge of town, he frequently met Ronnie when he was testing there. *'He was my hero then,'* said Eje. *'All drivers wanted to be like Ronnie; it was a combination of his driving skill and his charisma.'* Fast-forward ten years, and Eje was racing an ex-Gunnar Nilsson Formula Vee. Torsten Palm asked him to test his F3 Ralt at Silverstone, and Eje promptly went two seconds quicker than its owner. Torsten virtually handed the car over there and then. At this point Ronnie got involved, and took Eje to see Derek Bennett at Chevron. A deal worth £22,000 was struck, and the Plastic Padding and Marlboro sponsorship fell into place for 1977. *'I was in a dream,'* said Eje. *'F3 seemed so professional that it never seemed like getting into it would be a reality.'* He shared a flat in Maidenhead with Danish driver Thorkild Thyrring and then moved into the garage flat at Grey Thatch along with Åke Strandberg. Duties ranged from babysitting Nina and ferrying Ronnie to and from the airport. Eje got his first break in F3 at Oulton Park when, to his surprise, he led from flag to flag, narrowly beating Derek Warwick.

Next race was the Easter Monday meeting at Thruxton, and Ronnie promised him a present if he took pole position. Eje duly did just that, and Ronnie presented him with a new, highly fashionable Linea Sport pinstripe race suit – only Ronnie and Jody Scheckter had them at the time. *'I spent the evening sewing badges on it and probably slept in it too,'* said Eje. He looked unbeatable at Thruxton, and led the race from flagfall. Out of the corner of his eye, he became aware of his mentor's bright blue BMW jacket standing by the chicane observing his progress – Ronnie had the only such jacket in the country at the time. On the last lap he decided to take a better look and see if it was indeed Ronnie. But, in so doing, he struck the barriers, deranging the suspension. *'It wasn't a complete disaster,'* said Eje, *'I'd built up such a lead that I was able to cruise over the line with the wheels all pointing in different directions. Ronnie said to me before I'd even got my helmet off, "what the fuck did you think you were doing on that last lap?"'* Eje was only in the same race as Ronnie once. It was a Group 5 event at Vallelunga, when both were driving BMW 320 turbos, and although Eje did well, Peterson retired early. Two weeks later, he was dead.

The other driver to benefit from Peterson's patronage was Stefan Johansson, who lived for a while in a summerhouse in Ronnie's garden at Grey Thatch. Stefan Johansson's decade in F1 spanned 1980 to 1991; taking in 79 GP starts (and a few non-starts) for Shadow, Spirit, Tyrrell, Toleman, Ferrari, McLaren, Ligier, Onyx, AGS and Footwork (Arrows). Although there were several podium finishes, notably with Ferrari and McLaren in the mid-1980s, there were no wins. Johansson went to CART to drive for Tony Bettenhausen after that, and most recently, his Mike Earle-run Arena Motorsport Gulf Audi R8 contested selected rounds of the American and European Le Mans Series in 2001, and a win and a second place earned Johansson and Audi the Driver's and Manufacturers' 2001 ELMS titles respectively.

Apart from the Swedish F1 drivers who've already been mentioned – Jo Bonnier, Reine Wisell, Torsten Palm and Gunnar Nilsson – there were just three others: Conny Andersson, Bertil Roos and Slim Borgudd. More recently, the other great Swede of note is Kenny Brack, who pursued a successful career in the USA, winning the Indy Racing league title in 1998 and the Indy 500 for A.J Foyt's team in a Dallara in 1999. Brack, aged 37, spent 2000 to 2002 in CART with Bobby Rahal and Chip Ganassi Racing, and was reunited for the 2003 season with Rahal's Miller Lite/Pioneer-backed team to contest the IRL with a Dallara-Honda.

One of the best modern touring car pilots is Rickard Rydell, who won the BTCC in 1998, while Fredrik Ekblom drove a works BMW M3GTR with success in the ETCC in 2002. The latest batch of Swedish hopefuls in single seaters includes Robert Dahlgren in F3, with Stefan Soderberg doing well in Formula Renault and Richard Goransson stepping from Formula Ford to F3, while in F3000 we have Bjorn Wirdheim on the up-and-up.

Watershed

The death of Ronnie Peterson marked a watershed in motor racing. Reine Wisell spoke of a knock on effect that Ronnie's death had in Sweden: *'Back home, motorsport was seen very much with a negative slant after Ronnie's death as far as the public and commercial sponsors were concerned. This lasted for many years, and even now it is difficult to get companies interested in motorsport sponsorship because of it.'*

Torsten Palm made a similar observation: *'Motor racing in Sweden went completely downhill after Ronnie's accident. We lost F1 at Anderstorp, we lost all the sponsors, and we lost all the spectators. It took 15 years to get the interest back again, and now we are back to 15, – 20,000 for touring cars. Very tough. F3 is completely out of the picture as all the good young drivers go to Italy, the UK or Germany. We have Kenny Brack and Ricard Rydell; they are very good, but not in Ronnie's class. Stefan Johansson was in Ronnie's shadow. As far as I'm concerned, in Swedish racing, Ronnie is no 1, Brack is no 2, Reine is no 3, and no 4 is maybe Stefan.'*

Meanwhile, whenever motoring journalists seek an icon of speed from the past, the image of Ronnie barrelling through pre-chicane Woodcote at 160mph on full-blooded oversteer at the absolute limit springs to mind. As Max Mosley put it: *'In the old days when Woodcote was one big corner, Ronnie would think nothing of going into it with an oversteering car, getting opposite lock right round to the stop, and still keeping his foot flat to the floor when he had a couple of wheels on the grass.'* There are maybe one or two today who could do that, but it's very rare. He had an extraordinary talent.

Opposite: Fellow F1 stars (Watson, Scheckter Mass, Hunt, Emmo and Hulme) inspect Ronnie's helmet bag (or is it a Swedish reindeer herder's hat of some kind?) **Above:** Reine and Ronnie – Sweden's great F1 hopes of the early '70s.

Complete Race Entry Listing
Compiled by Kenneth Olausson

(Seen here relaxing with Ronnie at Kyalami in 1971)

NC= National championship, EC = European championship, WC = World championship, GP = Grand Prix

1952-1961 on track & around his Örebro home. Tractor with 50cc engine later re-built by father Bengt and exchanged for a more effective 125 cc engine.

During his karting career Ronnie represented his home town club Örebro Bil & MC-Klubb (Örebro Car & Motor Cycle Club)

	Race, event	Track, county	Result, comments
1962	Kart: Robardie, class D (Ardie 200cc engine) finished 2nd in national championship, class D.		
12 aug	Invitation, class	Höör, Skåne	1st
12 aug	Höörloppet	Höör, Skåne	4th
23 sep	NC	Laxå	2nd
7 oct	Invitation, class	Älmhult, Småland	4th
30 sep	Invitation, class	Kilafors, Hälsingland	retired
14 oct	Invitation, class	Skövde, Våstergötland	1st
14 oct	Skaraborgsloppet	Skövde, Våstergötland	4th
21 oct	Invitation, class	Malmö, Skåne	3rd
21 oct	Final race	Malmö, Skåne	4th
1963	Kart: Robardie, class D (Bultaco 200cc engine) won the national championship, class D special.		
5 may	Invitation, class	Gislaved, Småland	retired
12 may	Tivedsloppet	Laxå, 2 runs	1st & 1st
19 may	Road race	Falkenberg, Halland	1st
26 may	Malmöloppet	Malmö, Lockarp, Skåne	1st
3 june	Invitation, class	Höör, Skåne	1st
3 june	Hööerloppet	Höör, Skane	2nd
18 aug	Invitation, class	Älmhult, Småland	1st
25 aug	Invitation, class	Gislaved, Småland	1st
1 sep	Solnaloppet	Botkyrka, Stockholm	2nd (class A Special)
1 sep	Solnaloppet	Botkyrka, Stockholm	4th (class D)
8 sep	Grand Prix	Laxå	1st
22 sep	NC	Kilafors, Hälsingland	1st
1964	Kart, Bultaco/Parilla, Robardie, class A Sport (100cc engine) class D-Special (200cc m/c engine) won the national championship, class A-sport.		
5 april	Sydloppet, A, D & final	Malmö, Skåne	6th, 2nd & 4th
12 april	Vårloppet A & D	Höör, Skåne	2nd & 1st
19 april	Invitation A & D	Skövde, Västergötland	2nd & 1st
26 april	Invitation A	Gislaved, Småland	1st
3 may	Invitation A & D	Mölndal, Bohuslän	1st & 2nd
10 may	Invitation A, D, final	Stockholm	1st, 1st & 2nd
24 may	Jubileum A	Kristianstad, Skåne	2nd
31 may	NC, class A	Älmhult, Småland	5th
14 june	NC, class D	Kilafors, Hälsingland	retired
19 june	Invitation A & D	Håby Ring, Uppland	1st & 1st
28 june	Tivedsloppet A & final	Laxå	1st & 1st
12 july	EC, team	München, Germany	RP best Swede individual
26 july	Invitation A	Munkedal, Bohuslän	retired
16 aug	EC, team	Leidschendam, Holland	3rd individual
23 aug	Swe GP & Rundtursloppet	Lockarp, Malmö	1st & 7th
30 aug	Nordic challenge, D	Älmhult, Småland (3 runs)	1st & 1st & 1st
6 sept	NC, class D	Åmål, Dalsland	ret.
13 sept	B. Lundberg cup, A, D & BL-cup	Laxå, Örebro	1st, 1st & 1st
20 sept	NC, class A	Skövde, Västergötland	1st
27 sept	NC, class A	Höör, Skåne	1st
4 oct	EC, team	Villecoublay, Paris, France	not placed
11 oct	NC, class A	Åmål, Dalsland	1st
18 oct	Gulfloppet 2-hour	Gislaved, Småland	1st - 195 laps
25 oct	Invitation D & final	Ludvika, Dalarna	1st & 1st
8 nov	2-hour race, A	Stockholm	4th (with Rolf Skoghag)
1965	2nd in the national championship, class D special, 1st class C int. & D in the Nordic challenge championship, 3rd in the European team championship. Robardie/Parilla kart.		
11 april	Invitation, class A	Malmö, Skåne	1st
19 april	Invitation, class A	Höör, Skåne	1st
25 april	EC, team	Vevey, Switzerland	3rd indivdual, team Sweden 4th
2 may	Invitation, A, D & C+D	Munkedal, Bohuslän	1st, 2nd & 1st
9 may	Tivedsloppet, D	Laxå, Örebro, 3 runs	ret, ret & 1st
16 may	Invitation, A & D	Ludvika, Dalarna	1st & 1st
23 may	Vårdkaseloppet, A, D & final	Huddinge, Stockholm	1st, 1st & 4th
13 june	Invitation, A int & C int	Skövde, Västergötland	1st & 1st World premiere for a twin-engined kart in this event
20 june	EC, team	Leidschendam, Holland	team Sweden 5th
27 june	NC, class D	Hedemora, Dalarna	2nd
11 july	Invitation, A int & final	Hofors, SMK Storvik	1st & 1st
18 july	Invitation, C	Munkedal, Bohuslän	1st
8 aug	Nordic champ, class D	Knutstorp, Skåne	1st
22 aug	Invitation, A int	Åmål, Dalsland	2nd
29 aug	Nordic Champ	Laxå, Örebro	1st & 1st
19 sept	Aspoe Ring, NC. class A	Skövde, Västergötland	retired
26 sept	Pista d'Oro, WC. class A	Rome, Italy	14th
3 oct	EC. team	Villecoublay, Paris, France	Team Sweden 1st (RP 1st individual)
17 oct	Nordic champ, class C int	Malmö, Sweden	1st
24 oct	B. Lundbergs cup	Kallebäcksbanan, Göteborg	1st
7 nov	Invitation, A int	Handen, Stockholm	2nd
14 nov	Invitation, C int	Ludvika, Dalarna	1st

1966	Finished 3rd in the national kart championship, class A int, 3rd in the WC and did his 1st F3 season in the Svebe car.		
17 april	Ikealoppet, A Int	Stockholm	1st
1 may	EC, team	Vevey, Switzerland	2nd (Susy Raganelli won)
22 may	Duvnäsloppet, Duv. Kart Ring	Askersund, Örebro	1st
5 june	EC, team	Lissone, Italy	1st
12 june	Aspö Ring	Skövde, Västergötland	qual 3rd, final 1st
26 june	EC, team	Coo, Belgium	2nd
3 july	Inauguration race,F3	Dalsland Ring, Bengtsfors	3rd
july/aug	Djurland Ring, F3	Jysland, Denmark	7th
14 aug	Roskilde Ring, F3	Roskilde, Denmark	retired
21 aug	Kanonloppet, F3	Karlskoga	not placed
28 aug	NC, class A int	Hedemora, Dalarna	1st
4 sept	NC, class A int	Skövde, Västergötland	qual 1st, final ret., broken silencer
11 sept	NC, class A int	Laxå, Örebro	4th
25 sept	WC, class A, 3 races	Copenhagen, Denmark	3rd (7th, 3rd &4th)
2 oct	F4, 2 heats	Castiglioncello, Italy	4th & 6th (with Leif Engström)
9 oct	EC, team	Villecoublay, France	4th
16 oct	F3	Karlskoga	crashed
23 oct	Lundhagen Cup,	Törp, Kart circuit Skåne	1st

1967	Drove a Brabham BT18 in the national championship, his first full season in car racing, finishing 5th overal		
23 april	Ring Djursland, F3	Jylland, Denmark	6th
30 april	Ring Knutstorp NC. F3	Hyllinge, Skåne	retired
7 may	Skarpnäck, NC. F3	MS, Stockholm	7th
15 may	Dalsland Ring, F3	Bengtsfors	5th
21 may	NC F3	Karlskoga	4th
28 may	Keimola, F3	Helsinki, Finland	2nd
23 june	NC. F3	Skellefteå, Västerbotten	4th
2 july	NC. F3	Dalsland Ring, Bengtsfors	4th
9 july	Vila Real, F3	Portugal	not placed
6 aug	Västkustloppet, NC. F3	Falkenberg, Halland	3rd
13 aug	Kanonloppet, F3	Karlskoga	retired
20 aug	Skarpnäck, NC. F3	MS, Stockholm	retired
27 aug	Ring Knutstorp, F3	Hyllinge, Skåne, 2 races	1st & 2nd (in final)
3 sept	Finland GP, F3	Keimola Ring	retired
5 sept	F3	Hämeenlinna, Finland	4th
12 sept	Roskilde Ring, F3	Denmark	3rd
24 sept	Stockholmsloppet, F3	Skarpnäck, Stockholm	3rd
1 oct	Euro Cup, F3	Hockenheim, Germany	13th
29 oct	F3	Brands Hatch, GB	did not qualify
12 nov	Jarama, F3	Madrid, Spain	11th

1968	Squadra Robardie, National F 3 champion, Tecno Formula 3 car.		
31 mar	F3	Barcelona, Spain	retired, flat tyre
7 april	F3	Monza, Italy	4th
21 april	F3	Falkenberg, Halland	1st (fast lap)
28 april	F3	Ring Knutstorp, Hyllinge	1st (fast lap)
5 may	NC. F3	Karlskoga, Sweden	7th (2nd grid)
12 may	NC. F3	Skarpnäck, Stockholm	1st (fast lap)
19 may	NC. F3	Dalsland Ring, Bengtsfors	1st
25 may	F3	Monaco, Monte Carlo	3rd
2 june	F3	Hockenheim, Germany	1st
7 june	F3	Hämeenlinna, Finland	2nd (pole p)
9 june	F3	Keimola, Finland	ret., battery, (pole p)
16 june	F3	Anderstorp, Småland	ret., gearbox
7 july	F3	Vila Real, Portugal	ret., clutch, (2nd grid)
14 july	F3	Magny Cours, France	2nd (fast lap, 2nd grid)
21 july	F3	Hockenheim, Germany	1st
28 july	F3	Djursland Ring, Denmark	1st (fast lap)
4 aug	NC. F3	Falkenberg, Halland	1st (fast lap)
11 aug	Kanonloppet, F3	Karlskoga, Sweden	ret., brakes, (pole p)
18 aug	F3	Hämeenlinna, Finland	1st
25 aug	F3	Ring Knutstorp, Hyllinge	ret (broken cam follower, 3rd grid)
1 sept	F3	Skarpnäck, Stockholm	1st
8 sept	F3	Dalsland Ring, Bengtsfors	3rd (3rd grid)
15 sept	F3	Hämeenlinna, Finland	1st
22 sept	F3	Monza, Italy	1st
6 oct	F3	Montlhéry, France	4th
20 oct	F3	Brands Hatch, GB	ret., gearbox

1969	Squadra Robardie, National & European F3 champion in Tecno Formula 3 car. Ronnie was winner of 'Sportscar cup of the year' presented by 13 motoring journalists in Sweden.			
13-16 feb	Swedish KAK rally, WC	Värmland	VW 1600TL	went off twice
6 april	F3	Monza, Italy	Tecno	1st
13 april	F3	Vallelunga, Italy	Tecno	1st
20 april	F3	Falkenberg, Halland	Tecno	1st
27 april	F3	Ring Knutstorp, Hyllinge	Tecno	1st
4 may	NC. F3	Karlskoga	Tecno	1st
11 may	F3	Vallelunga, Italy	Tecno	1st
17 may	F3	Monaco, Monte Carlo	Tecno	1st
25 may	F3	Chimay, Belgium	Tecno	not placed
26 may	F3	Crystal Palace, GB	Tecno	2nd
1 june	F3	Keimola Ring, Finland	Tecno	ret. battery
8 june	NC. F3	Anderstorp, Småland	Tecno	1st
15 june	Le Mans 24 hours	Le Mans, France	Chevrolet Corvette	ret. gear box
22 june	F 2	Monza, Italy	Tecno	7th
29 june	F3	Anderstorp, Småland	Tecno	1st
6 july	F3	Vila Real, Portugal	Tecno	not placed
13 july	F3 & sports car	Magny Cours, France	Tecno & Lola T70b	2nd & 1st
19 july	F3	Silverstone, GB	Tecno	3rd
27 july	Österreichring, sportscars	Zeltweg, Austria	Lola T70 Mk3b	Accident
3 aug	NC. F3	Falkenberg, Halland	Tecno	1st
10 aug	F3	Kinnekulle, Västergötland	Tecno	1st
17 aug	EC, Kanonloppet, F3 & sp car	Karlskoga	Tecno & Lola T70b	1st & 3rd
24 aug	F3	Skarpnäck, Stockholm	Tecno	1st
31 aug	F3	Ring Knutstorp, Hyllinge	Tecno	4th
1 sept	Guard's Trophy, F3	Brands Hatch, GB	Lotus	not placed
7 sept	NC, F3	Dalsland Ring, Bengtsfors	Tecno	1st
14 sept	F 2	Albi, France,	Lotus 59	5th
21 sept	F3	Monza, Italy	Tecno	1st
28 sept	F3	Cadwell Park,GB	March 693	3rd
5 oct	F3	Montlhéry, France	March 693	accident

Ronnie's 5 remaining races at Vallelunga, Brands Hatch, 2 in Madrid and the last in Syracusa, Italy, were cancelled due to his injuries at Montlhéry.

1970

11 jan	Temporada1,000 km	Buenos Aires, Argentina	Lola-Chevrolet T70b	3rd
11-15 feb	Swedish KAK rally, WC	Värmland	Porsche 911	ret. gearbox, (with Torsten Palm)
12 april	EC F2	Hockenheim Germany	March 702	ret. crash
26 april	EC F2	Barcelona, Spain	March 702	ret. clutch
3 may	F2	Nürburgring, Germany	March 702	ret. crash
10 may	Monaco GP	Monte Carlo	March 701	7th
24 may	F2	Zolder, Belgium	March 702	ret.
25 may	F2	Crystal Palace	March 702	accident
30 may	F2, MK Scandia	Mantorp Park, Sweden	March 702	not placed
7 june	Belgian GP	Spa-Francorchamps	March 701	ret.
14/15 june	Le Mans 24 hours	Le Mans, France	Ferrari 512	ret. (with Derek Bell)
21 june	Dutch GP	Zandvoort	March 701	9th
28 june	EC F2	Rouen, France	March 702	6th
5 july	French GP	Clermont-Ferrand	March 701	ret. final drive
18 july	British GP	Brands Hatch	March 701	8th
26 july	EC F2	Paul Ricard, France	March 702	6th

Ronnie Peterson: Super Swede

Date	Event	Location	Car	Result
2 aug	German GP	Hockenheim	March 701	ret. engine
9 aug	Kanonloppet	Karlskoga, Sweden	Porsche 917	ret. drive shaft
23 aug	Nordic Cup	Keimola Ring, Finland	Porsche 917	3rd
30 aug	F2	Mantorp Park, Sweden	March 702	ret. petrol pump
6 sept	Italian GP	Monza	March 701	ret. camshaft
13 sept	F2	Tulln-Langenlebarn, Austria	March 702	5th
20 sept	Canadian GP	Mont-Tremblant	March 701	14th
27 sept	F2	Imola, Italy	March 702	4th
4 oct	United States GP	Watkins Glen	March 701	11th
11 oct	F2 & Sportscar	Hockenheim, Germany	March 702 & Lola	3rd & 4th

1971 Ronnie was voted 'Motoring Man of the Year' in Sweden

Date	Event	Location	Car	Result
10 jan	WC, 1,000 km	Buenos Aires, Argentina	Lola-Cosworth T210	11th (with J. Cupeiro)
6 mar	South African GP	Kyalami	March 711	10th
14 mar	F2	Mallory Park, GB	March 712	ret. accident
21 mar	F1 Non Ch. Race of Champions	Brands Hatch, GB	March 711	ret. brakes
28 mar	F1 Non Ch. Questor GP, 2 races	Ontario, Calif., USA	March 711	16th & 16th (18th overall)
4 april	EC. F2, Deutschlandtrofé	Hockenheim, Germany	March 712	2nd & ret. engine
12 april	EC. F2, Euro Trophy Meeting	Thruxton, GB	March 712	2nd
18 april	Spanish GP	Montjuich P., Barcelona	March 711	ret. ignition
25 april	GP Pau, F2	Pau, France	March 712	ret. rear wheel, suspension
2 may	EC. F2, Eifelrennen	Nürburgring, Germany	March 712	ret. puncture
8 may	F1 Non Ch. Daily Express Int Trophy	Silverstone, GB	March 711 (Alfa)	accident
16 may	EC. F2 Gran Premio Madrid	Jarama, Spain	March 712	ret. engine
23 may	Monaco GP	Monte Carlo	March 711	2nd
31 may	Hilton Transp Race, EC. F2	Crystal Palace, GB	March 712	3rd
6 june	Martini Trophy	Silverstone, 2 runs	Lola-FVC T212	2nd (4th & 1st)
13 june	Jochen Rindt Mem. F1 Non Ch.	Hockenheim, Germany	March 711	2nd
20 june	Dutch GP	Zandvoort	March 711	4th
27 june	EC. F2, GP Rouen	Rouen, France	March 712	1st
4 july	French GP	Paul Ricard	March 711 (Alfa)	ret. engine
17 july	British GP	Silverstone	March 711	2nd
24 july	Watkins Glen, 6 hours	Watkins Glen, USA	Alfa Romeo T33	1st (with DeAdamich)
1 aug	German GP	Nürburgring	March 711	5th
8 aug	EC. F2	Mantorp Park, Sweden	March 712	1st
15 aug	Austrian GP	Österreichring	March 711	8th
22 aug	F2	Kinnekulle, Sweden	March 712	1st
29 aug	Swedish Gold Cup, F2	Karlskoga	March 712	1st
30 aug	Rothmans Int. Trophy, F2	Brands Hatch, GB	March 712	1st
5 sept	Italian GP	Monza	March 711	2nd
12 sept	EC. F2	Tulln-Langenlebarn, Austria	March 712	1st
19 sept	Canadian GP	Mosport Park	March 711	2nd
26 sept	EC. F2	Albi, France	March 712	6th
3 oct	United States GP	Watkins Glen	March 711	3rd
10 oct	EC. F2	Vallelunga, Italy	March 712	1st
11 oct	Sports car race	Montjuich Park, Spain	Lola T212	1st (with Jo Bonnier)
17 oct	F2	Vallelunga, Italy	March 712	1st
24 oct	F1 Non Ch. WC Victory Race	Brands Hatch, GB	March 711	16th
31 oct	F2	Interlagos, Brazil	March 712	2nd
7 nov	F2	Interlagos, Brazil	March 712	10th
14 nov	F2	Porto Alegre, Brazil	March 712	ret.
21 nov	F2	Cordoba, Brazil	March 712	ret.

1972

Date	Event	Location	Car	Result
9 jan	1,000 km	Buenos Aires, Argentina	Ferrari 312P	1st (with Tim Schenken)
23 jan	Argentine GP	Buenos Aires	March 721	6th
6 feb	Daytona 24 hours	Florida, USA	Ferrari 312P	2nd (with Tim Schenken)
4 mar	South African GP	Kyalami	March 721	5th
12 mar	EC. F2	Mallory Park, GB	March 722	accident
19 mar	F1 Non Ch. Race of Champions	Brands Hatch, GB	March 721X	12th
25 mar	Sebring 12 hours	Florida, USA	Ferrari 312P	2nd (with Tim Schenken)
30 mar	Brazilian GP	Interlagos	March 721	2nd
3 april	EC. F2	Thruxton, GB	March 722	1st
16 april	BOAC 1,000 km	Brands Hatch, GB	Ferrari 312P	2nd (with Tim Schenken)
25 april	Monza 1,000 km	Italy	Ferrari 312P	3rd (with Tim Schenken)
1 may	Spanish GP	Jarama	March 721X	ret. fuel leak
7 may	Spa 1,000 km	Belgium	Ferrari 312P	ret. (with Tim Schenken)
14 may	Monaco GP	Monte Carlo	March 721X	11th
28 may	Nürburgring 1,000 km	Germany	Ferrari 312P	1st (with Tim Schenken)
29 may	F1 Gold Cup Non Ch	Oulton Park, GB	March 721X	crash
4 june	Belgian GP	Nivelles	March 721X	9th
11 june	EC. F2	Hockenheim, Germany	March 722	3rd
25 june	Austrian 1,000 km	Österreichring, Austria	Ferrari 312P	3rd (with Tim Schenken)
2 july	French GP	Clermont-Ferrand	March 721G	5th
15 july	British GP	Brands Hatch	March 721G	accident
22 july	Watkins Glen, 6 hours	Watkins Glen, USA	Ferrari 312P	2nd (with Tim Schenken)
30 july	German GP	Nürburgring	March 721G	3rd
6 aug	EC. F2, & touring car race	Mantorp Park, Sweden	March 722, Ford Capri RS2600	ret.(f2) 1st (touring car)
13 aug	Austrian GP	Österreichring	March 721G	12th
3 sept	EC. F2	Salzburgring, Austria	March 722	ret.
10 sept	Italian GP	Monza	March 721G	9th
16 sept	Oulton Park, F2	Great Britain	March 722	1st
24 sept	Canadian GP	Mosport Park	March 721G	ret suspension
1 oct	EC. F2	Hockenheim, Germany	March 722	3rd
8 oct	United States GP	Watkins Glen	March 721G	4th
15 oct	Rome, F2	Italy	March 722	not placed
22 oct	F1 Non Ch. JPS Victory Meeting	Brands Hatch, GB	March 721G	8th (lead early)
29 oct	F2	Interlagos, Brazil	Brabham BT 38	ret.
5 nov	F2	Interlagos, Brazil	Brabham BT 38	ret.
12 nov	F2	Interlagos, Brazil	Brabham BT 38	ret

1973 Voted 'Motoring Man of the Year' in Sweden

Date	Event	Location	Car	Result
28 jan	Argentine GP	Buenos Aires	Lotus 72	ret. oil pressure
11 feb	Brazilian GP	Interlagos	Lotus 72	ret. broken wheel
15-18 feb	Swedish KAK rally, WC	Värmland	Ford Escort Mexico	ret. crash (with Torsten Palm)
3 mar	South African GP	Kyalami	Lotus 72	11th
18 mar	F1 Non Ch. Race of Champions	Brands Hatch, GB	Lotus 72	ret.
8 april	F1 Non Ch. Daily Express Int Trophy	Silverstone, GB	Lotus 72	2nd
29 april	Spanish GP	Montjuich Park	Lotus 72	ret.
20 may	Belgian GP	Zolder	Lotus 72	accident
3 june	Monaco GP	Monte Carlo	Lotus 72	3rd
10 june	EC. F2	Nivelles, Belgium	Lotus 74	ret.. engine
17 june	Swedish GP	Anderstorp	Lotus 72	2nd
24 june	EC. F2	Rouen, France	Lotus 74	accident (fast lap)
1 july	French GP	Paul Ricard	Lotus 72	1st
14 july	British GP	Silverstone	Lotus 72	2nd
22 july	F2	Misano, Italy	Lotus 74	engine, not placed

Date	Event	Location	Car	Result
29 july	Dutch GP	Zandvoort	Lotus 72	ret. gearbox
5 aug	German GP	Nürburgring	Lotus 72	ret. ignition
12 aug	EC. F2	Karlskoga, Sweden	Lotus 74	5th
19 aug	Austrian GP	Österreichring	Lotus 72	1st
26 aug	EC. F2	Enna-Pergusa, 2 runs	Lotus 74	7th
2 sept	Knutstorp, 2 runs	Hyllinge, Sweden	Ford Escort	ret.& 4th
9 sept	Italian GP	Monza	Lotus 72	1st
16 sept	EC. F2	Albi, France	Lotus 74	ret. engine
23 sept	Canadian GP	Mosport Park	Lotus 72	ret. suspension
7 oct	United States GP	Watkins Glen	Lotus 72	1st
14 oct	EC. F2	Vallelunga, Italy	Lotus 74	ret. engine

1974

Date	Event	Location	Car	Result
13 jan	Argentine GP	Buenos Aires	Lotus 72	13th
27 jan	Brazilian GP	Interlagos	Lotus 72	6th
30 mar	South African GP	Kyalami	Lotus 76	ret. suspension
6 april	F1 Non Ch. Daily Express Int Trophy	Silverstone, GB	Lotus 76	ret. engine & tyres
28 april	Spanish GP	Jarama	Lotus 76	ret. (oil pressure)
12 may	Belgian GP	Nivelles	Lotus 76	ret. fuel leak
26 may	Monaco GP	Monte Carlo	Lotus 72	1st
9 june	Swedish GP	Anderstorp	Lotus 72	ret. transmission
23 june	Dutch GP	Zandvoort	Lotus 72	8th
7 july	French GP	Dijon-Prenois	Lotus 72	1st
14 july	Nürburgring	Germany	BMW 3.0 CSL	ret. (with H.Stuck)
20 july	British GP	Brands Hatch	Lotus 72	10th
4 aug	German GP	Nürburgring	Lotus 76	4th
11 aug	Kanonloppet, F2	Karlskoga, Sweden	March-BMW	1st
18 aug	Austrian GP	Österreichring	Lotus 72	ret. transmission
1 sept	Knutstorp, 2 runs	Hyllinge, Sweden	BMW 3.0 CSL	1st & crash
8 sept	Italian GP	Monza	Lotus 72	1st
15 sept	IROC, Michigan Speedway	Michigan, USA	Chevrolet Camaro	7th
22 sept	Canadian GP	Mosport Park	Lotus 72	3rd
6 oct	United States GP	Watkins Glen	Lotus 72	ret. fuel system
26 oct	IROC, Riverside Raceway	California, USA	Chevrolet Camaro	7th
27 oct	IROC, Riverside Raceway	California, USA	Chevrolet Camaro	8th
3 nov	Kyalami 9 hours	South Africa	BMW 3.0 CSL	crashed in rain (with J.Scheckter)
7 dec	Fuji Raceway, F1	Japan (non-WC race)	Lotus 72	fastest lap: 1.15 min.

1975

Date	Event	Location	Car	Result
12 jan	Argentine GP	Buenos Aires	Lotus 72	ret. brakes
26 jan	Brazilian GP	Interlagos	Lotus 72	15th
1/2 feb	Daytona 24 hours	Florida, USA	BMW 3.0 CSL	ret. piston conrod
14 feb	IROC Final	Daytona, USA	Chevrolet Camaro	ret. spun at 275 km/h
1 mar	South African GP	Kyalami	Lotus 72	10th
9 mar	Rallycross event	Gelleråsen, Karlskoga	Volkswagen	crashed in 3rd heat
15 mar	F1 Non Ch. Race of Champions	Brands Hatch, GB	Lotus 72	3rd
31 march	EC, F2	Thruxton, GB	March-BMW 752	accident
13 april	F1 Non Ch. Daily Express Int Trophy	Silverstone, GB	Lotus 72	failed to start
27 april	Spanish GP	Montjuich Park	Lotus 72	ret. crash
11 may	Monaco GP	Monte Carlo	Lotus 72	4th
25 may	Belgian GP	Zolder	Lotus 72	ret. accident
8 june	Swedish GP	Anderstorp	Lotus 72	9th
15 june	Rallycross event	Gelleråsen, Karlskoga	Volkswagen	6th
22 june	Dutch GP	Zandvoort	Lotus 72	ret. out of petrol
29 june	Norisring	Germany	BMW 3.0 CSL	ret. brakes
6 july	French GP	Paul Ricard	Lotus 72	10th
12 july	Watkins Glen 6 hours	Watkins Glen, USA	BMW 3.0 CSL	ret. tank leak (with Stuck)
19 july	British GP	Silverstone	Lotus 72	ret. engine
3 aug	German GP	Nürburgring	Lotus 72	ret. clutch
10 aug	EC, rallycross	Gelleråsen, Karlskoga	2.2 litre VW	5th D final
17 aug	Austrian GP	Österreichring	Lotus 72	5th
24 aug	F1 Non Ch. Swiss GP	Dijon-Prenois	Lotus 72	4th
7 sept	Italian GP	Monza	Lotus 72	ret. engine
5 oct	United States GP	Watkins Glen	Lotus 72	5th
2 nov	Kyalami 1,000 km	Kyalami, South Africa	BMW 3.0 CSL	ret. engine

1976

Date	Event	Location	Car	Result
25 jan	Brazilian GP	Interlagos	Lotus 77	ret. crash
6 mar	South African GP	Kyalami, South Africa	March 761	accident
28 mar	US GP West	Long Beach, California	March 761	10th
11 april	Jim Clark Memorial, F2	Hockenheim, Germany	March-BMW 762	ret. engine
2 may	Spanish GP	Jarama	March 761	ret. gearbox
9 may	Silverstone 6 hours	Silverstone, GB	BMW 3.2 turbo	ret. gearbox (with G. Nilsson)
16 may	Belgian GP	Zolder	March 761	accident
30 may	Monaco GP	Monte Carlo	March 761	accident
13 june	Swedish GP	Anderstorp	March 761	7th
27 june	Österreichring 6 hours	Zeltweg, Austria	BMW 3.2 turbo	ret. clutch
4 july	French GP	Paul Ricard	March 761	17th
10 july	Watkins Glen 6 hours	Watkins Glen, USA	BMW 3.2 turbo	5th
18 july	British GP	Brands Hatch	March 761	ret. engine
25 july	Österreichring, Gr5	Zeltweg, Austria	BMW 3.2 turbo	ret. clutch
1 aug	German GP	Nürburgring	March 761	accident
15 aug	Austrian GP	Österreichring	March 761	6th
29 aug	Dutch GP	Zandvoort	March 761	ret.engine
5 sept	Dijon Gr. 5	France	BMW 3.2 turbo	ret. (with Gunnar Nilsson)
12 sept	Italian GP	Monza	March 761	1st
3 oct	Canadian GP	Mosport Park	March 761	9th
10 oct	United States GP	Watkins Glen	March 761	ret. suspension
24 oct	F1 Non Ch. Fuji Raceway, F1	Japan	March 761	ret. engine
7 nov	Kyalami	South Africa	BMW 3.2 turbo	ret. petrol leak with (J.Fitzpatrick)

1977

Date	Event	Location	Car	Result
9 jan	Argentine GP	Buenos Aires	Tyrrell P34	ret. crashed
23 jan	Brazilian GP	Interlagos	Tyrrell P34	accident
6 feb	Daytona 24 hours	Florida, USA	BMW 320i	ret.engine (withDavid Hobbs, Sam Posey)
5 mar	South African GP	Kyalami	Tyrrell P34	ret. fuel pressure
20 mar	F1 Non Ch. Race of Champions	Brands Hatch	Tyrrell P34	10th
27 mar	Nürburgring, Gr. 5	Germany	BMW 320i	3rd
3 april	US GP West	Long Beach	Tyrrell P34	ret. fuel pipe
1 may	Nürburgring, Gr. 5	Germany	BMW 320i	ret.
8 may	Spanish GP	Jarama	Tyrrell P34	8th
15 may	Silverstone 6 hours	Great Britain	BMW 320i	4th (with H.Kelleners)
22 may	Monaco GP	Monte Carlo	Tyrrell P34	ret. brakes
5 june	Belgian GP	Zolder	Tyrrell P34	3rd
19 june	Swedish GP	Anderstorp	Tyrrell P34	ret. ignition
3 july	French GP	Dijon-Prenois	Tyrrell P34	12th
10 july	Watkins Glen 6 hours	USA	BMW 320i	accident (with David Hobbs)
16 july	British GP	Silverstone	Tyrrell P34	ret. engine
31 july	German GP	Hockenheim	Tyrrell P34	9th
14 aug	Austrian GP	Österreichring	Tyrrell P34	5th
21 aug	Mosport Park, Gr 5	Canada	BMW 320i	accident (with David Hobbs)
28 aug	Dutch GP	Zandvoort	Tyrrell P34	ret. ignition
11 sept	Italian GP	Monza	Tyrrell P34	6th

Ronnie Peterson: Super Swede

25 sept	Brands Hatch 6 hours	Great Britain	BMW 320i	accident (with Stuck)
2 oct	US GP East	Watkins Glen	Tyrrell P34	16th
9 oct	Canadian GP	Mosport Park	Tyrrell P34	ret. fuel leak
23 oct	Japanese GP	Mount Fuji	Tyrrell P34	ret. crash
5 nov	Kyalami, 6 hours, 2 runs	South Africa	BMW 320	1st & ret. gearbox (with H. Stuck)

1978

15 jan	Argentine GP	Buenos Aires	Lotus 78	5th
29 jan	Brazilian GP	Jacarepagua	Lotus 78	ret. accident
5 feb	Daytona, 24 hours	Florida, USA	BMW 320 turbo	ret. engine
4 mar	South African GP	Kyalami	Lotus 78	1st
19 mar	F1 Non Ch.Daily Express Int. Trophy	Silverstone, GB	Lotus 78	ret. poor handling
2 april	United States GP West	Long Beach, California	Lotus 78	4th
30 april	Nürburgring, Gr. 5	Germany	BMW 320 turbo	ret.
7 may	Monaco GP	Monte Carlo	Lotus 78	ret. gearbox
14 may	Silverstone 6 hours	Great Britain	BMW 320 turbo	ret. (with Hans Stuck)
21 may	Belgian GP	Zolder	Lotus 78	2nd
28 may	Nürburgring 1000 km	Germany	BMW 320turbo	7th (with Dieter Quester)
4 june	Spanish GP	Jarama	Lotus 79	2nd
17 june	Swedish GP	Anderstorp	Lotus 79	3rd
2 july	French GP	Paul Ricard	Lotus 79	2nd
9 july	Watkins Glen 6 hours	USA	BMW 320 turbo	ret. (with David Hobbs)
16 july	British GP	Brands Hatch	Lotus 79	ret. fuel pipe
30 july	German GP	Hockenheim	Lotus 79	ret. gearbox
6 aug	Knutstorp	Hyllinge, Sweden	BMW 320 turbo	ret. engine
13 aug	Austrian GP	Österreichring	Lotus 79	1st
27 aug	Dutch GP	Zandvoort	Lotus 79	2nd
3 sept	Vallelunga, Gr. 5	Italy	BMW 320 turbo	ret. (with Hans Stuck)
10 sept	Italian GP	Monza	Lotus 78	start accident

Appendices: Ronnie Peterson's Complete Race Entry Listing

Ronnie Peterson: Super Swede

A
Ahrens, Kurt	30
Aldridge, Geoff	141
Amon, Chris	34,44,47,48,50,52,55,56,66,68,74,78,153,154
Andersson, Sven	26,30
Andretti, Mario	10,13,44,47,48,56,65,66,74,84,85,87,95,126,136,137,141,145,149, 153,154,157,158,161,162,166,169,170,173,174,176,179,180,182, 183,184,187,188,190,192,193,194,197,199,200,202,203,204,208, 212,215,217,218
Attwood, Richard	55

B
Backman, Lasse	30
Bellamy, Ralph	115,118,179
Bell, Derek	47,47,52,56,62,69,92,95,133
Beltoise, Jean-Pierre	18,15,62
Berntson, Lars	21,22,23,29,106,141,142,169,173,205,215,218,221
Birrell, Gerry	9,49,73,76,109
Blodyk, Trevor	34
Bloor, Rodney	33,35
Bond, Bev	38
Bonnier, Jo	38,39,41,55,70,72,84,92,222
Brabham, Jack	30,33
Brambilla, Vittorio	15,33,134,141,149,150,153,157,158,161,169,202
Brise, Tony	141
Brodie, Dave	9,10,17,18,22,118,130,133,137,177,188,197,215

C
Cevert Francois	34,56,68,73,78,80,87,102,105,106,110,113
Cewrien, Per	19,34
Chapman, Colin	13,14,15,25,44,56,92,96,101,102,104,106,108,110,113,122,124, 128,129,133,134,137,138,141,142,145,146,173,174,176,182,184, 188,190,197,199,203,204,205,215
Clark, Jim	12,32,46,48,66,98,109,176
Coaker, Graham	42,43,44,56,70
Courage, Piers	33,55
Crawford, Jim	133,138,141
Crabbe, Colin	44,46,51,52,53,55,56

D
Dal-Bo, Patrick	34
Dance, Bob	47,51,173,176,180,182,190,194,200,203,205,212
Dennis, Eddie	212,215
Dennis, Ron	66,95,133
Depailler, Patrick	9,23,37,66,125,141,150,153,157,158,161,162,165,166,170,182, 183,184,187,190,194,203
Donohue, Mark	81,126,137,138
Doodson, Mike	56
Dreyfus, Rene	8

E
Ecclestone, Bernie	205
Edwards, Guy	15,71
Elgh, Eje	218,221,222
Elford, Vic	51,70,92
Elverskog, Gerth	22,35
Engstrom, Leif	24
Eriksson, Sveneric	14,17,25,26,30,35,48,58,61,62,73,81,88,92,96,99,102,105,106,113, 199,217

F
Faijersson, Sven	26
Fittipaldi, Emerson	8,10,11,12,20,21,34,35,37,41,44,55,56,65,66,69,73,74,76,78,81,83, 87,88,92,95,96,96,99,100,101,102,105,106,106,108,109,110,113, 114,115,117,118,126,133,134,146150,158,176,182,193,208,212
Fittipaldi, Maria-Helena	20
Foley, Barry	14,107
Follmer, George	15,64,129

Franklin, Bill	118

G
Ganley, Howden	17,18,21,28,35,41,44,50,76,80,106,125
Gardner, Derek	13,56,165,169,174
Gardner, Frank	33
Gethin, Peter	34,35,78,79
Granatelli, Andy	46,47
Guthrie, Sir Malcolm	49,50,51,55

H
Hailwood, Mike	76,78,81,95,102,104,110,125,133
Hart, Rex	48,96,105,113,115,117,137,165,180,183,184,188,193,203,204, 207,208,212
Hedlund, Ove	30,34
Henry, Alan	66,91,126,138
Henton, Brian	138
Herd, Robin	12,43,44,47,48,50,51,56,59,63,64,66,74,76,78,81,83,89,90,91,96, 141,146,149,190,216,217,218
Hermann, Hans	53
Hicks, Clive	46,179,180
Hill, Graham	15,21,33,37,40,44,52,55,66,69,76,91,92,99,109,134,142,176,203
Holmberg, Conny	26
Horsley, Bubbles	17
Hulme, Denny	48,70,87,106,107,109,110
Hunt, James	12,21,36,41,88,95,113,115,121,126,137,141,150,153,154,157, 158,161,162,165,166,170,173,180,183,184,190,202,208,211

I
Ickx, Jackie	15,38,52,55,66,69,70,72,78,84,85,86,92,95,101,105,117,118,121, 122,125,126,129,130,133,134,138,161
Irwin, Chris	33

J
Jabouille, Jean-Pierre	35,37,66,200
Jarier, Jean-Pierre	14,78,101,110,118,130,134,141
Jaussaud, Jean-Pierre	34,37,38,66
Jenkinson, Dennis	47,78,83,104,107,141
Johannsson, George	19

K
Kerr, Peter	37,47,65,67,73,88,91
Kinnunen, Leo	34
Kottulinsky, Freddy	34

L
Laffite, Jaques	36,133,137,138,153,205
Lanfranchi, Tony	35
Lauda, Niki	9,69,74,76,83,87,88,91,95,96,106,121,122,125,130,134,137,141, 150,153,157,158,161,165,169,170,182,183,187,190,197,202,208
Leighton, Keith	15,20,22,48,51,61,65,66,70,73,76,95,96,101,109,110,112,145, 174,218
Lincoln, Kurt	33
Lombardi, Lella	15,146,149
Lucas, Charles	30,33,41,47

M
Mass, Jochen	9,125,141,154,157,161,165,169,173
May, Stevie	15
Mazet, Francois	38
Miles, John	35,48,70
Mosley, Max	11,12,15,37,38,41,43,44,45,47,51,56,59,65,69,70,74,79,83,92,96, 99,149,150,157,158,182,207,218,222
Moss, Sir Stirling	6
Muller, John	17

N
Nichols, Don	129,130

Nilsson, Gunnar	146,149,150,153,154,169,170,173,176,179,182,221,222
Nunn, Mo	38
Nuvolari, Tazio	9

O

Ogilive, Martin	141,179,180,212
Olausson, Kenneth	21,30,34,37,52,217
Oliver, Jackie	38,52,54,129,176

P

Pace, Carlos	9,15,93,95,122,133,153,154,157,165,166
Patrese, Riccardo	211,212
Palm, Gunnar	34,106,176
Palm, Torsten	17,18,21,34,35,41,62,134,136,215,217,218,222
Parkes, Mike	55
Pederzani, bros.	35,49,109
Penske, Roger	130,138,153,154,157,158
Persson, Ake	26,29
Pescarolo, Henri	33,38,48,65,66
Peterson, Barbro	19,20,22,21,23,25,41,48,61,78,101,108,111,113,115,116,133,138, 145,162,169,180,199,204,217,218
Peterson, Bengt	25,26,29,30,34,105
Peterson, Maj-Britt	17
Peterson, Tommy	23,25,218
Phipps, David	157
Phillippe, Maurice	137,174
Pike, Roy	33,34
Piper, David	38
Pironi, Didier	37,187
Pyrce, Tom	129,130,133,134,149,153,154,157,161,166
Prost, Alain	13,37,113

R

Radio Luxembourg	9
Raganelli, Suzanna	28
Redman, Brian	38,84,92,95
Rees, Alan	33,37,38,43,44,56,59,65,66,73,87,129
Regazzoni, Clay	33,34,35,48,55,56,73,74,78,84,87,92,95,102,105,110,118,124,125, 136,137,141,153,154,157,158,161,162,166,169,182,205,217
Reutemann, Carlos	9,13,56,69,73,78,81,87,88,99,101,125,136,150,157,170,173,179, 180,183,184,190,194,197
Revson, Peter	32,87,106,108,110,113,115,121
Rindt, Jochen	17,33,37,38,40,43,44,47,48,52,55,65,67,73,78,95,102,161,197
Rodriguez, Pedro	52,56,70
Roebuck, Nigel	9,13,211
Rollinson, Allan	11
Rosberg, Keke	18
Russell, Jim	41

S

Scheckter, Jody	9,13,106,125,133,141,150,153,157,158,161,162,165,169,170, 173,174,182,183,187,190,193,194,202,203,208
Schenken, Tim	9,18,19,21,23,33,35,37,38,41,44,48,54,56,59,61,62,66,69,73,74,76, 78,79,81,83,84,85,87,92,95,94,101,126,216
Schumacher, Michael	12,176
Senna, Ayrton	13,115
Servoz-Gavin, Johnny	38,44,48
Siffert, Jo	43,44,47,48,51,52,55,56,62,70,74,76,78,80,92
Stanbury, Noel	14,108
Stewart, Sir Jackie	9,10,14,35,36,38,43,44,47,48,51,52,65,66,69,70,71,74,78,81,87,92, 99,102,105,106,110,113,114,117,118,158,182,190,215
Strandberg, Åke	30,86,87,145,199,203,205,208,216,217,218,221
Surtees, John	52,73,78,87,95
Svenby, Staffan	14,17,37,38,48,51,52,92,96,122,134,137,146,158,162,169,174, 176,199,203,204,216,222
Svensson, Ulf	30,34

T

Taylor, Sid	38
Thompson, John	47,48,
Troberg, Picko	21,33,34,55,56
Tyrrell, Ken	14,43,44,47,134,158,162,166,173,174

V

Villeneuve, Gilles	9,182,183,184,194,202,212,216

W

Waldegaard, Bjorn	38,41
Walker, Rob	44,52,205
Wardell, Ray	41,47
Warr, Peter	17,23,92,96,99,105,106,109,113,114,117,121,129,130,138,141, 145,174,176,203,207
Watkins, Sid	202,203,204,205
Watson, John	22,73,83,96,99,114,117,122,133,138,141,146,153,154,156,157, 158,161,162,165,169,170,180,183,184,187,188,190,197,208,215, 216,217,218
Westbury, Peter	35
Wheatcroft, Tom	55
Widdows, Robin	35
Wilds, Mike	15
Williams, Chris	34
Williams, Frank	9,18,33,65,66,68,74,145,146
Williams, Jonathan	33
Williamson, Roger	9,110
Wisell, Reine	17,18,28,29,30,32,34,35,37,38,41,44,48,55,56,65,66,69,73,76,83, 84,91,93,95,203,207,222,223
Wollek, Bob	9
Worred, Steve	30
Wright, Peter	47,179

Z

Zanon, Count Ghughie	17,146,162,174,176,182,187,188,194,211,217

Ronnie Peterson: Super Swede

Acknowledgements

Many thanks to everyone who's helped with research for this book, given interviews and provided photographs. In particular, I want to thank Nina Kennedy (Peterson) for her hospitality and lending pictures from her family albums. I am most grateful to Max Mosley for the apposite Foreword. The comprehensive race entry list was compiled by Kenneth Olausson, and is an invaluable record of Ronnie's career. Kenneth also helped with research into Ronnie's early racing days and with the Swedish translation version of the book.

Ronnie's competitors, team-mates, mechanics, employers and friends who kindly shared their opinions and reminiscences include Picko Troberg, Reine Wisell, Torsten Palm, Eje Elgh, Tim Schenken, Howden Ganley, Dave Brodie, Sir Jackie Stewart, Alan Rees, Peter Kerr, Max Mosley, Robin Herd, Sir Malcolm Guthrie, Peter Warr, Mario Andretti, John Watson, Martin Ogilvie, Bob Dance, Eddie Dennis, Keith Leighton, Åke Strandberg, Rex Hart, Glenn Waters, Derek Gardner, Alistair Caldwell, David Phipps, Professor Sid Watkins, Lars Berntson, and Nigel Roebuck.

I had a wonderful time in Sweden meeting with Ronnie's managers Staffan Svenby and Sveneric Eriksson, as well as photo-journalists Kenneth Olausson, Robert Petersson, George Johansson and Gunnar Elmgren. I would also like to mention sculptor Richard Brixel, creator of Ronnie's statue to be un-veiled in Örebro in 2003, his partner Ylva, and Anders Fasth and Michael Olsson from Örebro Läns Museum.

As always it was a pleasure to get together with Noel Stanbury, and catch up with former colleague Mike Doodson, as well as Jan Hedegård, who translated a lot of material for me from Swedish sources. Paul Fearnley, Liam Clogger, David Tremayne and Laurie Caddell helped with liaison and I also spoke to Dr Simon Donnell, Chrissie Leighton, Per Cewrien, Tommy Peterson and Emerson Fittipaldi. Although a proposed meeting with Emmo never materialised: All I have to offer is a good-humoured quote from him at the Goodwood Festival of Speed 2002: *'You can't write a book about Ronnie without some words from me!'*

Photographic sources were primarily Kenneth Olausson who provided many images from his extensive collection of *"Ronnie"* images. Also, Ian Catt, William Taylor, Ford Photographic Archive (Fran Chamberlain), Ferret Fotographic (Ted Walker), Classic Team Lotus (Clive Chapman), Grand Prix Foto (Peter Nygaard), LAT, BMW Archive, Charles Briscoe-Knight, Jerry Booen, Richard Spelberg, Robert Petersson, Giles Chapman and David Marshall.

Rupert Harding got the project off the ground, but it was left to William Taylor at Coterie Press to bring it to fruition – thanks to William, Jim and Lesley.

Bibliography

- *Ronnie - racerföraren by Rune Månzon (Förlags AB Marieberg, 1978)*
- *Ronnie Peterson: la race des seigneurs by Martine Camus (SIPE, 1978)*
- *The Viking Drivers by Fredrik Petersens (William Kimber, 1979)*
- *Ronnie Peterson: SuperSwede by Alan Henry (Haynes, 1978)*
- *Life at the Limit by Professor Sid Watkins (Pan, 1996)*
- *Colin Chapman: The man and his cars by Jabby Crombac (Patrick Stephens, 1986)*
- *James Hunt biography by Gerald Donaldson (Virgin, 2003)*
- *Ronnie! By Sveneric Eriksson (Sport Promotion AB, 1971)*
- *Motor blandning by George Johansson (Natur och Kultur, 2000)*
- *Grand Prix: Ronnie Peterson och hans sport by George Johansson (Teknikens värld, 1974).*